RHETORIC, INC.

RSA·STR

THE RSA SERIES IN TRANSDISCIPLINARY RHETORIC

Edited by
Michael Bernard-Donals *(University of Wisconsin)* and
Leah Ceccarelli *(University of Washington)*

Editorial Board:
Diane Davis, *The University of Texas at Austin*
Cara Finnegan, *University of Illinois at Urbana-Champaign*
Debra Hawhee, *The Pennsylvania State University*
John Lynch, *University of Cincinnati*
Steven Mailloux, *Loyola Marymount University*
Kendall Phillips, *Syracuse University*
Thomas Rickert, *Purdue University*

The RSA Series in Transdisciplinary Rhetoric is a collaboration with the Rhetoric Society of America to publish innovative and rigorously argued scholarship on the tremendous disciplinary breadth of rhetoric. Books in the series take a variety of approaches, including theoretical, historical, interpretive, critical, or ethnographic, and examine rhetorical action in a way that appeals, first, to scholars in communication studies and English or writing and, second, to at least one other discipline or subject area.

Other titles in this series:
Nathan Stormer, *Sign of Pathology: U.S. Medical Rhetoric on Abortion, 1800s–1960s*
Mark Longaker, *Rhetorical Style and Bourgeois Virtue: Capitalism and Civil Society in the British Enlightenment*
Robin E. Jensen, *Infertility: A Rhetorical History*
Steven Mailloux, *Rhetoric's Pragmatism: Essays in Rhetorical Hermeneutics*
M. Elizabeth Weiser, *Museum Rhetoric: Building Civic Identity in National Spaces*
Chris Mays, Nathaniel A. Rivers and Kellie Sharp-Hoskins, eds., *Kenneth Burke + The Posthuman*
Amy Koerber, *From Hysteria to Hormones: A Rhetorical History*
Elizabeth C. Britt, *Reimagining Advocacy: Rhetorical Education in the Legal Clinic*
Ian E. J. Hill, *Advocating Weapons, War, and Terrorism: Technological and Rhetorical Paradox*
Kelly Pender, *Being at Genetic Risk: Toward a Rhetoric of Care*
James L. Cherney, *Ableist Rhetoric*
Susan Wells, *Robert Burton's Rhetoric: An Anatomy of Early Modern Knowledge*
Ralph Cintron, *Democracy as Fetish*
Maggie Werner, *Stripped: Reading the Erotic Body*

Timothy Johnson

RHETORIC, INC.

Ford's Filmmaking and the Rise of Corporatism

THE PENNSYLVANIA STATE UNIVERSITY PRESS
UNIVERSITY PARK, PENNSYLVANIA

Library of Congress Cataloging-in-Publication Data

Names: Johnson, Timothy (Timothy S.), 1984– author.
Title: Rhetoric, Inc. : Ford's filmmaking and the rise of corporatism / Timothy Johnson.
Other titles: RSA series in transdisciplinary rhetoric.
Description: University Park, Pennsylvania : The Pennsylvania State University Press, [2020] | Series: The RSA series in transdisciplinary rhetoric | Includes bibliographical references and index.
Summary: "Examines motion pictures produced or sponsored by Ford Motor Company from a rhetorical perspective, demonstrating how the films reveal a long-term rhetorical project that has helped embed corporations into many of the social systems guiding societies today"—Provided by publisher.
Identifiers: LCCN 2020024094 | ISBN 9780271087900 (cloth)
Subjects: LCSH: Ford Motor Company—In motion pictures—History. | Industrial films—Social aspects—United States—History. | Automobile industry and trade—Social aspects—United States—History. | Rhetoric—Economic aspects—United States—History. | Corporate state—United States—History.
Classification: LCC HD9710.U54 F637 2020 | DDC 070.1/8—dc23
LC record available at https://lccn.loc.gov/2020024094

Copyright © 2020 Timothy Johnson
All rights reserved
Printed in the United States of America
Published by The Pennsylvania State University Press,
University Park, PA 16802-1003

The Pennsylvania State University Press is a member of the Association of University Presses.

It is the policy of The Pennsylvania State University Press to use acid-free paper. Publications on uncoated stock satisfy the minimum requirements of American National Standard for Information Sciences—Permanence of Paper for Printed Library Material, ANSI Z39.48–1992.

For Katie and Owen

Contents

List of Illustrations | ix

Acknowledgments | xi

Introduction | 1

1 Spreading the Industrial Aesthetic in Ford's Education Films | 27

2 Ford's Montage Films and the "Rhetorical Economy" | 62

3 Ford's Cinematic Production of Economic Space | 92

4 Spectacle and Spectatorship in Ford's World's Fair Films | 122

5 War, Industrial Globalization, and the Managerial Gaze | 153

Conclusion | 185

Notes | 193

Bibliography | 205

Index | 219

Illustrations

1. Ford Motion Picture Laboratory, still from *Luther Burbank*, 1922 | 35
2. Ford Motion Picture Laboratory, still from *Luther Burbank*, 1922 | 35
3. Ford Motion Picture Laboratory, stills from *Olive and Orange Growing*, 1920 | 40
4. Ford Motion Picture Laboratory, stills from *Bubbles, I'm Forever Using Soap*, 1919 | 40
5. Ford Motion Picture Laboratory, stills from *Sugar*, 1919 | 40
6. Ford Motion Picture Laboratory, stills from *Democracy and Education*, 1921 | 49
7. Ford Motion Picture Laboratory, still from *The Henry Ford Trade School*, 1927 | 55
8. Ford Motion Picture Laboratory, still from *The Henry Ford Trade School*, 1927 | 56
9. Ford Motion Picture Laboratory, still from *As Dreams Come True*, 1921 | 64
10. Ford Motion Picture Laboratory, stills from *As Dreams Come True*, 1921 | 75
11. Ford Motion Picture Laboratory, stills from *As Dreams Come True*, 1921 | 88
12. Ford Motion Picture Laboratory, stills from *Good Roads*, 1921 | 100
13. Ford Motion Picture Laboratory, stills from *Village-Industries*, 1932 | 107
14. Ford Motion Picture Laboratory, stills from *Village-Industries*, 1932 | 108
15. Ford Motion Picture Laboratory, still from *A Visit to Yellowstone National Park*, 1922 | 114
16. Ford Motion Picture Laboratory, still from *A Visit to Yellowstone National Park*, 1922 | 115

17. Ford Motion Picture Laboratory, stills from *Fairy Fantasy in Stone-Bryce National Park*, 1937 | 118
18. Ford Motion Picture Laboratory, stills from *Ford and a Century of Progress*, 1934 | 132
19. Ford Motion Picture Laboratory, still from *Ford and a Century of Progress*, 1934 | 132
20. Ford Motion Picture Laboratory, stills from *Ford and a Century of Progress*, 1934 | 135
21. Ford Motion Picture Laboratory, stills from *Ford and a Century of Progress*, 1934 | 137
22. Ford Motion Picture Laboratory, still from *Rhapsody in Steel*, 1934 | 142
23. Ford Motion Picture Laboratory, still from *Rhapsody in Steel*, 1934 | 142
24. Ford Motion Picture Laboratory, still from *Harvest of the Years*, 1940 | 149
25. Ford Motion Picture Laboratory, stills from *Women on the Warpath*, 1943 | 159
26. Ford Motion Picture Laboratory, still from *Women on the Warpath*, 1943 | 161
27. Ford Motion Picture Laboratory, still from *Women on the Warpath*, 1943 | 162
28. Ford Motion Picture Laboratory, stills from *Around the World with Ford Motor Company*, 1948 | 169
29. Ford Motion Picture Laboratory, still from *Ford Bombay, India*, 1948 | 179
30. Ford Motion Picture Laboratory, still from *Ford Alexandria, Egypt*, 1948 | 180

Acknowledgments

I would like to thank the English Departments at the University of Louisville, the University of Madison–Wisconsin, the University of Illinois–Chicago, and Roger Williams University for their support and intellectual cultures over the years. In particular I would like to thank Jim Phelan, Gerald Graff, Christa Olson, Morris Young, Jim Brown, Mark Garrett Longaker, and Michael Bernard-Donals for their guidance and encouragement on this project and others at various points in my academic career.

I would also like to thank the series editors, reviewers, and editorial staff at Penn State University Press for all of their help in making this book possible. An earlier version of chapter 3 appeared as "Paving the Way to Prosperity: Ford Motor Company's Films, Interstitial Rhetoric, and the Production of Economic Space in the Interwar Period" in *Rhetoric Society Quarterly*. I thank them for letting me use this material.

To my parents, I cannot express enough how thankful I am for your kindness and patience and for modeling what it is to work hard and balance a life lived happily. To my brother, Ben, you have been a wonderful role model over the years, and I owe you more than I can say. Most of all, I would like to thank my wife, Katie. You have endured my strangeness while I wrote this book and offered joy and support and love all along the way. You are simply the best. To my son, Owen, thank you for being the most joyous child.

Introduction

On December 4, 2008, the CEOs of Chrysler, General Motors, and Ford Motor Company sat before the Congressional Banking, Housing, and Urban Affairs Committee to persuade the panel of senators to provide loans to an American automotive industry teetering on the edge of bankruptcy. Similar bailout funds had been given to major banks only months before, prompting a debate over whether taxpayers should be responsible for propping up private corporations. The trio, just two weeks before, had been widely criticized for arriving to the first hearing in expensive private jets and for not presenting clear plans for restructuring their companies. Many saw these actions as evidence of the unchecked privilege of corporate actors in the years leading up to economic turmoil, and the vote was suspended.[1]

At the second hearing (to which the CEOs each drove), a theme developed in the executives' rhetoric defending the bailouts. Rick Wagoner, CEO of GM, declared that "GM has been an important part of American culture for a hundred years, and most of that time as the world's leading automaker."[2] Bob Nardelli, CEO of Chrysler, reiterated this notion by pointing out that he was "here representing the one million people who depend on Chrysler for their livelihoods." Finally, though noting that Ford was still solvent, Alan Mullaly, CEO of Ford, declared that "Ford is an American company, and an American icon, we are woven into the fabric of every community that relies on our cars and our trucks." He further argued that to allow Ford (or Chrysler or GM) to fail was to jeopardize the livelihoods of the senators' constituents by damaging such an integral figure of civic life and national identity.[3]

These arguments would prove successful, and Congress later allocated $75.9 billion to help keep the American automobile industry solvent. Notably, this was only one part of the Troubled Asset Relief Program's $363.8 billion set aside for securing the financial well-being of corporations considered crucial to the health of the American economy.[4] The reasoning behind this remarkable federal aid was that the companies were "too big to fail," that their size and significance ensured that both economy and nation could not thrive without the continued presence of its three largest car companies.

This book asks how we arrived at this point. How did corporations take on such an integral role in American society? How were these CEOs able to position their companies as central to the economy and, in turn, the economy as the defining feature of the nation? What role have appeals to size and interconnectivity played in this perception that economic institutions have become "too big" (and what does this designation mean for our collective imaginaries of the power of the nation-state)?

In responding to these questions, I argue that the rhetorical appeals positioning the corporation at the center of national, economic, and even personal systems of meaning have been long in the making—a century for car companies, but centuries for corporations generally. In this sense, I have opened with the bailout hearings as one notable (and expensive) moment in a much longer rhetorical history in which the corporation has enjoyed considerable advantages over other actors.

Indeed, a century before these bailout hearings, there were no giant car companies—let alone three big enough to be defining figures in the national economy. At the turn of the century, Ford Motor Company was a small but developing manufacturer in Detroit, Michigan. While it began by producing vehicles for recreational racing, in 1908 the company began producing the Model T for use by the general public. By 1911, the recorded number of cars sold in the United States was just over 200,000; in 1914, Ford began use of the moving assembly line, and by 1921, this number had ballooned to nearly 1.7 million—55 percent of which were Fords.[5] The company became so ingrained in the national economy in just under two decades that Ford's decision to stop production for six months in 1927—in order to switch from production of the Model T to the Model A—led to a national economic downturn. By 1934, the company, along with its two largest competitors (the same pair that joined Ford at the bailout hearings), replaced steel and railroads as the defining industries in America, and cars quickly became more than just a mode of transportation. Cars were, instead, presented as an important technological symbol for understanding the ebbs and flows of American society—economically and socially. In the words of an observer of the company in 1937,

> Americans cannot, however, help noticing the great impersonal corporations which dominate the American scene. And then, if they make comparisons, they find that the Ford organization is a corporation like other

corporations. To study it is to study the ways of all big enterprises. More, it is a model for corporations, a model of how to maintain a good repute and a lawless spirit at the same time.⁶

This part of Ford's story is well known; it may be one of the most well-documented and influential narratives in American economic history. Robert Jessop has argued that, for economists, the idea of "Fordism" that took shape over this period has come to represent "a particular configuration of the technical and social division of labor involved in making long runs of standardized goods" that resulted in an economy-defining "macro-economic regime" based on "a virtuous circle of growth based on mass production and mass consumption." To this day, this "virtuous circle" remains one of the most prominent narratives in economic and social imaginaries, particularly in the United States. This narrative has helped guide what kind of labor is imagined at the center of the economy (industrial workers and, especially, their managers rather than teachers, scientists, and farmers). It has been used to define what the purposes and responsibilities of corporations are. (Corporations are still imagined as the domain of producers/consumers and not entities bound to an investor class.) Finally, the story of Ford has defined many theories about what drives economic productivity (efficiency, competition, scale). For some, however, this economic narrative is mythologizing at its most insidious. John Kenneth Galbraith, for example, has argued that "the Ford myth is the first of the industrial fairy tales—not in total of course, but in considerable part. If we resolve, as we must, that the purveyors of fiction and bamboozlement not get the better of us, then we must start right there."⁷

Many have heeded Galbraith's advice. Jessop notes that Ford's story has had a profound impact on how we have come to understand the economy as a vast "mode of regulation" that consists of "an ensemble of norms, institutions, organizational forms, social networks, and patterns of conduct."⁸ In this latter framework, for cultural historians, Ford's story has been used to examine a number of similar principles: Michel Foucault's disciplinary "episteme" (McKinlay and Wilson), Thomas Kuhn's "paradigm" materialized (Lipietz, Roobeek), Max Weber's "bureaucratic" nightmare (Ray and Reed), and an ideal case for studying Joseph Schumpeter's and Karl Marx's separate accounts of "creative destruction."⁹ These theories share a perspective that reads history through the ebbs and flows of powerful systems that bring together knowledge, institutional practice, and personal systems of meaning that dominate for a period of time but are eventually replaced. From this perspective, Fordism rose to epistemic significance because the company collected a remarkably diverse array of objects, ideas, and people and organized them into something that could be understood as a salient, economically driven society. It fell (or, perhaps, is falling) when these networks were replaced or disrupted.

For all of this attention to the emergence of corporate culture, the role rhetoric played in producing this system has largely remained a conceptual touchstone rather than a point of detailed textual analysis. However, as Martin Sklar has pointed out, throughout the twentieth century, "the growth of the corporation was not 'organic' . . . capitalists and like-minded political and intellectual leaders fought hard and consciously, with 'doctrine and dogma' and with economic, political, and legal stratagem, to establish the large corporation, in a historically short period of time, as the dominant mode of business enterprise, and to attain popular acceptance of that development."[10]

Over this period of growth, Ford Motor Company produced and distributed thousands of texts—newspaper articles, pamphlets, photographs, and speeches. Most importantly, for this work at least, the company produced hundreds of motion pictures ranging from in-factory safety films to educational shorts to travelogues to full-length feature films. In fact, for a brief period of time in the late 1910s, the company boasted that it was the largest film producer in the world.[11] (In terms of financial investment and circulation, it probably was.)

In 1963, William Clay Ford presented the U.S. National Archives with nearly 300 hours of this film content.[12] Though only a fraction of the total output of films produced by the company, the films arrived at the National Archives as right around one and a half million feet of celluloid film spanning four decades of production and a number of cohesive rhetorical projects deployed by the company. With a few exceptions, the archive is composed of three kinds of motion-picture texts: complete and publicly circulated films, complete and internally circulated films, and hours of stock footage. After an appraiser labeled the films "priceless" but suggested around $200,000 for restoration, Ford donated the films and $200,400. Archivists sorted the materials into 2,425 entries in what is officially named the "Collection FC: Ford Motor Company Collection, ca. 1903–ca. 1954."[13]

These films represent a period of intense ideological inculcation that branched out in all directions, at once aligning social institutions (schools, community centers, homes), conceptions of labor and capital, the nature of commodities, roads, national parks, ideas about the home and community, senses of the global, senses of citizenship, the rise of movie stars, and even internal plumbing. Nothing seemed to escape the cameras at Ford as it brought all of these features under an expansive visual rubric. The connection of these many entities on-screen worked to expand a Fordist way of seeing in an increasingly wide sphere of influence spreading outward from Detroit, Michigan, to the American Midwest, to the whole of the United States, and to a number of global settings. In this sense, Fordism, for all of its material and economic might, was also a visual phenomenon—a mass configuration of new images and objects organized around a shifting conception of corporate capitalism.

Examining, through these films, the rise of Ford Motor Company from a small producer of hobbyist machinery to the face of corporate hegemony, this book presents a "rhetorical study of historical events" spanning the four decades captured in the archive. This was a particularly important period that witnessed vastly accelerated mass production, economic depression, war, and global reconstruction.[14] In the face of these events, Ford produced or sponsored films narrating and re-narrating a version of society in which corporate and industrial life was central. In examining these films, I argue that economies are powerful rhetorical constructs built to a large degree by large corporate institutions and produced as controlling narratives "incorporated" to their core.

Ford's films are also an opportunity to study the expanding rhetorical practices that developed during the first half of the twentieth century. Ford's story raises questions about the relationship between rhetoric and changing ideas about the aesthetic, new economic imaginaries, new configurations of space, new understandings of the sublime, and new structures of power as these relationships shifted in the face of changing media technologies and the rise of mass culture. In this sense, this book also serves as a "history of rhetorical events" that seeks to understand rhetoric in the early twentieth century, particularly as it was impacted by the motion picture.[15]

In exploring this history, this book pairs film, critical, and rhetorical theory to ask a number of questions about rhetoric and film: how does a concept like mise-en-scène, applied to read Ford's films, help unpack the impact of these films on debates over education in the Progressive Era? What effect did the cinematic technique of montage have on conceptions of the economy in the 1920s? How did the mobility of cameras and the motion in motion pictures help create "economized" spaces out of a national landscape in the interwar period? How did the spectacle of film, when paired with elaborate World's Fairs, work to combat doubts about mass culture after the Great Depression? Finally, how did depictions of Ford factories and workers around the world, as they were shown to the company's growing managerial class, impact the shape of post–World War II globalization by generating a corporate "world picture" filtered through the "managerial gaze"? What can we learn from these questions about the expanding nature of economic rhetoric at the time? What of corporations as rhetorical actors? Of rhetoric itself? In answering this second set of questions, Ford's films make it possible to study what I call "incorporational rhetoric."

Incorporational Rhetoric

As a broad theoretical framework, incorporational rhetoric is an approach to analyzing the large, distributed configurations of materials, texts, and ideas brought together by immense corporations like Ford. As Michael Warner has argued, "Our lives are minutely administered and recorded, to a degree unprecedented in history; we navigate a world of corporate agents that do not respond or act as people do."[16] There are many reasons, then, to approach corporate rhetoric as unique enough to warrant a bracketed, named iteration of rhetorical practice. Incorporational rhetoric is the work of a massive, distributed system of actors and producers; it is often executed simultaneously across a number of coordinated media; and it can sustain a consistent and cumulative presence for decades. But perhaps the most significant difference is that incorporational rhetoric's baseline rationalities lie in two concepts essential to economic reason: connection and coordination. Such an uncommon case, then, leads to an uncommon place to find a theory of rhetorical criticism: the intellectual legacy of Antonio Gramsci's theory of hegemony.

Notably, Gramsci's theories of political economy were positioned as a direct response to Ford Motor Company's rise. Throughout the early 1930s, from a cell in the Turi prison in southern Italy, Gramsci reflected on a pair of phenomena marking the changing relationship between, in the terms of Karl Marx, *societas rerum* (the society of things) and *societas hominem* (the society of men).[17] Gramsci called these new social relations "Americanism" and "Fordism," and they represented the organizational structures that developed from two institutions—one a nation, the other a corporation. When the nation and the corporation worked in concert, he suggested, they were able to produce "the biggest collective effort to date to create, with unprecedented speed, and with a consciousness of purpose unmatched in history, a new type of worker and of man."[18]

Highlighting both the textual and polysemic nature of how these institutions "compose," Gramsci argued that Ford's process of "making men" and "composing demographics" consisted of "a skillful combination of force (destruction of working-class trade unionism on a territorial basis) and persuasion (high wages, various social benefits, extremely subtle ideological and political propaganda) and thus succeed[ed] in making the whole life of the nation revolve around production."[19] Naming this process, Gramsci coined the term "hegemony," but rather than treating hegemony as an end product (i.e., simply pointing to Fordist hegemony), Gramsci presented the concept as an analytical tool for understanding the societal movement toward economic reason. As a method, Gramsci suggested the pairing of "historiography" and "the concept of hegemony" to create readings of social development that could identify the ideologies of capitalism and thereby "combat economism."[20]

Through these methods, Gramsci calls for a reading of history in which the ideological structures of economic power must be understood through the textual and, conversely, texts' meanings must be read through the material workings of immense institutions, state and company alike. In short, he points his readers' attention to the potential of rhetorical criticism when applied to totalizing arguments and massive rhetorical actors. (Notably, he also positions a wide array of concepts including wages and social benefits as textual in nature.)

Gramsci's approach argues that the rhetorical work of corporations is unique in that it goes beyond persuasion. Rather, corporate rhetoric relies on a network of "skillful combinations" that draws together humans, material objects, and ideas to create systems of meaning that appear to be closed, circular, and definitive. For incorporational rhetoric, success is a new perceived "reality" composed of a new kind of reason, new identities, and new spaces. Incorporational rhetoric thus produces entire systems of economic reason and action that appear natural and are ubiquitous.

This rhetoric, once applied, positions its user beyond the reach of traditional rhetoric. One needn't be persuaded of an idea; rather, one is simply positioned to see no other alternative (a concept that, notably, Margaret Thatcher would deploy decades later to describe the market economy and that would be at the heart of the "too big to fail" designation). In calling this process incorporational rhetoric, rather than hegemonic rhetoric, I follow a handful of scholars who have continued this work to describe an active and more readily observable process of producing hegemony.

Taking up Gramsci's framework, Raymond Williams has elaborated on the concept of incorporation as the process through which hegemony takes shape. Williams explains that "hegemony," as a critical term, "goes beyond ideology" in that it names "the whole lived social process as practically organized by specific and dominant meanings and values," whereas "ideology" is more simply "a relatively formal and articulated system of meanings, values, and beliefs."[21] Hegemony, then, "is always a more or less adequate organization and interconnection of otherwise separated and even disparate meanings, values, and practices, which it specifically incorporates in a significant culture and an effective social order."[22] Analyzing this "process of incorporation," Williams theorizes that true power takes shape when "the processes of education; the processes of much wider social training within institutions like the family; the practical definitions and organizations of work; the selective tradition at an intellectual and theoretical level ... are involved in a continual making and remaking of an effective dominant culture."[23]

Alan Trachtenberg continued this line of reasoning by arguing that the concept of incorporation "gives a name to visible signs of change and to less than visible causes and agencies of change."[24] He uses incorporation as "both a descriptive and an explanatory term ... braiding together of several stories into a single narrative of change." Writing of the eighteenth and nineteenth centuries, he notes the coordination between the "colonization of the West, standardization of time, accelerated mechanization of the means of production and the circulation of goods, the rise of metropolis, of department stores, railroad terminals, and tall office buildings."[25] More than this, his work reveals that these material configurations led to a collection of "less tangible outcomes," such as "new class formations and antagonisms, extreme polarization of the propertied and the property-less, a changing middle group increasingly comprised of managers, office workers, and professionals—and not least, altered meanings of keywords such as *land, work, city, civic,* and *incorporation* itself."[26]

In many ways, Williams's and Trachtenberg's works are groundbreaking for the study of incorporational rhetoric, though they largely provide broad readings of cultural trends. David R. Shumway's review of Trachtenberg's book *The Incorporation of America Today* highlights some of the generative places to expand the study of incorporation, however. For Shumway, Trachtenberg's work provides important broad strokes on the history of social change but maintains "a deep want to maintain Emersonian individuality at the center of cultural studies where a corporate-driven society denies any such desire" as well as "a lack of emphasis on 'monied corporations' as the source of a massive new kind of political and social domination that remains with us to this day."[27]

Rhetoric, I argue, is particularly useful for addressing Shumway's concerns for two reasons. First, rhetorical theory has a long history of naming specific textual effects that produce ideas, connection, and coordination that can explain the nature of a "corporate-driven society." Concepts like metonymy, synecdoche, and chiasmus all rely on connecting parts and wholes conceptually. Aesthetic rhetoric has a number of terms that describe the bringing together of ideas through style: mimesis, consonance, emulation, and analogy. Rhetorical studies of the sublime have inquired into the ways that ideas like amplitude and megethos can work to bring together wide configurations of people and ideas. In his work on identification, Kenneth Burke considered a variety of ideas that led to "consubstantiation"—the making of one from many—and this has led to the study of how texts create publics and counterpublics. In more recent scholarship, scholars of new materialism and ecological rhetorics examine how texts can serve as an entry point for studying networks of social and rhetorical action that are complex and dynamic. Applied to the work of Ford Motor Company, these concepts illuminate the active work of one "monied corporation" in the active, historical making of corporate culture.

Second, pairing rhetorical criticism with existing theories about incorporation presses rhetoric to move beyond approaching texts as a readable set of general appeals that can be identified, ordered, and applied from classical texts or traditions or as the work of producing mere ornamentation. Rather, incorporational rhetoric considers how rhetoric has been used to shift notions of what is "available"—both materially and recognized as appropriate—in a given period. For some, attending to these systemic networks surrounding persuasion serves as a wholesale reconceptualization of rhetoric itself. Ernesto Laclau has recently argued that we might understand rhetoric as a process for creating "the ideological effect *strictu senso*; the belief that there is a particular social arrangement that can bring about the closure and transparency of the community." He explains that this process is necessary for understanding not only why a text is persuasive to its audience but also how rhetoric is "inherent to . . . 'hegemony.'"[28] Michael Kaplan, extending Laclau's project, argues that this kind of rhetoric studies the "contingent, discursive, and fundamentally tropological process that brings objective reality into existence by imposing on an array of heterogeneous elements the semblance of a structure within which they acquire identity/meaning."[29]

In this frame, what gets studied as the rhetorical is the result of networks or systems of meaning either guided by powerfully supported actors (philosopher-tutors like Aristotle looking to the agora, theologians like Thomas Aquinas looking to examine and communicate the will of God, college professors like Kenneth Burke looking to understand the place of motive in deliberative democracy, or corporations looking to produce economized subjects) or understood through accounts of distributed action (rhetoric as it exists in the ever-fluid relationship among texts, meaning, mores, and the material context of cultures, particularly within specific historical periods). The former defines rhetoric's hegemonic nature—its propagation of structures of power—and the latter its dynamic fluidity—how individual actors work within and against these ideological structures to achieve more personal, and sometimes collective, goals. In this book, I study Ford's films in this former hegemonic framework for rhetorical action, working to account for how rhetoric was used to align society with the needs of corporate capitalism. When the three CEOs argued that their companies were instrumental to the lives of so many, they drew attention to the success that corporations have achieved in becoming such a "social arrangement" that has brought "objective reality into existence."

As a field tied intimately to texts, however, rhetoric is also useful for its commitment to textual histories. Most rhetorical appeals were developed in relation to a text or set of texts, and for every text there is a history that is integral to understanding how that text responds to the rhetorical challenges of its particular moment. As Gramsci's notes were being smuggled out of a prison hospital in southern Italy, for example, Ford's films had been in circulation for nearly two decades. As he wrote, then, thousands of Americans were sitting in theaters, churches, and YMCAs taking in images of Yellowstone National Park, assembly lines in Detroit, and a World's Fair in Chicago produced by Ford whose direct purpose was to enact the very structures of power being theorized. It is to these questions of circulation and accumulation that I turn next.

The Rise of Corporate Film

Ford Motor Company opened its Motion Picture Laboratory, one of the earliest and largest in-house corporate film departments of its kind, on the whim of the company's founder. Seemingly persuaded of the public potential of motion pictures (likely by his friend Thomas Edison), at some point in April 1914, Henry Ford walked into his advertising department and put Ambrose B. Jewett in charge of producing public films for the company.³⁰ Film was particularly well suited to Ford's needs for a few reasons. First, as Ford began investing heavily in the technology, many were touting the potential for film to have a revolutionary impact on educating the public. As Orgeron et al. have noted, Ford's rapid rise came in a period rich with "faith in educational reform and the betterment of society," and this optimism "was perfectly matched with the educational capabilities of the motion picture."³¹ Second, film was particularly amenable to replicating Fordist reason because, as Elspeth Brown has argued, "film decomposes and recombines movement into standardized, individual units (the film frames, the shot)." For this reason, she argues, film was an ideal tool "for espousing industrial ideology," which was predicated on the combination of many moving parts.³² Finally, film was capable of mass distribution rivaling newspapers and radio. The medium not only could depict hundreds of concepts in a related fashion, it also could present these related items around the country through coordinated distribution processes.

Using this medium, the company was able to expand its rhetorical influence to include texts on innumerable subjects being depicted to millions of moviegoers around the world. While it would be a stretch to argue that without film there would be no Fordism, the emergence of the medium certainly played an important role in the economic shape of the world, an idea Lee Grieveson has recently studied in depth as he positions Ford's films as integral texts in a larger movement of films that "explicated and extolled the advantages of the new technologies, economic practices, and infrastructural and circulatory networks of the second-stage industrial revolution and the ascendant corporate and monopoly stage of capitalism."³³ Ford's films worked across decades and faced many, often interrelated rhetorical challenges, the first of which was to answer why the public shouldn't be deeply skeptical of films being produced by a company designed to build and sell cars.

Soon after Henry Ford's appearance in the advertising department, the newly formed Ford Motor Company Motion Picture Laboratory began distributing *The Ford Animated Weekly*, a series committed to projecting seemingly innocuous narratives of Americana (e.g., baseball games, visits to American cities, celebrities motoring about) as extensions of an emerging Fordist way of life. In many ways, *The Ford Animated Weekly* was indiscernible from other newsreels of the time, offering up simple depictions of day-to-day life in America. The fragments of this series that made it into the National Archives depict football games at the University of Michigan, parades on Detroit streets, and sightseeing trips to cities around the country. Ford's earliest motion pictures appeared in the lives of many Americans as simply one more innovation from the company that had already provided the moving assembly line, the five-dollar-a-day profit-sharing plan, the Ford English School, and an in-house Industrial Sociology Department (all introduced in or around 1914).

In this sense, the earliest films were experienced as a process of gradual immersion—a seemingly hands-off depiction of the world to the public and a bit of good fun. For the company, however, the newsreels' purpose was more pointed. The *Ford Times*, one of the company's many newspapers, suggested that these early films "are used as one of the important mediums to disseminate the Ford idea [in manufacture and social and industrial welfare] in a very big and broad way. And incidentally they instruct and entertain by putting the public in touch with world events."[34] While Ford's films were openly ideological texts for the company, seeking first to inculcate and only "incidentally" to entertain, entertain they did.

Remarkably, at a time when there were considerable concerns over the ramifications of most commercial films and in spite of the internal goal of disseminating the "Ford Idea," Ford's films were praised for their ability to resist overtly commercialized material. In one account of the films early in their distribution, film critic Gladys Bollman wrote that "[t]he best of industrials contain little or no specific advertising matter. The *Ford Weekly*, for instance, contains no reference to the Ford Car except in the title 'Produced by Ford Motor Company.' It is one of the best one-reel picture shows now on the market, and was welcomed ... at almost all theaters."[35]

Rapidly capturing the attention of roughly one in ten moviegoers with its weekly offerings, Ford's Motion Picture Laboratory would go on to develop a remarkably diverse collection of films: full-length feature films, travelogues, educational films, sales and marketing materials, war propaganda, safety instruction films, and films explaining the nature of production practices. Ford's films were also part of a far more expansive set of texts within the company—built environments (factories, roads, mines) captured by the films, coordinated media efforts to promote and frame their reception, and competing narratives produced by other organizations.

Helping to set the tone for corporate communication at the time, other prominent industrial organizations took up the practice of having utility films produced and circulated as well. Examples of these series include training films by Western Union, *The Chevrolet Leader News*, *The Goodyear Newsreel*, and a series produced by the Jam Handy marketing firm for General Motors. Collectively, then, private corporations were producing and distributing hours of cinematic material dedicated to keeping the public informed about news, innovations, and economic "realities."[36]

By the early 1920s, Ford's motion pictures were integral elements of a number of public exhibitions; they traveled as offerings screened by civic entities and played in YMCAs nationwide. The films also were distributed to dealerships to help with promotional series, were used to teach safety to workers in theaters built within Ford's factories, and served as feature presentations in mainstream theaters across the country.[37] Through this extensive distribution scheme, over the first six years of the Laboratory's work (1914 to 1920), Ford's films were reportedly shown in more than 4,000 venues to five million people, or "roughly one-seventh of the nation's weekly movie-going audience"; translated into eleven different languages; and shown internationally.[38] In the early months of 1920, a story ran in newspapers around the country declaring that Ford Motor Company's films enjoyed the "world's largest circulation," an argument that remains to this day a part of the films' narrative. At the apex of their relative circulation in 1920, *Film World and A-V News* reported that the *Ford Animated Weekly* was being "shown in 2,000 theaters to 4 million U.S. visitors weekly," while the *Ford Educational Weekly* was being shown regularly "in 7,000 theaters across the country and reached between 10 and 12 million viewers."[39]

The first ten years of film production might be considered a long honeymoon period for Fordism. John Kenneth Galbraith called this the company's "ecstatic" phase, explaining that "Ford's view of Ford was widely accepted at face value."[40] The work taking place at the company was heralded around the world. The combination of this wide circulation and framing the films as yet another Fordist innovation would help the company spread a vast aesthetic framework that would further normalize machinery and production while also positioning them as powerful extended analogies for understanding knowledge, economies, and the idea of a well-lived modern life. More than this, the very presence of these films argued that one could "see" the Fordist economy—allowing for the company to convince its many viewers to accept the wholesale shifts in economic relations taking place at the time.

If the first decade of Ford's films highlights the ability for the medium to introduce and then embed industrial capitalism into much of society, the next fifteen years was a period of rhetorical work dedicated to defending this system—Galbraith would call these the "doubtful" years.[41] Two events make clear the need for such defense. In 1924, Henry Ford disrupted the work of Ford Motor Company, the institutional rhetor, by sponsoring an abhorrent series of anti-Semitic articles published in the *Dearborn Independent* between April 1924 and May 1925.[42]

The powerful executive, national icon, and figure perceived as an industrial savant was quickly forgiven and distanced from the articles, which in many ways indicates the power economism already held in the United States. Economic ideology insulated the idea of Fordism from the prejudices contained both in its infrastructure and in the ideas of its figurehead, and the public was unwilling to condemn a man and a company already so integral to its own prosperity. In this sense, the "Jewish campaign" is just one more example that, particularly in America, perception of economic acumen cures all sorts of ills, but we don't need deep rhetorical analysis to understand this point. What the stain of the events did do was remove the perception that both the company and man were pure champions of the everyman and cast considerable doubts on the other media the company was producing. In his oral history of the company, E. G. Liebold, Henry Ford's longtime personal secretary (and a figure also closely associated with the anti-Semitic publications), explained the fallout by saying "they had men all around the world, I think, who were taking motion pictures . . . As soon as the Jewish campaign came on . . . sources immediately banned the Ford films, and we discontinued that."[43]

Company records suggest, however, that while Ford's films would never reach the same proportion of public exposure after this, the medium still maintained significant circulation and continued to play a variety of important roles throughout the first half of the twentieth century. The Ford Film Laboratory still produced a number of films in the late 1920s, but the archive contains far fewer films from this period when compared to the first half of the decade. When that economic buffer collapsed with the onset of the Great Depression, however, Ford would not so easily avoid criticism.

Ford fared particularly poorly during the Great Depression. Murmurs nationally suggested that the company's Security Department, run by Harry Bennett, was running amok and that Henry Ford had lost touch. The pair consistently clashed with unions, and tensions escalated throughout the 1930s, culminating in the Battle of the Overpass in 1937, wherein Ford "security" forces violently suppressed a crowd marching on its factory. The episode virtually erased any goodwill the company had built up over the previous two decades.

As Douglas Brinkley has described the situation, "Ford Motor Company of the mid-1930s is typically regarded as a dark, almost gothic place, with a shadowy administration, activities shrouded in mystery, and a roster of dubious characters running rampant on the premises."[44] Making matters worse, the company could not simply tout its economic acumen as a defense for the righteousness of its actions or its superiority over unions. The company was faring poorly financially, General Motors had outpaced Ford for some time, and Chrysler had overtaken Ford in overall production in 1933. Watching Ford's films, however, one would never know any of this. Due to this economic pressure, rising distrust in Ford's management, and the rise of "soundies," the company shut down its in-house film laboratory in 1932 and turned instead to outside agencies to create and distribute visual materials on its behalf (with the exception of a set of films produced by the company for the Department of the Interior). Script approval, however, remained with the company.[45]

Where Ford's earliest in-house films had worked to attune the public to industrial life, the company's contracted films in the 1930s worked to quell concerns over capitalism after the Great Depression and used a new set of rhetorical frameworks to do so. These films are predominantly longer and more complex than the short, serially released films that appear earlier in the archive. Three genres of film were prominent in this period: travelogues, World's Fair films, and a set of Hollywood-like feature films. Collectively, these films would circulate as a growing series distributed by Ford's dealers to a wide variety of local institutions throughout the 1930s.[46] The purpose of these films is hard to miss. They make up a collection of films designed to distract and dazzle. This change from education to entertainment was a response to a set of competing visual projects deeply critical of Fordism and sweeping shifts in legislation—particularly the New Deal—attempting to jump-start a damaged economy by sheer force of scale and will. This was an era of grand industrial and infrastructural spectacle (attempting to compensate for economic depression), and its visual culture offered up similarly scaled texts.

As I interpret them, the films produced in this period worked to deflect the initial damage wrought by the Great Depression and gradually nurture the public's faith in the mass industrial organization—and capitalism more generally. Over time, these appeals worked to bring the public back to corporate actors as important figures not just in economic relations nationally but in their personal and political lives as well. Company reports show that nearly ten million people viewed this collection of films in 1940, and nearly six million attended screenings of these films at various branch locations around the country in just three months (January to March) of 1941.⁴⁷

As a result of this rhetorical work to keep faith in industrial capitalism in the 1930s, the nation was primed to embrace arguments that World War II was an industrial war and eventually a victory for the productive economic power of the United States. During the war, many corporate actors created films that played on the theme of the "Arsenal of Democracy," which argued that the United States' production practices were the defining feature of a free, capitalist world. This theme would carry throughout the war as corporate actors consistently used wartime production as a pretense for arguing that the United States' true power lay in its productive powers and that these powers were made possible by two features: visionary and efficient managers and prideful but pliant workers.

In the 1950s, industrial films flourished. A *New York Times* article from 1954 quotes J. R. Bingham, president of Associated Films, Inc. (a distributor), declaring that "[t]he growth of the sponsored film field has been tremendous since the end of World War II . . . our roster of film-using organizations . . . has grown from 36,000 non-theatrical exhibitors in 1946 to more than 90,000 today."⁴⁸ Industrial capitalism was back in the limelight as the driving feature of global reconstruction. Ford continued to be an important part of this rise. A 1955 company memo suggests that Ford was working hard to reach the same circulation as its chief competitor GM, which was enjoying a yearly film circulation of seventy million viewers, and by 1961, just two years before the collection was donated to the National Archives, Ford Motor Company captured an annual film audience of sixty million.⁴⁹

While chapters of this book take up these periods of rhetorical development individually, when they are taken collectively, part of the rhetorical force of Ford's films came from the sheer quantity of films produced and circulated as well as the consistency with which they were screened for the public over a long period of time. Attending to this force becomes particularly important when addressing institutions with deep pockets and wide reach that can create a sustained presence in the public sphere for years. With such considerable circulation, these films developed into a shared experience for many Americans—in both the act of attending a screening and the acquisition of knowledge held therein. Throughout the first half of the twentieth century, millions took in Ford-sponsored or Ford-produced films. To accept the cumulative narratives presented in these films meant identifying oneself as an active member of a larger public that was responsible for the upkeep of a society built around immense economic institutions.

Rhetoric has used a number of ideas to understand this kind of sustained and distributed rhetorical process. First, Ford's films make clear the importance of attending to circulation in understanding rhetorical force.[50] Working to define and direct the public amid these various challenges, Ford built a vast distribution system for its films throughout the twentieth century and surrounded this system with a number of supplementary messages framing the value of the films. Ford, in this sense, had far more control over who would see its films and in what context than most. Because of this control, the company was able to treat distribution as part of the rhetorical process—making where, when, and how the films were seen an extension of the meanings being proffered.

Second, these films point to the potential of studying channels that develop via what Michael Warner has called a "concatenation of texts over time."[51] These channels lead to a number of rhetorical advantages not necessarily recognized when studying single events and texts. For these individuals, the company kept a powerful industrial aesthetic in circulation for decades; narratives about roads that were crucial for decisions made in 1930 began in 1914; eventual suburbanization in 1945 depended on films explaining decentralization in 1930; and postwar globalization relied on forty years of films, photographs, and narratives that presented the world as a site for economic development. More than any of these individual threads, however, this history highlights that children who watched Ford's educational films in the 1910s took to the roads in the 1920s, bought homes in the 1930s, and provided an immediate pool of middle managers readily prepared to take up the mantle of global superpower via the military-industrial might of the nation. Corporations suggest that we might better consider generational time frames for understanding rhetorical practice.

Finally, in addition to offering insights into the temporal elements of sustained arguments on a single topic, the sheer volume of texts produced by the company creates what Christa Olson has termed "agglutination," a term that recognizes the "cumulative force" accrued by serial texts. Many of Ford's rhetorical projects required rhetorical tasks dependent on size and networked action.[52] Building roads or industrializing the national landscape required enormous coordination between communities and economic sectors. Sometimes the company simply relied on the argument that bigger is better; at other times it relied on the production of sizable publics attuned to witnessing its economic developments. The sheer quantity and geographical spread of the films make important contributions to these projects.

In sum, these films—their circulation, their concatenation, their agglutination—all highlight the impact of a massive corporate filmmaker on visual culture in the earliest, foundational years of cinema's rise. Ford's films had an important role to play in shaping what Charles R. Acland and Haidee Wasson have called "the middle period of American film history," which took place within what Orgeron et al. have called the "cinematic century"—a period marked by the rise of mass publics and considerable shifts in ideas about the visual.[53] Jonathan Beller, however, takes these features a step further, arguing that as a result of this proliferation of film production and circulation, "machine-mediated perception now is inextricable from . . . psychological, economic, visceral, and ideological dispensations. Spectatorship, as the fusion and development of the cultural, industrial, economic and psychological, quickly gained a handhold on human fate and then became decisive." For this reason, he concludes that "[n]ow, visuality reigns and social theory needs to become film theory."[54] Beller's point, as I read it, is that Ford's films contributed to sweeping shifts that would challenge spoken and written argument as the defining constructs for making meaning in the period. Indeed, the motion picture provided a wide variety of affordances that have been integral to the rhetoric used by the company over this period. Film's ability to overlay images, sounds, motion, and pacing helped the company to present industrial life as a unified, understandable, and often attractive whole. In Ford's films, specifically, this whole was presented as a vision of "the economy"—a knowable system worthy of allegiance and a system in which the corporation is the defining entity.

Film Rhetoric

Rhetoric and film have a considerable shared history, and a number of frameworks have been developed to unpack the rhetorical nature of cinema. As David Blakesley has argued, however, the study of film is strengthened when scholars approach films using "competing perspectives." Some of these perspectives have included approaching film as a collection of texts that can be drawn on to produce more complex meanings (Plantinga); rhetoric as a lens in an Aristotelian sense—the application of classic terms about persuasion to film (Bordwell); and the application of a Burkean frame (which examines how films produce identifications) to film criticism (Blakesly). My hope is that this book continues this interdisciplinary work in two ways.

First, it contributes to the growing literature on industrial and sponsored films. In spite of their considerable circulation, consistent use across decades, and role in larger cultural shifts, films like Ford's have been a footnote in historical accounts of capitalism, in studies of rhetoric, and in analyses of film. Reversing this oversight in film studies, Vinzenz Hediger and Patrick Vonderau have argued that industrial and utility films of this kind have served as a set of important "interfaces between discourses and forms of social and industrial organization" in which "what is at stake . . . is the complex interrelationship of visuality, power, organization and specifically how film as a medium creates the preconditions for forms of knowledge and social practice."[55] For this reason, Hediger and Vonderau argue that "films made by and for the purposes of industrial and social organizations constitute the next big chunk of uncharted territory in cinema studies"—they also, I argue, offer important challenges to rhetorical studies of the economy.[56]

During this period, film allowed the company to treat images as it did resources—as objects to be captured, manipulated, aligned with other images, and ultimately disseminated as a produced way of seeing the world but also to accumulate and distribute a particular model of publicity—a steadily growing and largely complacent collective of witnesses to industry's rise. These various genres of film had an impact on many important debates: how to educate the public, how to understand the nature of the economy, how to interpret both the Great Depression and World War II, and how to expand globally. Studies of visual culture in this era are incomplete without some attention to the visual work of corporations, but, conversely, I contend that rhetoric is an important framework for approaching films of this nature.

Second, I see the idea of "incorporational rhetoric" as a useful "perspective" for approaching this kind of film. Debra Hawhee and Paul Messaris have recently suggested that visual rhetoricians have been excellent at providing "broader theoretical conclusions about the power of images" but have been much less successful in exploring "what makes images *special*, in comparison with words and other means of communication."[57] A brief overview of theories about film suggests that motion pictures are "special" rhetorical objects for their ability to connect and combine different objects with greater speed and complexity than written texts, speeches, and photographs.

Filtering film scholarship through the "perspective" of incorporational rhetoric reveals that when film scholars have written about film, they have done so using language that depends less on ideas of persuasion or identification and more on the concept at the heart of the incorporational—"skillful combination." Mise-en-scène has been described as the bringing together of many elements of film production to produce discrete "shots." Montage describes the incorporation of these "shots" into sequences. Deleuze's theory of movement-images describes how these sequences produce particular configurations of space—cohesive mental maps that often organize the world beyond the film. Spectatorship moves beyond the film itself to describe how these collected cinematic features encourage identification within viewers (singular) and between audiences/publics (plural). Finally, gaze theory considers how vision itself can be used to produce homogeneity out of complexity. As general observations, these features of making many textual features condense into one cohesive narrative are interesting in their own right. However, when applied to the case of a corporation, whose central goal was to rope together as much of society as possible under the confines of its ideological positions (that is, to produce hegemony), these features become undeniably rhetorical.

———

On Corporate Archives

A final word on the method and scope of this work: if rhetoric is an analytical framework used to "read" a society through the texts it produces, then the discipline itself has archival properties as it collects and organizes a wide collection of texts and then draws from them a series of observable effects. However, these readings are always partial, and while historically rhetoricians have been less inclined to explain why particular texts have been selected as the corpus for developing theories of rhetoric, contemporary rhetoricians point to the importance of attending to the study of textuality itself—that is, supplementing close reading with accounts of where and how the studied texts, and the analytical approaches used to understand them, became available.

In the case of archival work like this, Lynée Gaillet has argued that "[h]istorians of rhetorical practice examine archives in an effort to seek nuanced, complicated tales—ones moored to their own times and cultural exigencies."[58] Indeed, I entered my archival work seeking to understand the nature of corporate rhetoric, and this guided many choices about where and how to look at these materials. However, in seeking these tales, rhetoricians have also argued that researchers must recognize that, as Cara Finnegan has put it, "archives—even seemingly transparent image archives—function as terministic screens, simultaneously revealing and concealing 'facts,' at once enabling and constraining interpretation."⁵⁹

The material in this book largely drew from the content of two archives that have been particularly important to the production of an economized account of Ford's history and also illustrate the difficulty of historical work with such powerful corporate rhetoricians. These sites are very much material places that I read as contributing to a third, abstract archive—a mental depository that holds the collective of events and artifacts as they have been organized into the social structure called, variably, Fordism or "managerial" capitalism. As a stored collection, Ford's films already work to, in Charles Bazerman's terms, "draw together heterogeneous pieces from heterogeneous circumstances" and give them the appearance of a unified narrative, which I have, in turn, used to generate a seemingly unified rhetorical history.⁶⁰

The first archive is an outpost of U.S. National Archives located in College Park, Maryland. While the archive itself looks like a relatively innocuous suburban depot (with an above-average food court, if you ever get the chance to visit), inside sits what Jacques Derrida has called the *archontic*—a location that contains not just the laws of a society but its history and identity; a site where a cultural imaginary is made. Derrida suggests in *Archive Fever* that texts, when archived, become powerful by "existing in this uncommon place, this place of election where law and singularity intersect in *privilege*" and help to valorize particular understandings of the culture doing the archiving.⁶¹

In these terms, the presence of Ford's films in the National Archives is itself one form of enunciation declaring that the corporation holds a place in the *archos* of American history.⁶² The very possibility of the present work is, in this sense, just one more arrow in the spacious rhetorical quiver proffered by corporate and economic actors. The ability to first store the films in a private archive and then gain access, through extraordinary financial means, to the historical depository of a nation positions the film archive itself as simply one branch in a grand rhetorical apparatus available to corporate actors.

In seeking to contextualize these films and to unearth this development, I turned to a second archive. This one appears to be far less common, though no less important, to cultural constructions of the past. It lies just outside the gates of Greenfield Village, an Americana-themed amusement park and historical reenactment site adjacent to Ford Motor Company's manufacturing site in Dearborn, Michigan. (Greenfield Village is another story that has fallen to the cutting-room floor of this text.) I entered the small work area to the marches of John Philip Sousa, having walked past a statue of Henry Ford and picked my way through school field trips and tourists. I bought a mug in the gift shop on my way out.

The company's public archives, as these anecdotes suggest, are much more clearly a site designed to use history rhetorically—to engage in the economization of national memory. If the films' presence in the National Archives positions Ford's story as a narrative of national importance, the work of the Ford archive highlights another of Derrida's points: an archive can function both "as accumulation" and as the "*capitalization* of memory on some substrate and in an exterior place."[63]

The entire Greenfield Village complex serves as a material history of the American economy, and the archives adjacent to it tell the documentary history of this tale. In collecting, storing, and ordering a century of advertising materials, internal correspondence, and general miscellany, Ford's archive retains an important documentary history of Ford Motor Company. Functioning in conjunction with the Benson Ford Research Center, these films function as more than just a set of texts designed to entertain and inform and as one integral node in a much more expansive economic treatise documented by the company: a treatise distributed across decades and genres. As I read them, these are just two of many institutions—corporate, academic, and national—that have saved and circulated millions of texts integral to the proliferation of economized narratives of history. In short, they are just one more act of incorporation.

All of this is to say that while I position the Ford Motor Company collection as a rare opportunity to analyze a corporate actor at work in the production of symbolic material as it accrues over time, it would be a mistake to view these films as striations stacked on top of one another to reveal a transparent set of economic narrations from the first half of the twentieth century. Rather, Ford's film archive is itself a rhetorical act—it, like all archives, suggests connections, materializes particular forms of history, and exists within material structures that produce many extra-textual messages.

Perhaps the most obvious way that this archive has functioned as a rhetorical entity is, as Cara Finnegan has pointed out, the erasures that come about when official history is written only using recognized or sponsored archives. Housed in the National Archives, these films present a curated history, an anesthetized historical account of the stories Ford hoped to tell. To accept this archive as it is is to hear its sponsored voices; to see these films is to also see the power dynamics that stamp out the voices and bodies, the frameworks and rhetorics that did not have the kind of institutional support required to create and sustain expositions, films, and archives to keep their memory alive. I am afraid I contribute more often than I would like to this process. At the same time, this will make up one of the running themes in this book: meaning-making practices often work through omission.

There are, in this sense, many stories not told in the archive: stories of Ford's complicated racial relations, Henry Ford's anti-Semitism, or Harry Bennett and the violent suppression of union members, for example. These issues, unsurprisingly, appear only tangentially in the company's films: the negative narratives featuring bankers and financiers or Bolsheviks appear as thinly veiled codings of Henry Ford's anti-Semitism, a handful of unedited clips of manager strikes, and the sporadic mention of "calamity howlers" and labor troublemakers.

The film collection's unbalanced historicity is particularly clear when looking at proportion across the archive. For example, there are two entries in the collection involving labor strikes (an integral part of the era of Fordism), yet there are more than ten entries related to "threshing" (a less integral part). As a rhetorical history in situ, however, these omissions and inclusions tell a compelling story about the construction of history itself. In the ethos of a corporation being constructed by Ford Motor Company, what happened to grain harvesting was revolutionary; what happened with the strikes was ancillary.

The chapters that follow, then, represent threads that I observed across the archives' contents. Some of these were organized formally by Ford (as in the case of the official series of educational or management training films); others, however, cut across the archive itself (as in the case of Ford's "rhetorical economy" or space films). My goal, then, follows Jeremy Packer's argument that "thinking about the archive via the apparatus means thinking outside questions of signification and spectatorship, of the adequacy, effectiveness, and fidelity of meanings and messages. Rather, it is to address communications and media as mechanisms for linking things together, as articulations in networks, as the glue and the infrastructure of apparatuses."[64]

In this sense, these sites contribute to a very different kind of archive in American history. Existing somewhere between historiography and foundational myth, the history of market-mediated capitalism oriented around increasingly large corporate entities guided by visionary figureheads has been buttressed by an expansive depository of stories, commonplaces, data points, and acts of economic proselytizing. Each of these archives might be further understood as examples of what Derrida has explored as an "eco-*nomic* archive" that "keeps, it puts in reserve, it saves, but in an unnatural fashion, that is to say in making the law (*nomos*) or in making people respect the law."⁶⁵ For Ford's films, this "law" amounts to a collective argument over the importance of economic reason and the industrial corporation.

In this sense, even as a partial account of historical events, there is much to learn about the rhetorical shape (and shaping) of the contemporary, economized world through these texts. This abstracted understanding of an "archive" is one way Michel Foucault used the term when describing his methodological framework of "archaeology." Archeological research is a critical approach to understanding regimes of truth; an archive, he explains, is "the set (l'ensemble) of discourses actually pronounced" in a given epistemological period.⁶⁶ For Foucault, then, archeological methods function to "show how certain things—state and society, sovereign and subjects, etcetera—were actually able to be formed, and the status of which should obviously be questioned."⁶⁷ In turn, this means treating the objects in an archive—material or abstract—"not only as events having occurred, but as 'things,' with their own economies, scarcities, and (later in his thought) strategies that continue to function, transformed through history and providing the possibility of appearing for other discourses."⁶⁸

Throughout this work, I argue that Ford's films present small glimpses into the historical project of reconfiguring a nation (and eventually many nations) into an economic entity guided by industrial corporations. In this sense, this work contributes to an ongoing conversation in rhetorical studies concerned with understanding how economies have been presented to the public as a set of frameworks that are central to understanding the world. The chapters that follow, then, examine what I see as a particularly important episode in a long and complex history, a history that economic rhetoricians seek to unearth (to follow Foucault's metaphor) in order to observe how a society built on economic reason and organized around corporate power was "actually able to be formed."

Chapter Overview

A number of threads run through this text with the goal of addressing a wide disciplinary audience. For those coming to this text looking for film history, the book might be approached as a work that sorts the "industrial film" into five genres (education films, "rhetorical economy" films, spatial films, World's Fair films, and management training films). These films, in turn, provide an opportunity to revisit a handful of important historical debates. Chapter 1 examines debates over American public education in the Progressive Era; chapter 2, a national debate over the nature and direction of the interwar economy; chapter 3, a struggle over conceptions of the national landscape; chapter 4, a struggle over the nature of the public in the wake of the Great Depression; and chapter 5, questions over how to develop post–World War II globalization. Notably, each of these debates was seemingly won by corporate interests (that is, at each of these points, an important part of social life was incorporated into industrial capitalism).

For those approaching this book as a work analyzing film rhetoric, within these historical contexts each chapter presents a different pairing of film theory and rhetorical theory. Chapter 1 combines studies of mise-en-scène with rhetorical studies of "similitude." Chapter 2 combines montage theory with rhetorical analysis concerned with "topics" or *topoi*. Chapter 3 combines ideas of cinematic mobility with theories of spatial rhetoric. Chapter 4 considers a shared approach to spectatorship in film and rhetorical studies grounded in the idea of affect. Chapter 5 aligns these various approaches with the idea of producing a "gaze."

Putting these together with greater detail, chapter 1 examines Ford's educational films as they circulated between 1918 and 1927 using two analytical frameworks: similitude and mise-en-scène. By producing a uniform industrial aesthetic and applying it to a wide variety of ideas, by emulating the structure of arguments being made by educational theorists like John Dewey, and by collapsing distinctions between schools and factories, the company successfully mapped what has been called the "corporate image of society" onto public education—the effects of which are still in effect today.

The second chapter examines the idea of montage rhetoric, particularly as it was integral to the company's ability to produce what I explore as a "rhetorical economy" by addressing and connecting a number of economic *topoi* on-screen. Using a 1921 film titled *As Dreams Come True*, I argue that economies are rhetorical constructs predicated on aligning ideas of imagined futures, labor, value, and capital while also embedding these concepts in terms drawn from the everyday lives of their intended audience.

The third chapter takes up the idea that the motion picture (as its name more or less gives away) is a particularly powerful medium for making spatial arguments. The movement of cameras, the selection and positioning of landscapes, and the interplay of these spaces and perspectives to create setting are all done to enhance the film's rhetorical power. In Ford's films, I argue, the company used this mobility to generate a sense of "interstitiality" that remapped the United States as an economic space. This process of producing the interstitial involved breaking down traditional boundaries (between the local and the national, between industry and agriculture, and between the natural world and consumption) and replacing them with an immense interconnected system of economically based spatial dynamics—marketplaces, decentralization, and spaces of middle-class consumption. Through this extensive network of films, then, Americans were led to reconceive their relationship to one another, their neighborhoods, and their relationships with the natural world.

In the fourth chapter, I turn to theories of spectatorship to better understand a set of World's Fair films that accompanied massive events conducted by corporate actors throughout the 1930s. Responding to critiques of corporate capitalism, corporate actors complexly reconfigured the core of the economy to become about witnessing and consuming the development of the economy itself rather than viewing it as purely a system of production. An important step in this process was to (re)produce a public that could happily witness the comings and goings of mass production–mediated capitalism on-screen. Applying a series of concepts drawn from rhetorical registers that account for audience-making practices—*theoros, megethos, amplitude,* and *hyperbole*—I argue that Ford's World's Fair films animate a number of critical theories describing the effects of this kind of economic sublimation (Walter Benjamin's "phantasmagoria," Guy Debord's "Society of Spectacle").

Finally, the fifth chapter draws on the line of critical analyses of film working outward from "gaze" theory to understand the powerful rhetorical construct generated during and after World War II to produce a neocolonial way of seeing in which the white male Western executive exerted tremendous power over the development of global economic and social development. *Women on the Warpath* enacts, at once, Althusserian hailing and the application of the managerial gaze. *Around the World with Ford Motor Company*, on the other hand, operationalizes this managerial gaze to train an internal set of middle managers to enact particular forms of global capitalism.

When taken collectively, these chapters display a growing network of corporate influence that used a wide variety of rhetorical and cinematic techniques to incorporate a larger and larger network of ideas, people, and objects. It is this network upon which the modern corporate structure and economy are based.

1

Spreading the Industrial Aesthetic in Ford's Educational Films

Ford's ability to expand beyond its status as a producer of cars was, in many ways, a matter of fortuitous timing. At the beginning of the twentieth century, questions of industry, national identity, and education were being presented to the public as interrelated pieces in a larger discussion over the values that would guide a nation—all of this has been written into history as the Progressive Era. Describing the period, John Dewey identified three systems vying for centrality at the time: "industrial competency" (a nation guided by economic production), "civic efficiency or good citizenship" (a nation guided by democratic decision-making), and a "cultural" approach (a nation dedicated to "cultivation with respect to appreciation of ideas and art and broad human interests").[1] Many Progressives at the time would argue in similar systemic terms but add an all-or-nothing framework to the discussion. Herbert David Croly, for example, argued that any "genuinely national system must possess unity as well as inclusiveness; and the unity can be obtained only by active cooperation of its different parts for the realization of a common purpose."[2] In this frame, the most successful argument for how to educate in American public schools would not necessarily be the most rational, or even ethical, but the approach that could most clearly connect education to its vision of national development. In this sense, the debate over Progressive education is, in its own right, an interesting case for studying incorporational rhetoric as the nation self-consciously debated which of a number of social systems could most effectively guide a new era of progress.

This period is interesting for a second reason, however. Visual materials and performances circulated throughout these debates to create a set of competing aesthetic arguments. Leslie A. Hahner, for example, has extensively studied how "Good Citizenship" Progressives produced a "'Republican aesthetic'—an eye-catching style that highlighted the virtues of nationalism and the need for collective action." Nathan Crick and Jeremy Engels have analyzed how at least one cultural Progressive sought to use the aesthetic affordances of poetry to produce "a new rhetorical practice which would call the citizen to be a certain type of person, a type of community, a type of nation," and Carol Quirke has noted that the "industrial competency" Progressives, in part, produced "a populist aesthetic that suffused America's visual culture" by drawing on narratives of the down-and-out laborer toiling honorably.[3] Such attention to the aesthetic as a rhetorical practice was fitting in the face of these systemically minded debates because, as James Porter has argued, "[a]esthetics, and notably the aesthetic dimensions of rhetoric, are the materials through which [fundamental ideologies and beliefs about meaning and experience] are 'sutured': through these, culture appears to cohere, and its subjects can form passionate attachments to their culture."[4] Similarly, for Alan Singer, the aesthetic defines far more than a pure sensory act of enjoyment. Instead, the aesthetic is "a presentation of sensuous particulars that compels a reconfiguration of conceptual wholes," and these conceptual wholes impact "rational choice-making and ethical subjectivity."[5]

It is in this context that I begin a chapter on Ford's educational rhetoric with one the most vivid of its visual performances. On a July afternoon in 1916 in Detroit, Michigan, the company invited a crowd of more than 2,000 to form around an odd tableau. On the lawn of Ford Motor Company's massive manufacturing plant, a facade painted to look like a steamship served as the backdrop to a massive black cauldron with the words "Ford Motor Company English School" painted on the front. Amid murmurs of interest and excitement over this strange scene, one of the dozens of "Melting Pot" ceremonies conducted by the company over the second half of the 1910s would begin. This, at least, is how the *Ford Times* described the affair in the article titled "Assimilation through Education: A Motto Wrought into Education." The article explains that the crowd, "including representatives of many prominent business concerns," looked on as

> [f]rom the deck of the steamship came the preliminaries of docking the ship and then suddenly a picturesque figure appeared at the top of the gangway. Dressed in a foreign costume and carrying his cherished possessions wrapped in a bundle suspended from a cane, he gazed about with a look of bewilderment then slowly descended the ladder into the "Melting Pot" holding aloft a sign indicating the country from which he had come. Another figure followed and then another—"Syria," "Greece," "Italy," "Austria," "India" read the cards, as the representatives of each of the different countries included in the class filed down the gangway into the "Melting

Pot." From it they emerged dressed in American clothes, faces eager with the stimulus of the new opportunities and responsibilities opening out before them.⁶

At the end of the ceremony, these graduates stood on risers in neat lines around the melting pot in uniform business suits (their "American clothes," apparently), American flags raised, with the phrase E PLURIBUS UNUM—"out of many, one"—painted overhead.

While the phrase had already been adopted as the unofficial motto for the nation, *e pluribus unum* was an ideal slogan for Ford Motor Company in 1914. The company repeatedly showed that from many natural resources came automotive parts, from many regions and countries came workers, from their many acts of labor came a single production process, and through this process resources and labor produced a single object—the car. Further, from this expanding configuration came a company. Unlike its application to the nation (and certainly by Deweyan humanists), however, "the many" would become "one" in this system not by embracing diversity to form unity but by manufacturing homogeneity.

The Melting Pot Pageant is particularly useful for identifying the ideological positions central to the company's arguments about education and citizenship in the period: it positioned education as a logical extension of the industrial organization (and, therefore, made students subject to its deeply paternalistic management practices); it presented Ford's guiding vision for homogeneity as a preferred state not just for its workers but for the world itself; and, finally, it shifted the broad cultural trope of the "melting pot" from a coming together of various cultures to a technology dedicated to the production of homogenized national subjects. In short, the ceremony was a celebration of education as a pathway to sameness rather than a system for embracing and integrating difference. Through this performed argument about uniformity, Ford invited the public to see industrial living as the easiest way to become an American citizen—not just for newly arriving immigrants but for anyone seeking a place in a changing economic and social landscape. In the process, the company argued that the industrial corporation was more than just an economic entity but an institution capable of producing new knowledge sets and producing new national subjects.

The pageant was the culmination of a program that, by contemporary standards, was one of the more dystopian of Ford's practices in producing this homogeneity. Beginning in 1914, the company engaged aggressively in an industrialized version of social engineering with its workers by using superior compensation as leverage for increased social demands. The program consisted of a system of policies that allowed for "qualified" workers to receive nearly double the average pay for line work at the time (famously, five dollars a day), while Samuel Marquis, Henry Ford's personal pastor, dean of the English School, and head of the company's "Sociology Department" inspected the homes and bodies of these workers to ensure an appropriate level of "American-ness."

In turn, the company's English School taught all-but-compulsory courses in both citizenship and language acquisition for immigrant workers. Workers who did not adhere to these policies were excluded from the increased pay and benefits or fired. Workers who completed the program were granted citizenship and stepped into a newly minted industrial middle class. The company widely publicized the program both to the public and to policymakers. In a 1916 address to the National Education Association, Samuel Marquis explained that "[t]he impression has somehow got abroad that Henry Ford is in the automobile business. It isn't true. Mr. Ford shoots about fifteen hundred cars out of the back door of his factory every day just to get rid of them. They are but the by-products of his real business, which is the making of men."[7]

A *National Magazine* article titled "Give Men a Chance—Not Charity" similarly presented all of this as part of Henry Ford's grand vision for society, declaring that "[t]he great mechanical genius [Ford] had evolved a system so unique and so remarkable that his plans and dreams blend together, making a practical whole which has actually benefitted over fifty-thousand homes. They are based on a foundation of education and Americanization."[8] In this way, the pageant also displays that the company was making these arguments by presenting manufacturing as an aesthetic—a set of visual cues about how objects, ideas, and persons could be cultivated through strategic and procedural planning (resulting in "a practical whole" as Bushnell described it). In the pageant, elements of this aesthetic included the use of external features (clothes, hygiene, posture) to gauge internal value (American-ness, stick-to-itiveness, ambition); the application of visual conventions associated with producing cars to its "making of men" (quick, uniform, and in a line); and the fusion of industrial and educational spaces.

The images in the *National Magazine* article, for example, presented an integral complementary argument to the written support of Ford's program.

Pictures of orderly classrooms and workers' bodies displayed to the reader a tidy network designed to take immigrant bodies ("the serious conditions" of the day, it seems) and convert them into more recognizably "American" workers. Throughout these images, visual order and homogeneity were running themes. In images of classrooms, no papers were askew, all chairs were equidistant from tables, and the tables were frequently long and thin so that the students as they were seated in the classroom bore a remarkable resemblance to workers on an assembly line. The students flanking these tables wore uniform wool suits and paid undivided attention to a single figure, the teacher.

In this sense, more than just an extreme form of labor management, the entire Sociology Department and English School were an aesthetic boon—an opportunity for the company to put on display the power of homogeneity and the expanded potential for the industrial corporation in society. Over time, however, increased backlash from stifled workers and the threat of emerging unions caused the company's "hands-on" approach and restrictive definition of Americanization to lose favor as a method for institutionally shaping individuals. In Henry Ford's recounts of these policies, he recast the Sociology Department as "a sort of prosperity-sharing plan. But on conditions." In a stunning act of understatement (or, more likely, revisionist history), Ford further explained that while "[n]othing paternal was intended!—a certain amount of paternalism did develop, and that is one reason why the whole plan and the social welfare plan were readjusted."[9] The Sociology Department was disbanded in 1919, and wages were no longer tied directly to the company's opinion of a worker's American qualities. This, however, did not mean that the company's goals to produce a homogeneous workforce or to impact education had subsided. Rather, Ford simply shifted strategy by creating an extensive network of educational endeavors related to the company including hundreds of educational films, the construction of schools and colleges, and the sponsorship of technical programs.

It should come as no surprise, in this context, that one of the most prominent collections in the Ford film archive is a series of educational films produced between 1918 and 1925. These films were dedicated to continuing the project set out by the Sociology Department to argue that knowledge could be manufactured through (film) spectatorship, character could be manufactured through industrial education, and worker-citizens could be manufactured by schools integrated directly into industrial corporations. They were, in this context, integral texts in the company's project to develop and circulate what educational historian Joel Spring has called the "corporate image of society," an image that "turned American schools into a central social institution for the production of men and women who conformed to the needs and expectations of a corporate and technocratic world."[10] This overall image of education would, in turn, produce "the dominant institutional style for more than the next half of the century." While Spring uses the idea of the "corporate image" metaphorically, closer analysis of Ford's films suggests that there is tremendous power in the production and circulation of literal "corporate images"—pageants, photographs, and films that replicate economic sensibilities guided by corporations.

To better understand the visual nature of this "corporate image," this chapter examines these films through three overlapping frameworks. The first positions Ford's educational films as a set of historical and material moments that organized bodies in seats, that were the subject of extensive media coverage, and that traveled around the world as a coordinated series. Each of these material features was important to the company's larger aesthetic project to position the films as sites of knowledge. The second framework draws on the work of Michel Foucault, who studied the power of generating "similitude" as a way of organizing a society's understanding of knowledge. From this perspective, these films functioned by producing a vast visual network of similarities that both normalized industrial life and extended this life as a broader analogy for understanding much of the world.

Finally, to understand the particular power that film afforded the company when engaging in the production of these similitudes, I read Ford's films via the language of mise-en-scène. Thinking through the appearance of Fordism using the same principles that guide readings of style in film analysis (from the basic—color and angle—to the more complex—elasticity and proxemics) draws on a half-century of debates about the nature of film style as well. Indeed, it is surprising how many descriptions of mise-en-scène and descriptions of Fordism overlap. When Jacques Rivette described "mise-en-scène" as "the creation of a precise complex of sets and characters, a network of relationships, an architecture of connections, an animated complex that seems suspended in space," he could just as easily have been describing the economic rhetoric of Ford as it staged organized bodies, imbued objects with greater meanings, and projected social needs as extensions of industrial capitalism.[11] As the next section shows, however, before viewers sat down to view any of these arguments, they had already been encouraged to view the films as an act of corporate altruism, of modern learning, and of nationally important forms of knowledge.

Ford's Turn to Educational Films

The earliest version of Ford's educational motion pictures, the *Ford Educational Weekly*, featured more than 190 films produced by the company's Motion Picture Laboratory and distributed using the company's dealers.[12] Eventually, however, the series was distributed more widely by the Goldwyn Distributing Corporation. Generally, when shown in theaters, *Ford Educational Weekly* films were presented as an "augmenting feature" in a program typically consisting of a Hollywood feature film and some combination of "augmenting" newsreels and industrial/educational films.[13] They gained popularity quickly, with Ford reporting in 1920 that "[e]ach week ten million people see 'The Ford Educational Weekly.' It is shown in seven thousand—nearly half—the moving picture theatres in the United States and has gained for the Ford Motor Company the distinction of having the largest circulation of motion pictures in the world."[14]

Reports on the films described them as "intensely interesting" and as "particularly valuable because of their high moral and educational value."[15] The films did wonders for the perception of the company and its founder. An article in the *New York Times*, for example, explained that "Mr. Ford is many things to many men, but ... if they know anything about the Ford films, [they know] that he is decidedly valuable as a public producer of pictures."[16]

When early showings of the films were marred by a rumor that theaters and patrons were being charged per showing (removing their altruistic nature), theater owners were quick to defend the films. A Virginia theater owner, for example, wrote in the local newspaper that the films were "one of Henry Ford's free contributions to the public ... for the purpose of educating the people along certain lines which they are unable to obtain except by this method."[17]

The series' production became a form of spectacle in itself, and the films were positioned as an integral part of national projections of American power abroad. The article "Ford to Furnish Films for U.S. Propaganda in Europe," for example, explained that "[t]he Ford educational weeklies have become of such significance that they have reached the attention of the president, and in casting about for an efficient American Propaganda for foreign countries he came to inspect a series of Ford weeklies ... nearly 300,000 feet have already been shipped to Russia, France, Italy, and Spain."[18]

On the heels of these successes, the films produced for the *Ford Educational Weekly* were collected, supplemented with new material, and repackaged as the *Ford Educational Library* in 1921. This second film series was distributed to schools, universities, and prisons by a second publicity firm, Fitzpatrick and McElroy. Presenting these films as purely educational rather than edutainment or domestic propaganda, the new distribution company explained in a number of educational trade journals that *Ford Educational Library* films were serious pedagogical materials. In *Visual Education,* for example, the firm noted that the films were "prepared, edited, and titled by some of the leading educational authorities in the United States" and, to further create this educational distinction, claimed that the *Library* films "are not to be confused with the 'Ford Educational Weekly' which is entirely a separate production, intended for use in theaters. The films are being prepared by educators who are acknowledged experts in their own subjects, to meet all conditions and requirements of the school curricula."[19]

To further accentuate their educational nature, the *Ford Educational Library* films were organized into a variety of disciplines—Regional Geography, Industrial Geography, Agriculture, and Civics and Citizenship, for example—and presented a distributed curriculum expressed through a set of textbook-like chapters that happened to be captured on film. Mimicking the look of places where knowledge was traditionally stored, each film opened with a book cover—emblazoned with an oil lamp to represent enlightenment—being thrown open to reveal the films' content (see figure 1).

This twofold distribution system for getting Ford's educational films into both theaters and educational institutions is significant on two counts. Through its immense distribution system, millions of Americans encountered Ford Motor Company's motion pictures as a set of educational texts and the company as a reputable distributor of knowledge. At the same time, the films provided a homogenized national experience of visual learning as theatergoers, workers, and students received identical lessons. The films also actively set out an argument about what was worthy of observation in the industrial age. As one of the films (chronicling the work of horticulturalist Luther Burbank) put it, the company wanted the public to understand that "Motion Pictures preserve for us the history of interesting persons and events" (see figure 2). What made these persons and events interesting, however, was consistently the subject matter's position as important economic and technological innovation.

The company would continue to escalate its claims over the potential for the series to teach for a number of years. A 1923 edition of *Ford News* perhaps best sums up the tone the company was using to bolster the educational potential of its films by positing that the company had solved a long-standing educational challenge. The article declares that "[f]or two hundred years, Orbis Sensualium

1 | Ford Motion Picture Laboratory, still from *Luther Burbank*, 1922.

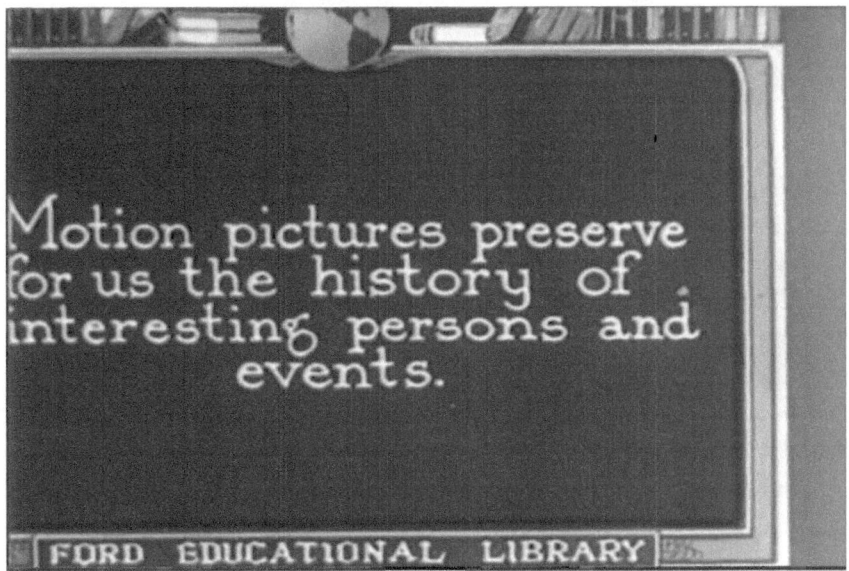

2 | Ford Motion Picture Laboratory, still from *Luther Burbank*, 1922.

Pictus: interested the people, but it was not until that handsome hero, Motion Pictures, touched the Sleeping Beauty, Visual Education, that she awoke, moved about and became a power in the world ... The Ford Educational Library is the result of this happy union."[20]

For much of the early 1920s, then, Ford Motor Company touted this broad celebration of seeing-as-knowing by producing and promoting a steady stream of films depicting distant cities, natural wonders, zoomed-in shots of beehives, the inner workings of watches, internal plumbing systems, and the factory floor—all the while working to fashion these various objects into a cohesive visual curriculum. Using these films, the company systematically attuned the public to see like an industrialist—to see the natural world as a collective of resources, to see geography as a series of maps chronicling how resources become products and how products appear in the lives of consumers, to see knowledge as intimately connected with machine-aided production, and to see diverse humans as a single moldable resource to produce laborer-citizens.

Mirroring this homogeneous package for the educational experience, the films' disparate subject matter was drawn together further by a consistent set of cinematic techniques. In general, the films in both collections were created using brief, simple shots of machinery, landscapes, animals, and/or laborers. These snippets were then organized into a procedural whole using text-based intertitles to explain the images' content and these contents' place in the larger economic system. In this sense, the films worked to create what Michel Foucault identified as "similitude." In general, similitude names a process wherein a given period's system of knowledge has been organized around an ever-expanding set of similarities that "tell us how the world must fold in upon itself, duplicate itself, reflect itself, or form a chain with itself so that things can resemble one another." In such a theory, social systems are guided by a connection to a central referent—in the twelfth century, for example, this was the divine (knowledge and ethics relied on their resemblance to godliness) or the idea of connection itself. In the sixteenth century, Foucault notes, this meant a broader system of connections wherein physical resemblance was translated into conceptual relations ("the earth echoing the sky, faces seeing themselves reflected in the stars").[21]

Ford's educational films suggest that Ford's use of *similitude* was a matter of presenting manufacturing as a central referent that organized the order of the world. For Foucault, there are four main similitude-based appeals that allow for such a system of associations to expand. *Convenientia* names connections drawn between already similar or "close" concepts as they can be understood via "the world in which they exist"; *emulation* expands this way of seeing to related but not immediately comparable ideas; *analogy* allows for such a system of knowledge to extend across conceptual systems to ideas otherwise considered distant; and finally *sympathies* promotes a more general way of looking at the world in which just about anything can be assimilated into a system of knowledge. Where medieval and Renaissance versions of similitude relied on natural resemblances to produce these similitudes, the technology of the film—with its ability to stage and organize the appearance of many different objects—could manufacture these relationships.

In this theory of similitude, in order for Ford's aesthetic project to work on a national scale, the public would need to understand—or, perhaps, to "recognize"—the visual conventions of industrial production as the defining feature of its similitude-based arguments. On-screen, the company first needed to produce these close linkages through *convenientia*, which produced a collection of visual contiguities between manufactured objects. Taking up this challenge, amid the more traditional subjects like geography and history, the Motion Picture Laboratory produced a series of films dedicated to presenting industrial manufacturing. Regardless of the subject matter, these films featured condensed depictions of the assembly line processes involved in making any commodity. When placed under the uniform visual rubric, these various objects became parts of one expansive and important system. Highlighting this, the core of nearly all of the industrial production films used similar cinematic techniques to present the sequential processes involved in manufacturing. Analyzing these techniques, then, is the work of attending to mise-en-scène.

As a mode of analysis, attending to mise-en-scène means reading films for the composition of specific shots or uncut scenes. This means looking at how bodies and objects are ordered in space on-screen; how lighting and color are used to enhance meanings; and how actors, objects, and the camera all move through the scene to "stage" time and space for the viewer. More than this, reading a film's mise-en-scène means working from the perspective that these various features cohere to create a recognizable (and replicable) "style."

Whereas mise-en-scène has often been used to understand the artistic contributions of a film—whether this is a director's or genre's particular style or a way of appreciating technical artistry—here we might consider the rhetorical capacities of these cinematic features. Circulating during an extant debate over the nature of knowledge, I read these films as an extended argument put to the public that the films did more than teach viewers how commodities were made or what cities looked like; rather, they were changing the nature of knowledge itself. In the Fordist era, then, knowledge consisted of recognizing the regimented fragments of a process and how those fragments could be ordered sequentially until the various pieces were compiled into a final product.

In this way, Ford's use of mise-en-scène raises questions like: How might the positioning of bodies and machines in a cinematic frame convey messages about values like order and efficiency? How might the contours and geometrical lines work as responses to existing arguments about the nature of knowledge? What might the overall aesthetic production of a film argue about the shape and direction of education? Ford's educational films worked to naturalize industrial production practices as the next step in a set of organic and/or historical developments; using color, lighting, depth, and angle, these films highlighted the ability of interconnected and orderly bodies, objects, and ideas to manufacture nearly anything.

Convenientia and the Experience of Industrial Knowledge

Students and frequent visitors to theaters, churches, and YMCAs would see a variety of pun-titled production films, including *Bubbles, I'm Forever Using Soap*; *Sweetness, Giving You a Taste of the Sugar Industry*; *Cut It Out: The Story of Making Cut Glass*; and *De-Light: Making an Electrical Lightbulb*. Across these films, there were many examples of *convenientia* at work. Films such as these made up roughly one-third of both the *Educational Library* and the *Educational Weekly*. The first consistent feature worked to naturalize relations and stretch traditional understandings of setting by drawing a link between economic production and society.

The films consistently did this by presenting industrial development as an extension of activity that could be directly observed in nature and/or in the historical development of humankind. Most of these films opened with stylized intertitles (the backdrop of the text slides featured drawings of historical scenes or prominent historical figures), which placed production in natural or historical contexts. The mass production of paper is prefaced by the point that "[t]he hornet changes wood into a pulp with which it makes a paper nest" and "[t]he Egyptians made paper of this plant, the papyrus, from which paper is named." For sugar: "The first cane sugar was made in China many centuries ago. Shortly after the discovery of America, sugar cane cultivation began in the West Indies which now produce more than one-fourth of the world's sugar." For soap: "Soap was originally invented by the Gauls says Roman History. But Cleopatra used soft soap in abundance, so there's a chance for an argument." Using these opening titles continued the work of mapping an educational aesthetic onto production carried over from the distribution and public framing practices but also shifted perceptions of the images to come. While these moments do communicate knowledge about their subject, they also position the production process as an important part of progress in civilization (broadly conceived) and as an organic part of the natural world.

While there are minor additions to the presentation of manufacturing—soap has an extended laboratory scene where scents are developed and sugar, oranges, and olives have extended orchard scenes—the films move relatively quickly from "seeing" production as historically significant to the factory floor. The primary outcome of Ford's cinematic decisions in this particular series was to demonstrate visual consonance. To illustrate this, figures 3, 4, and 5 feature still shots from three separate educational lessons in the *Educational Library*. The subjects of these films—oranges, soap, and sugar—are largely indistinguishable, and this is exactly the point. It is also, however, a matter of mise-en-scène.

As one of the principal features of mise-en-scène, film scholars have examined how the use of color can serve as an important resource for establishing mood or shifting perceptions of objects and characters. In Ford's educational films, color, or the lack thereof, contributed to the larger project of creating cohesion by removing many individual products' unique color schemes. At the precise moment the company needed the relatively colorless world of manufacturing to be legible, if not attractive, to the public, the medium of the motion picture was spreading its new configurations of the visual in grayscale.

Rather than a hindrance to the rhetorical capacities of Ford's educational films, the limitation to black and white helped to further two elements of its *convenientia*-based arguments: first, the lack of color helped to generate cohesion between products being created (one way to make the production of an orange and an olive appear uniform is to make them both gray). Second, however, this use of grayscale contributed to two alternating effects that were

3 | Ford Motion Picture Laboratory, stills from *Olive and Orange Growing*, 1920.

4 | Ford Motion Picture Laboratory, stills from *Bubbles, I'm Forever Using Soap*, 1919.

5 | Ford Motion Picture Laboratory, stills from *Sugar*, 1919.

integral to the films' visual order—highlighting the perfect geometry involved in manufacturing and manipulating focal points on the production floor.

In these effects, color coordinated with the use of lighting. Under the bright glare of heavy lighting in closely shot scenes, the machines and products pop. Conversely, for longer shots of production, the lack of lighting and muddled color scheme generate indistinguishable processes that blurred the specifics of what was taking place. Often, scenes of manufacturing combine these elements, drawing the focus to one element of a scene over others by positioning the camera and lighting close to one part of the industrial process. This sharp contrast between whatever the lights were hitting and what was cast to the shadows helped isolate manufacturing as a collection of perfectly geometrical shapes (the parallel lines of a vertical distributor of paper pulp, the precise angles of a machine filling packages, the perfect proportions of a sorting machine moving oranges). Figure 4, for example, features a machine working at the end of sugar production. The bright white and perfectly angular figure of the filling machine is punctuated against the gray backdrop of other machinery. The line of bags beneath the triangles and rectangles marks a uniform line prepared for packaging.

The visuals in the film make up a relatively seamless montage of similarly ordered scenes: Fordson tractors working their way across a field in perfectly parallel lines give way to shots of a full cast of machines as they work "separating the sugar crystals from the remaining syrup by whirling" or moving the sugar "from the centrifugal to be dried by hot air in the revolving drum" where "the melted sugar is formed into plates." Each of these scenes is notable for its attractive geometry—rotating cylinders and perfectly rectangular plates all jump out from their darkened, fuzzy backgrounds. The result of these features is a film that visually punctuates perfect order and the sequential simpatico of machines designed to complete their task discretely and efficiently. While human workers appear frequently (particularly in harvesting scenes early in these films), they are almost always supplementary figures to the mechanical actors of industrial capitalism.

Gunther Kress and Theo Van Leeuwen have considered the rhetorical capacities of such geometrical composition, pointing out that in Western structures of symbolic meaning, angular shapes (squares and triangles, in particular) represent order for both their symmetry and their potential to more easily interlock (as they can be easily stacked and paired).[22] However, Ford extends this geometry outward, converting this vision of control to order the (usually not-so-geometrical) humans as well. In scenes that combine machinery and humans, the various points of contrast highlight both a complex configuration of tasks and a fully incorporated network of bodies and machines that go into the making of products, even seemingly natural objects like oranges.

For example, figure 3 appears after oranges have been picked by humans and washed by machines. As a basic "plot" point, the purpose of the scene is to display that the oranges are inspected for any oddities or blemishes. In the first shot in this scene, machinery takes up the central position and is composed of symmetrical lines branching out from a mechanical spine. At the margins, three workers, only partially pictured, shuffle back and forth between the central machine and off-camera bins where imperfect fruit is disposed of. The next scene is organized as an even split, and the assembly line bisects the shot, with the workers making up the right half while the bins of quality fruit appear on the left. The workers—all women, all dressed in white, all wearing their hair in a bun—work to box the fruit while the machine and fruit churn in a dark contrast to the well-lit workers.

The primary motion in the scene is the workers' arms snapping out from their torsos to snatch an orange from the line. The result of this movement is that the workers' arms produce a wave that pulses from the front of the scene to the back over and over. Perfect oranges, perfect symmetry, and perfectly homogeneous workers all, the film argues, guarantee quality. These cinematic uses of space, or proxemics as film scholars have called them, were mimetic as they worked to convey that Fordism itself was in part a rational partitioning of space and order. If these coordinated acts had been performed on a studio lot by actors, they would have been lauded as a masterpiece of directorial precision. Positioned as nonfiction, the scenes were even more powerful.

Compounding the effects drawing on color, lighting, and spatial configuration, the films also rely on perspective by rapidly alternating between medium and close shots—using what film scholars have called "elasticity"—so that viewers of these films are rarely given a specific account of the mechanics that govern the machinery. Rather, the film creates a sense of procedural continuity by rapidly alternating shots that bring the viewer closer than traditional safety would allow and broader shots capturing the majority of the machine. No single machine or worker can be described as making soap or sugar, but they all contribute a contained yet connected task. This effect is further produced by framing choices. As each of the images in figures 3 through 5 highlights, few of the shots in these films captured the totality of any given machine. Instead, the machines spill out of the frame, and any one part or raw material is on-screen for only a few seconds. A viewer is given a general sense of how, for example, in figure 5, the mechanical dynamics of this collection of machines turned a chemically based substance into uniform bars of soap. The content of this particular film features neither human laborers nor the commodity in question but a system of mechanical characters like "the digester" (a rake-like object working its way into a bin) and "the beater" (a large circular tank) as they accumulated into a largely automated process of production. Moving too quickly for the audience to fully digest much of what is happening, the film more readily conveys that amid the blur of this white substance making its way through the indiscrete machine parts and passing rows of uniform employees watching this process, a bar of soap is miraculously made.

We might note, then, that these films worked as a doubled form of *convenientia*. On the one hand, these films relied heavily on perspective to generate contiguity between the objects and people on any given factory's floor, thereby drawing together all elements of production into equal and largely indistinguishable entities. On the other hand, when carried across films, these perspectives drew similarities between industries and products as well—suddenly, all sorts of previously distinct commodities were "like" in nature, and so were their workers. The films also worked, however, to present these similarities as revealing the "real" nature of the commodity.

Perspective has been theorized as having a number of potential rhetorical effects related to producing the "real" in this way. Kress and Van Leeuwen, for example, argue that central perspective is perceived as the most authentic perspective because it replicates the natural gaze of the viewer.[23] This, however, assumes that the goal of knowledge is to understand the single, discrete object in question from a uniform, embodied perspective rather than to understand systemic wholes. Ford's production films use perspective differently.

In the educational films, the assembly line makes up the central feature of many production shots but is rarely positioned perpendicular to the camera; instead, the line appears on-screen most often at an angle between forty-five and sixty degrees. In one sense, this generates a more dynamic image, as the objects move through multiple dimensions simultaneously. In another sense, this allows for greater emphasis on the collective motion of the production process. The movement of the many parts varies—at times moving toward the camera, at other times away. In general, however, the objects tend to move from left to right. This movement throughout the factory floor serves, in many ways, as the traditional "plot" for a production film.

Additionally, as these films move the viewer through their respective processes, this left-to-right motion is broken up using scenes shot from a high angle, positioning the specific mechanical feature as one part of a factory floor but also as a fully observable and discrete object rather than as itself a configuration of smaller mechanical features. In this way, the production films framed manufacturing at the level of entire machines—beaters, sorters, packers—rather than gears, springs, and hydraulic lines. Using a similar aesthetic framework for presenting the otherwise disparate objects these machines are producing, the film incorporates all of these objects into a massive industrial regime as well as an economy in which nearly anything is manufacturable, accessible, and therefore exchangeable with one another.

The implications of such a depiction have been considerable. For labor historians, these kinds of fragmentation and distribution were important shifts in the gradual devaluing of craft labor. By positioning human workers as equal parts or marginal features of machines and by suturing together many sites and labors as nodes in a single production process, the primary lessons of the films about where products come from quickly give way to secondary arguments about the nature of labor value and the importance of interconnection as an economic principle. More than this, however, knowledge is positioned as the work of piecing together the many interconnected parts that produce final products. Further still, knowledge of an individual product is not unique but one variation on a theme.

To the contemporary viewer of these images, the rotating metallic shelves, the steel girders and piping, and the imposing packaging apparatus would hardly be exciting visions of knowledge at work. However, the inaugural issue of *Visual Education* provides some evidence of the power in these regimented depictions at the time. A study conducted at Northwestern University in 1919 sought to understand the effectiveness of educational films and used Ford's educational films as nearly a quarter of its visual curriculum. Responses from the study include a fifth-grade teacher's observation that "[p]ictures of the different industries have been especially valuable to the pupils who are studying geography." Judging by the content of the films in question, however, we might understand his point to be that students now better understand the regional economies of the world through the resources they provide and the products they manufacture. More striking is one student's observation that "[b]efore I saw movies here at Lincolnwood, I knew almost nothing of the outside world."[24] This world, we might imagine, is now populated by objects that are the end point of a system of perfect order, mechanical production, and resource acquisition as it has taken on the appearance of a cohesive network of similar tasks.

Visual *convenientia* is important for understanding such a reaction in two ways. First, by presenting so many disparate ideas through a network of similar visible components, these production films made Fordist industrial manufacturing a recognizable style—and style can often serve as shorthand for more complex arguments about what constitutes knowledge. One could know the nature of soap or oranges as manufactured goods and, in knowing about the manufactured nature of these objects, could understand a remarkable number of other ideas from this same perspective—ideas about labor, about where any of the products one buys come from, about what modernity looks like. Second, however, this similarity provided a way for manufacturing to become a visual network that could be emulated in order to "know" other social processes in a similar procedural manner. Cities were brought under a similar visual rubric as the company repositioned places around the world as sites of equivalent industrial development—panoramas of bustling central squares flanked by steel, multistory buildings; of workers weaving in and out of traffic to deliver goods and labor; of resource collection.[25] Historical events were portrayed using a uniform set of narrative and visual conventions. And, most importantly, all acts of production and many of the resulting products took on a similar structure. The result of such a network of *convenientia* represents one integral part of Ford's similitude-based rhetoric. The films argued that this act of knowing by sequential observation was applicable almost universally—this manufactured product could be a plant, a city, a car, anything that could be bought or sold.

But if this were the totality of Ford's similitude-based argument, it would have had a limited scope—extending only to material objects as they could be integrated into the industrial economy. And so, the company moved on to produce the next step in Foucault's accounts of similitude-based constructions of knowledge—emulation—to expand its homogenizing vision of the world.

For Foucault, "emulation is a sort of natural twinship," so that if *convenientia* forms a "chain," the use of emulation creates "a series of concentric circles reflecting and rivaling one another."[26] Emulation is, on the surface, a seemingly simple rhetorical appeal. One rhetor must only replicate the style or tactics of another in order to borrow the force of the original, to attempt to outshine the original, or to mock the original through satire. Ford's use of the concept in its educational films lies somewhere between the first two of these rhetorical effects as, for example, handwriting could be mapped into this industrial world as one more technology for production.

The mise-en-scène of Ford's production films would be a useful rhetorical resource for the company because it could carry many of the arguments about homogeneity and order to sections of the company's educational films not immediately dedicated to mechanical production. In these non-production films, the same aesthetic features associated with the production of material commodities—naturalization, visuality, order, and interconnectedness—were extended to define the production of human sensibilities. Indeed, aligning these various cinematic techniques into a recognizable form of film style, Ford could press beyond arguing that manufacturing itself was a form of important knowledge to also argue that many educational principles were kindred production technologies capable of manufacturing particular kinds of pupils.

Emulation and the Spread of Industrial Knowledge

Perhaps the clearest example of Ford's use of emulation in the educational collection appeared as a direct response to John Dewey's *Democracy and Education*. The film, as I read it, works through a dual act of emulation. On the one hand, the film emulates the argumentative structure of Dewey's claims about the power and potential of education. On the other hand, the visual style of the film emulates the simultaneously circulating depictions capturing industrial production on the assembly line. The result of this fusion is, as Lee Grieveson has explained, a film that produces a "history and civics lesson [that] works to update the liberal capitalist citizenship that was historically allied to ideals of autonomy for the new machine or mass assembly age."[27]

Initially offered as one of the 190 publicly circulated *Ford Educational Weekly* films and released just two years after Dewey's landmark work, the film was eventually revised in 1922, renamed *Democracy in Education: Penmanship*, and placed in the "Civics and Citizenship" section of the *Ford Educational Library*. Both the original *Educational Weekly* and the revised *Educational Library* version of the film were widely distributed. The *Ford Educational Weekly* film was shown, for example, as the penultimate feature at a Parent-Teacher Association meeting in Juneau, Alaska, in December 1921.[28] The revised *Ford Educational Library* film was shown to the newly formed National Education Association. Reflecting this new administrative audience, the later film focused more on presenting ideal instructional practices.[29]

Responding directly to Dewey's work, the films reify the popularized notions that "public" knowledge could be deeply ingrained in the construction of healthy national identity and thus that a thriving nation could be achieved through education. They also, however, highlight the role that the manufacturing aesthetic played in these educational films by using a set of familiar visual cues to adjust the terms of such an argument. It is through the visual conventions of the film, then, that literacy acquisition is placed within a more expansive frame of Fordist relations. On the surface, *Democracy in Education: Penmanship* and the collection of manufacturing films appear to have little in common: the former a film connecting education to citizenship, the latter displaying how products are made. However, when approached as a pair of aesthetically driven texts, they are very much part of the same project.

In one sense, Dewey and Ford Motor Company shared a number of opinions on the potential of the industrial. Dewey maintained that "industrial life . . . so intimately affects all forms of social intercourse, that there is an opportunity to utilize it for development of mind and character."[30] They agreed that public education must serve democratic ends and should be a national rather than local endeavor. They were also polar opposites in how to understand these broader ideas. For Dewey, "[a] progressive society counts individual variations as precious since it finds in them the means of its own growth." For Ford, homogeneity was key. Throughout his arguments about education, Dewey worked to align the institution to democracy through a general narrative about how civilization grows by passing knowledge from experienced members of a society to immature members. As the ideal form of civilization, he explains, democracy must, in turn, develop ways of passing on not just its knowledge but its underlying ways of interacting to maintain "free interchange, for social continuity."[31]

In response, and much like the manufacturing films, the film *Democracy in Education: Penmanship* sought to draw out its own naturalized context for fusing education with the nation. To do so, the film fuses nationalist imagery with economic imagery. Generating a narrative that mirrored traditional discourses of Progressive education, the *Democracy and Education* films begin by fusing the educational storyline with that of a fledgling nation. The opening intertitle of the films declares that "[i]n the early days of our country the labors and hardships of pioneer life in the open developed a sturdy race of resourceful, independent, clear-thinking men, who rebelled against tyranny."

Juxtaposed with this written narrative is a series of shots replicating American iconography—three men stand before a forest where smoke has been blown into the background. They are dressed in costumes representing the Continental Army fife and drum corps of the American Revolution—the fife player's head bandaged from a wound. Both films then cut to an extreme close-up of the Declaration of Independence. Setting the tone for the logical link between handwriting and citizenship to come, the 1922 *Educational Library* revision of the film prefaces the appearance of this document (and the extreme close-up on the signatures) with the instruction that "[t]his is a picture of the original document written by Thomas Jefferson. Note the quality of the writing here, and in the signatures which follow. And established a democracy in which life, liberty and the pursuit of happiness are guaranteed to all."

The film then shifts this narrative into economic terms by declaring that "the new republic grew, prospered and became a rich, mighty nation." Visually, this maturation process from fledgling "republic" to recognizable "nation" is further developed in economic terms as both "rich" and "mighty" through the images of urbanization and industrialization. Because other subjects weren't immediately related to economic or production practices, Ford's nonindustrial films routinely make use of another visual convention—juxtaposition—to draw out connections between particular educational subjects and their "practical" counterparts. This strategy is put on display in the middle sequences of the films.

After the declaration that "school training must result in the development of those qualities which are essential both to the happiness of the individual and to the strength and vitality of the nation," the word "Readin'" (via a title slide) is visually recast as keeping up with the news. The image directly associated with attaining literacy in the *Educational Weekly* consists of six individuals reading newspapers on two park benches—one for men, the other for women. In the *Educational Library* version, a more traditional educational image appears, but with equally telling visual cues. In the later film, the camera is placed just behind the teacher's desk, positioning the viewer to gaze outward into a classroom featuring five perfectly straight rows of schoolchildren slanting at a sixty-degree angle to fully show off the uniformity with which they sit, heads bowed, reading.

Next "'ritin'" is followed by images of Ford executives signing a military contract and posing with uniformed officers. The implications of the smiling group chronicling a major industrial/military merger is the suggestion that writing itself allows an individual access to contractual relations and a new form of economic output. The "R" that garners the most attention in this sequence is "'rithmetic," which is closely associated with engineering (see figure 6). The images juxtaposed with this concept feature a man puzzling over a set of blueprints as he stands in front of the wooden frame of a building. He then takes up a ledger and begins to calculate—periodically glancing up at the structure. The shot then cuts to a close-up of the man's equations as they are being written on the page depicting both the complexity and the detailed nature of knowing how

6 | Ford Motion Picture Laboratory, stills from *Democracy and Education*, 1921.

to write with numbers. This sequence not only features the visual translation of academic work into economic action but aligns the three R's in a uniform configuration—staying aware of current affairs, engaging in transactions, and contributing to production—that adds up to citizenship.

Notably, two of the three images share the visual convention of producing lines that extend beyond the frame of the shot. Just as the assembly lines generating paper and oranges extended beyond the frame, the lines made up of newspaper readers and building infrastructure extend indefinitely. Just as the "beater" or a rotating metallic drum was positioned as an integral technological figure in the production of commodities, the *Democracy in Education* films position the three key pillars of education as technologies of subject production. More than this, these early images of a healthy republic suggest that such a concept is the result of a set of human products with particular capabilities. Producing these figures, it follows, was the work of manufacturing sensibilities.

It is no coincidence that Ford would organize this section of the film in this way. Rather than a problematic misappropriation of Dewey's sentiments, the film's aesthetic argument uses visual cues to shift the terms on which Dewey rested one of his central themes. Dewey, in accounting for the changing nature of education in the United States, had written previously that "[r]eading, writing, and arithmetic, the three R's, were to be taught because of their utility. They were needed to make individuals capable of self-support, of 'getting on' better and so capable of rendering better economic service under changed commercial conditions." More than this, the Three R's served as key aptitudes that could create a "flood of light upon the prevailing ideas of learning and knowledge," a theory that relied on the more fundamental argument that "[k]nowledge consists of the ready-made material which others have found out, and mastery of language is the means of access to this fund."[32]

Emulating these themes, the film presented an expansive historical narrative in which "America" and "American" were entities that could be upheld by systems of public education while also contesting that "American," "history," and "society" should be understood as extensions of mass-production paradigms. It does so by presenting notions of productivity, cultural uniformity, and economic prosperity as iterations of more traditional conceptions of deliberation, democracy, and civic engagement through the cinematic features of its manufacturing aesthetic as well as a set of juxtapositions.

By the end of part one of the film, public education has been charged with the task of developing the skills of "self-direction, self-appraisal, [and] self-control," thereby affiliating public knowledge with those mental and bodily features most closely associated with life on the production line. The film then argues that it is only through the formation of these attributes that the American way of life can prosper (a notion driven home more overtly in the 1922 re-release of the film, which depicts a troop of Boy Scouts assembling a wagon collectively, much in the way a Model T would have been put together before the appearance of the moving assembly line).

It is in part two, a section of the film added to the *Educational Library* version, that the company's argument relies more heavily on the cinematic emulation of the manufacturing aesthetic. In the 1922 version of the film, this extensive narrative aligning citizenship with commerce is labeled, simply, the "prologue," and the real work of bringing democracy into education takes place directly in the classroom. The opening intertitle of an added second section called "Putting Democracy into the Teaching of Handwriting" explains that the "film was prepared to demonstrate to teachers the spirit and the technique of using the Courtis Standard Practice Tests in Handwriting to develop self-appraisal, self-direction, and self-control as well as ability in handwriting." After identifying the time and place of the lesson, the teacher declares "time for the writing lesson," and the paired scene shows students in near-unison snap to attention, open their desks, and pull out the Courtis handwriting handbook. Not to let the visual cue go unnoticed, the next slide asks the viewer to "Note the excellent habits of work—Desks in order, Writing material put away in good order ready for instant use."

The film then follows a single student—Ralph—through the patterned lesson, using a telling set of cinematic properties. After a slide declaring "Self-Direction," Ralph looks at his daily record card to find out what part of the term's work he has already completed. In turn, the film shows Ralph trace his daily lessons down a prepared card with an extended index finger. An intertitle then declares: "Finds he has completed lesson 7 and is ready for lesson 8." Ralph then puts down the card and picks up his workbook. The next intertitle says: "Locates lesson 8," and a tight shot of a pencil scans down the pages of an open notebook until pausing at what is, ostensibly, lesson 8. The next slide: "Looks up standards to find out what a sixth grade boy should do." And after locating the particular standard in a sizeable chart, Ralph gets to work.

Here we see the manufacturing aesthetic circulating in films about producing oranges and paper extended out to the manufacture of Ralph—while there are no "beaters" or "digesters," the structure of the film and the nature of the interaction between human and technology (handwriting) are much the same. Through a set of systemic, efficient, and centrally planned steps, Ralph could be manufactured as a student capable of "Self-Direction." Using standardization as an aesthetic feature as well, however, the film next notes that Ralph is not alone. Rather, a slide states: "The whole room goes to work at once without any further direction from the teacher. *Note the concentration.*" The scene accompanying this claim returns to the orderly desks as students carefully follow their lines. This pattern is repeated for "Self-Appraisal" ("Frances can't get her H's to look like the copy"; they are "too scrawly"). No attention is directly given to "Self-Control," the third stated goal; rather, the film pivots to explain institutional control—a series of tests, statistical analyses, and explanations of accomplishment for the "half of Detroit Schools" that had taken up the method.

Part two of the film depicts a network of text-driven technologies: workbooks, progress reports, standards, desks, pencils, erasers, endless sheets covered with the letter *H*. It promises teachers, parents, and administrators two points: first, perfect order in their classrooms, which, it argues, frees them up to attend to individuals falling behind; and, second, a material way of displaying progress toward the mechanical and aesthetic elements of literacy. It suggests that knowledge itself is a kind of performable aesthetic—one's *H* must look proper, one's ledger must be orderly, one's desk must be aligned. Moreover, through this one in a larger network of texts dedicated to the manufacturing aesthetic, a viewer is encouraged to see the making of sugar and the "making of men" via literacy as part of a larger movement of incorporation capable of cumulatively defending and extending democracy. All of this is reduced, in Ford's films, to a set of visual similitudes that align quality in the rows of sugar and oranges with rows of students and rows of handwriting produced in near-factory form as one model for warding off national decline.

Through *Democracy in Education: Penmanship*, the company worked to incorporate systems of economic production and national ethos through the institution of education by positioning education primarily as a precursor to other institutional constructs (legal, political, militaristic). This is accomplished, in part, by extending its manufacturing outward from factories to schools, from paper to letters. In this regard, the broad application of this set of visual conventions allowed for the institutional constructs of schools to be cast as mass material institutions capable of contributing to the existing arguments over education. In the process, the film simultaneously takes up and attempts to exceed the arguments circulating in discussions of Progressive education by figures like Dewey (or, in this case, Dewey).

Literacy, however, was just one of many core subjects that the company worked to incorporate into its manufacturing aesthetic. In time, Ford would present the entirety of the educational experience through this system of similitudes by depicting the material site schools. Indeed, the archive also contains a number of films produced to capture a number of schools that represented

Fordist pedagogy in action.³³ These films, then, used the industrial factory as an extended analogy for not just education but the complete process of subject production.

―――――

Analogy and Model Schools

In Foucault's account of similitudes, it is the work of analogy that moves a system of knowledge one step further out than emulation. He explains that, in analogy, "*convenientia* and *aemulatio* are superimposed. Like the latter it makes possible the marvelous confrontation of resemblances across space; but it also speaks, like the former, of adjacencies, of bonds and joints. Its power is immense."³⁴ For rhetoricians, analogic rhetoric works by aligning two disparate concepts by suggesting that they function "according to the same kind of way." As Barbara Stafford has pointed out, "analogy is the vision of ordered relationships articulated as similarity-in-difference . . . analogues retain their individual intensity while being focused, interpreted, and related to other distinctive analogues and the prime analogue. We should imagine analogy, then, as a participatory performance, a ballet of centripetal and centrifugal forces lifting gobbets of sameness from one level or sphere to another. Analogy correlates originality with continuity, what comes after with what went before, ensuing parts with evolving whole."³⁵

Ford's educational films highlight that for institutions seeking power, becoming the "prime analogue" in a wide network of analogies is largely the goal of incorporational rhetoric. The more the world looks, or is understood to look, like a given institution, the more integral this institution becomes to that world. Notably, this was not an incidental observation but a central discussion to Progressive education. In no small part because of John Dewey, a set of model schools were being positioned as microcosms for the world itself.³⁶ Making the school function more like the factory, then, would prove one of the most powerful and effective elements of Ford's educational rhetorics and an integral moment in the instantiation of a "corporate image" of society.

In a 1927 film titled *The Henry Ford Trade School*, the core purpose of the school was identified as allowing for its students to "produce, while learning, contribute to their own support, and become an asset to the community." The film engages in three acts of similitude that align with those produced by the company's earlier educational films. First, the company presents the curriculum of the school as a sequential line—each course building on the last, each year building on the last. Second, it uses the industrially based *convenientia* to collapse distinctions between elements of industrial production and knowledge acquisition. Finally, it presents work itself as a form of character- and knowledge-building practice.

After an opening sequence explaining the school's history and showing hundreds of students flooding out of its front doors, the film focuses more directly on a specific pupil by following a young man who arrived at the school "to help support [his] mother and learn a practical trade." After a sharp cut from his arrival and registration, the boy is immediately shown how to roll up the sleeves of his shirt, tuck in his tie, and wear a protective bandanna as he heads off to his first class. In visual form, the boy literally puts on the physical demeanor of the Ford Man—a juvenile rendition of the industrial worker.

The film subsequently lays out for the viewer, without visual interludes, the full curriculum for each of the four years required to graduate—a curriculum that, aside from minor adjustments, mirrors traditional educational structures. However, as the film turns to the classroom directly using images, it works to show how this traditional curriculum has been incorporated into industrial sensibilities. The film depicts the combined lessons of industrial manufacturing with lessons in physics and trigonometry. For example, in one scene, a student is positioned between a piece of machinery and a blackboard. As he works through assembling, repairing, or explaining the mechanisms of an engine, he also records the equations that explain its nature on the blackboard in the background. Collapsing manufacturing and educational experience, the film argues that the use of a micrometer to "compute gears on Indexing Head to show how milling cutter forms a drill" becomes a lesson in "solving shop trigonometry" and "the operation of a gas engine" combines with a class in physics that is subtitled "measuring the expansion rate of a steel bar" (see figure 7).

In keeping with *Democracy in Education: Penmanship*'s earlier treatment of "readin', 'ritin', and 'rithmetic," the success of the film comes in its ability to collapse the distinctions between traditional educational structures and features of manual labor; however, in this later film, the relationship is inverted. Rather than providing meaning to education through a civic framework, by the late 1920s, the company was presenting narratives in which industrial production was itself both the impetus and the method for education, lending the

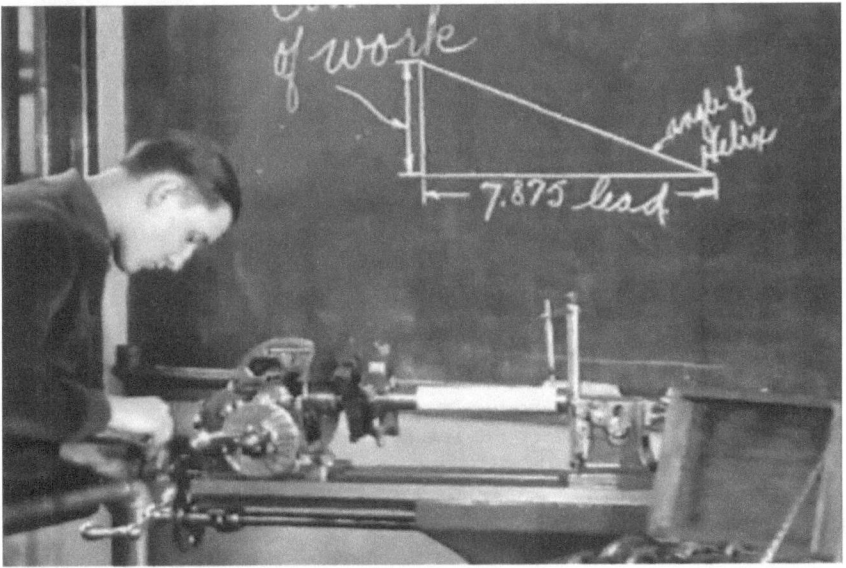

7 | Ford Motion Picture Laboratory, still from *The Henry Ford Trade School*, 1927.

all-important prestige of intellectualism to the work of constructing a car. The film is, in this sense, the capstone of Ford's cinematic project to present industrial knowledge as a subject worthy of academic attention.

By part three of the film, the civically minded education of earlier films, like *Democracy in Education: Penmanship*, all but disappears, and the incorporation of education appears largely complete. The final sequences of *The Henry Ford Trade School* explain that, structured as an extension of Ford's factories, the school uses punch cards to keep attendance and pays the students a "scholarship" of $7.20 per week (a figure that increases depending on performance). The school day lasts for seven hours and takes place fourteen weeks out of the year.

The students, insofar as they can still be referred to as such, work in a factory producing tools and smaller parts for Ford's larger factories. The scope of the film itself shifts away from both instructor and student to focus, instead, on the shop floor and products (see figure 8). The focus on the "making of men" by generating these products, however, does not change. Instead, films depicting schools argued for just what kind of individual is being generated and how an education in mass production achieves some of the goals of Progressive education.

8 | Ford Motion Picture Laboratory, still from *The Henry Ford Trade School*, 1927.

Expanding well beyond just immediate "shop" theory, students are shown learning to sew, cut hair, landscape, and garden. (In the notable enforcement of traditional relations between gender and labor, these tasks are labeled as "the time when thoughts of 'dear old mother' weigh heavily on the heart.") The visual depictions throughout the film are punctuated with interspersed text that draws constitutive power out of manual labor. In this, the film inverts the rhetorical strategy deployed by *Democracy in Education*, allowing for the images to capture the didactic and orderly activities and the intertitles to explain the invisible and loftier changes taking place.

Taking a sampling of these arguments, the film argues that "[a]s the stubborn metal is hammered into useful form, so is the developing character of the boy forged into the strength of manhood" and "[i]n removing the weeds that contaminate and destroy the good in plants, the boys are drawing for themselves an example of worth." Even during lunch, students enter the cafeteria "[w]ith an appetite that a growing boy must have, yet never forgetting for a minute the value of perfect order." In this way the symbolic circuit is closed through the complete fusion of bodily production and structures of culturally acceptable knowledge and sociality. The film concludes, then, with a wholly different vision of the enlightened "Ford Man" as it claims that "skilled mechanics at eighteen; non-employment has no terrors for these boys ... instruction in mathematics and mechanical science makes it easy for the boys to master shop problems." By positioning both mechanical knowledge and physical know-how at the intersection of the school/factory divide, Ford's many films concerned with education worked to legitimize the industrial as the knowledgeable, the work of the assembly line as skilled, and the role of education systems as the inculcation of this valued set of skills and knowledge.

This collapse was not simply a mapping of the industrial onto the educational, however. Rather, the films concerned with depicting the trade school also mapped the educational onto production practices in order to combat characterizations that this form of bodily labor was a lesser form stripped of knowledge. Instead, the company used these broad analogies to braid the bodily and mechanical with the ethical, social, and theoretical to create the concept of an education in "shop theory" (the namesake of the school's textbook). In doing so, Ford presented a vision of a miniaturized social structure, the factory, as a promise for not just the ends but the means of education. Students would receive consistent and internally applicable lessons to prepare them for an emerging industrial economy based in mass, mechanical production. Ford's films present the inverse proposition—that the social conditioning of the individual through these tasks, insofar as they could be intellectualized accordingly, was unleashing tremendous intellectual and social power as well.

While there was not a constructed melting pot or any other overt analogy, these cinematic arguments worked much in the same way as young men entered into the Henry Ford Trade School and exited as largely homogeneous figures of national economic power. Applying such an industrial aesthetic to education allowed the company to narrate the complexities involved with its production practices as work infused with both intellectual and societal complexity. Using a film like *The Henry Ford Trade School*, then, a Ford worker represented a particular kind of knowledgeable worker in the face of arguments that sought to position labor in the Fordist system as "unskilled," precisely because of its fragmented nature. The company argued that the designation of "unskilled," however, doesn't inherently mean a less skillful workforce, but an extensive rhetorical construction of what constitutes "skillful." More importantly, education as a shared institution for so many provided a set of rhetorical substances that could materialize elements of ideology to the public.

Conclusion

There are several ways that we might consider the significance of Ford's educational films in the early decades of the twentieth century. One is the impact these arguments had on the structure of education itself. Writing in 1914, Dewey suggested that "[t]he reasons thus far advanced for making industrial training an organic part of public school education are an undigested medley."[37] Writing again in 1930, Dewey reflected that the direction of public education and the aims of American society were "undigested" no longer. Instead, he wrote, the United States was witnessing "what happens to the isolated individual who lives in a society growing corporate."[38]

Indeed, by many accounts, institutions like Ford Motor Company won the debate over public education, placing the aims of industrial and corporate capitalism in control of educational and social development for decades. E. C. Lagemann suggests that "one cannot understand the history of education in the United States during the twentieth century unless one realizes that . . . John Dewey lost." D. F. Labaree suggests that "the administrative progressives trounced their pedagogical counterparts." Samuel Bowles and Herbert Gintis similarly suggest that "[i]n the end, the role of education in capitalist expansion and the integration of new workers into the wage labor system came to dominate the potential role of schooling as the great equalizer and the instrument of full human development."[39] They add that "the legacy of this period . . . is not exactly what John Dewey had in mind."

Framed as an important moment in the intellectual life of a nation, the rhetorical landscape surrounding education in the 1910s is worthy of attention in its own right. This chapter has explored some of what happened between 1914 and 1930 that contributed to American society "growing corporate." Rather, however, than lamenting that Dewey's humanism and rational deliberation did not win the day, this chapter has asked why this has happened. The debate over education is also, however, an important example of the power of visual rhetoric—in particular the power of the aesthetic to shape matters of important national development.

Barry Brummett has argued that "we live in a world that looks, feels, and sounds like machines and technology," and this remarkable network of similarities is not, he notes, some passive observation of an objective reality but the rhetorical work of "machine aesthetics." Through this aesthetic, we experience and shape the world as a place and set of social configurations that can be modeled on the order and logics of the industrial corporation.

Brummett is not alone in noting this powerful confluence of the visual and the industrial. A number of scholars have highlighted the gradual spread and tremendous power of "industrial realism"—a way of seeing the world as a set of substances useful primarily for their place in human production.[40] David Gartman has argued that "Fordism transformed the visual order and sensibilities of society through its revolutionary mass-production process."[41] Stuart Ewen and Elizabeth Ewen similarly note that Fordism represented "a new aesthetic of power: calibrated, plainly geometric, unadorned, predicated on the synchronicity of moving parts."[42]

Alan Trachtenberg has argued that industrial aesthetics led to "[t]he momentous event of mechanization" that "reproduced itself in ambivalent cultural images of machines and inventors, and in displacements running like waves of shock through the social order." The result, he argued, was an epistemological shift in which "*thought*," once the domain of the specialized worker, "now appears often in the dumb, mystifying shapes of machines, of standing and moving mechanical objects as incapable of explaining themselves to the unknowing eye as the standing stones of ancient peoples."[43]

Ford's educational films highlight that while the mechanical objects were, in a literal sense, unable to explain themselves, the institutions deploying those machines are a very different story, and their purposes were anything but ambivalent. Instead, Ford presented a networked collection of technologies to the public as part of a project working to position the machine-mediated assembly line as a grand metaphor for human potential. In this frame, the public's apparent turn to associating thought and machinery was part of an active aesthetic movement that positioned machines and inventors as symbols of thought that could be systematized and reproduced in public education—one that can be understood through the concept of *similitude* as an expanding argument contending for the public's sense of the "real" and mise-en-scène as the specific vehicle for doing so.

Throughout the early decades of the twentieth century, the conduit between these entities was an extensive rhetorical argument that hinged on visual equivalences between machine-mediated production and knowledge—a complex system of *similitudes* projected at hundreds of screening sites. In this linkage, knowledge meant understanding how various pieces of the world fit together; being educated meant becoming one of many; and schools became knowledge factories in which subjects were compiled with remarkable efficiency to literally produce the figure of the pupil-worker socialized for work on the assembly line. In the process of executing this argument, the company drew on a number of rhetorical conventions—consonance, emulation, and analogy—as they could be executed in terms film scholars have explored through the term "mise-en-scène"—through lighting, angle selection, pacing, and spacing.

For rhetoricians, then, this chapter has worked to understand an idea like mise-en-scène from a rhetorical perspective (and asks how such an idea expands rhetoric in return). Adrian Martin has argued that mise-en-scène is less a discrete, defined concept and more a shared idea that has existed largely within the definitions of film scholars.[44] More often than not, however, these cinematic features have been considered for their visual poetics—as a way of explaining film's artistic properties, its particular "magic" or moments of genius. While several film scholars have equated the concept with "visual rhetoric," a detailed account of what makes the idea particularly rhetorical has been elusive.[45] From this rhetorical perspective, the idea of mise-en-scène maps well onto the kind of work corporate actors—Ford in particular at this moment—engage in to produce economic arguments. Essentially, companies make the style of the lived world align with the various ideological constructs underlying economic imperatives. This requires elaborate visual coordination. Ford's films, as I read them, display the rhetorical potential of mise-en-scène when paired with a concept like similitude to understand the rhetorical nature of style.

There was, however, one last major similitude not addressed in this chapter—the largest, most powerful of the group. Foucault called this the *sympathies*, "which excites the things of the world to movement and can draw even the most distant of them together ... an instance of the *Same* so strong and so insistent that it will not rest content to be merely one form of likeness; it has the dangerous power of assimilating, of rendering things identical to one another, of mingling them, of causing their individuality to disappear—and thus of rendering them foreign to what they were before."[46] This power, as the next chapter will explore, was reserved for depictions of the economy itself. In this frame, the educational films contributed to attempts at a wholesale shift to Fordism in part by converting laboring bodies into props (notably, not characters) that could only be understood in the context of a more expansive drama of economic change. One's job, they communicated, was no longer the domain of the local and no longer separable from a vast interconnected network of resources and labors spanning the globe, and (perhaps most importantly) the industrial corporation was the defining institution for mediating this network.

For viewers of these educational films, then, the day-to-day work of producing and earning suddenly became something more: a set of tasks that represented collaborative knowledge and machine-oriented aptitudes, parts of a larger systemic wave of economic change sweeping across many regions and professions. More important than any of this, perhaps, they established going to work as a process worthy of showing others and discussing as a matter of national interest.

2

Ford's Montage Films and the "Rhetorical Economy"

At the same time that Ford's educational films were producing similitude-based arguments that directly addressed debates over education, they were also contributing to a larger project by the company to reconfigure the economy itself. It is hard to understate, in this context, the importance of Ford's educational films being produced serially and distributed nationally at a time when the nation was trying to come to terms with the nature of its economy as well.

In a single month, an educational film like *Cut and Dried: The Lumber Industry* depicted the logging industry as dynamic and changing to loggers throughout the Pacific Northwest at the same time that dockworkers in Louisiana were being shown their roles in national commerce in a film like *Sugar Cane Growing, Louisiana* (a film that circulated amid debates over changing the state's constitution because "a new era of industrial and commercial economy has come into being").[1] In that same month, coal miners and their children in Kentucky were watching *The Ford Way of Mining Coal*, a film that tied work in the mines with a massive distribution system to the Northeast, while ranchers and their children in Texas and Oklahoma were watching *Roundup on the U*, which presaged the rise of the mass cattle farm. More than this, these figures were seeing each other's industries as, at once, part of a larger, shared, and rapidly changing economy.

In this sense, these films were providing partial glimpses into what Woodrow Wilson was repeatedly describing to the nation as "nothing short of a new social age, a new era of human relationships, a new stage-setting for the drama of life" in which "a new economic society has sprung up, and we must effect a new set of adjustments."[2] This chapter asks a number of questions about this historical moment: How were these individuals being asked to understand the scale and scope of these purported changes? How were these groups being encouraged to think of the shifts in their local industries in terms of a grand, nationally experienced collective known as "the economy," let alone a "new economic society"? Further, how were they to integrate seeing other regional economic activities as part of the same grand trend in the changing nature of manufacturing, resource production, and labor?

One answer to these questions was for all of these figures to head, once again, to the local movie theater (or any of the many places Ford's films were being shown) to catch a particular genre of film being circulated by the company. Working alongside the educational films, there were a number of films designed to produce what I will explore in this chapter as a "rhetorical economy"—a narration that worked to give its audience the sense that they have seen and can understand the nature of this otherwise ephemeral social construct that is evoked by the term "the economy."

We might, then, imagine these loggers, dockworkers, coal miners, and ranchers amid crowds across the country in 1921 congregating in theaters, in public squares, at YMCAs, and at "industrial caravans" as they wait in anticipation for the films to start. The lights would dim or the sun would set, the projector would begin to whir, and the screen would illuminate with the image of a fisherboy clad in overalls and a straw hat gazing longingly at a gleaming, spired castle (figure 9). The words "As Dreams Come True" would fade into the foreground, and a film intended to sweep these figures up into a narrative of economic development would begin. This narrative would be nothing short of a fairy tale–like vision that appeared when discourses of American "bootstrap" ingenuity met with the still-fresh mechanical prowess of American industry in the wake of mass production's appearance in Ford's factories.

As Dreams Come True

In part because of its goal to capture the sum of an industrial regime—but also because of silent films' reliance on written intertitles to offer context—*As Dreams Come True* is made up of short, abrupt chunks of reenactments of the past, panning depictions of landscapes, close-ups of laboring workers, and footage from Henry Ford's personal life. The film is, formally, a montage of montages: a series of brief vignettes made up of sharply cut scenes that work to narrate the complete life of Henry Ford in just over ten minutes. Yet within this sleek biographical framework, the film presents an expansive set of images that worked to narrate the internal logics of the Fordist economy.

9 | Ford Motion Picture Laboratory, still from *As Dreams Come True*, 1921.

Broken into a collection of "chapters," most with a running time of between one and two minutes, *As Dreams Come True* depicts Henry Ford's upbringing, the array of resources and production practices that go into the creation of a Ford automobile, the role of Fordist production in World War I, the social nature of doing business (from farm chores to large corporate mergers), the life of leisure enjoyed by Henry Ford and friends, and the formation of the Henry Ford Trade School. Collectively, these vignettes create a visual narrative that ties new forms of education, class, labor, and leisure to mass production and mass production to both national and personal advancement. When layered one after the other, this compilation of scenes generates a set of part-to-whole relations outlining the potential of a society based on Fordist production. All of this, in turn, is embedded in a frame narrative positioning these developments as part of Henry Ford's meticulously planned and lifelong vision for society.

To capture all of these elements, the film progresses at a blistering pace, flooding its viewers with disparate images. In three minutes, the sum of Henry Ford's childhood and the birth of Fordism unfold on-screen; in three more, this grows into an unmatched industrial regime; in three more, Ford is a middle-aged, contented man enjoying the fruits of his revolutionary labors with friends and family. Concluding this trajectory in terms of immediate use to its audiences, one of the closing intertitles of the film provides a quote from Henry Ford that reads: "My ambition is to employ still more men; to spread the profits of this industrial system to the greatest possible number, to help them build up their lives and their homes."

Left with this message, viewers across the country left their respective viewing sites having been shown a structural vision that tied industrial action with the full trajectory of a human life, with an industrial version of Progressive national pride, and with a clearer sense of how production and consumption could guide their own lives. This vision worked by presenting the public with new imagined futures, by converting bodies and minds into particular forms of labor, and by pairing this new labor with access to new forms of classed consumption. Serving as a model for the Fordist "economy," *As Dreams Come True* argued that everyone could have access to a better economically driven existence should they choose to accept Ford Motor Company's invitation to become a part of its industrial vision.

As an example of the montage-driven film at work in the narration of an economy, *As Dreams Come True* transforms elements of the everyday into symbols for a budding economic system. In particular, the company presented the aspirations of its figurehead to naturalize a larger, and often turbulent, boom-and-bust structure for economic cycles; it used the combination of fracturing and suturing made possible by the montage to obfuscate elements of labor on the assembly line; and it used the layering of scenes to recast an influx of money into new forms of capital including military prowess, mass consumption, and leisure.

When organized into a single narrative, these ideas created the appearance of a cohesive "Fordist economy" on-screen. This cohesion, in turn, justified the prospect of standing in one place and conducting the same task thousands of times as "labor," re-humanized this labor by positioning it as simply one station in the "line" of one's life—a period of time justified by the equal gains in both leisure and social mobility—and presented the production of a material commodity—the car—as setting in motion the production of countless material and immaterial forms of valuable capital: citizenship, order, and the advancement of civilization itself.

Through closer attention to the rhetorical economy produced by *As Dreams Come True*, I argue that what gets codified as "the economy" is a contested set of rhetorical affiliations that take shape as a variety of actors, from governments to nonprofits to economic competitors, work to convince the public of the accuracy and effectiveness of their vision. The film uses two important rhetorical strategies in the production of its visualized economy. First, it depicts a number of key economic concepts—or *topoi*, in rhetorical terms—as they cohered to create the appearance of a closed system of meaning. Second, these *topoi* were placed in increasingly complex and interrelated textual structures using montage. Before returning to the film for closer analysis, I will address each of these concepts as analytical tools.

Economic *Topoi*

One of the interesting side effects of trying to figure out how Ford had shaped economic sensibilities in its earliest years demands that we first address a more fundamental question: What are economies? Rather than a stable structure, a number of scholars have argued that economies are imagined configurations that animate the material distribution of rights and resources. For example, Christian De Cock, Max Baker, and Christina Volkmann have claimed that "[a]ny time we try and deal with 'the economy' or 'finance capital' we confront the non-representable . . . we then have to map and explore the imaginaries in order to identify the type of images and allegories that have been invented or mobilized."[3]

When rhetoricians encounter such a "non-representable" concept that exists, instead, at the intersections of many ideas and opinions, they have analyzed the idea of meaning through the idea of *topoi*, or "commonplaces." Exploring a spatial account of the concept, Lynette Hunter explains that "[a] topic provides a general setting for a discussion, a framework for arguments rather than a fixed set of rules, standards or axioms. Those involved in the discussion need to agree that the setting is appropriate."[4] The purpose of *topoi*, then, is to make individuals with different perspectives and experiences capable of speaking with one another productively or acting in accordance with one another. Christa Olson continued the evolution of *topoi* as rhetorical tools by defining them as "nodes of social value and common sense that provide places of return for convening arguments across changing circumstances."[5] She adds that "visual images are ... frequent and natural carriers of the commonplace."[6]

This kind of topical criticism is useful for understanding economic relations in two ways. First, the "economic" itself serves as a powerful commonplace that individuals often return to (or rarely leave these days) in order to define and invent meanings. The repeated circulation of economic films like *As Dreams Come True* presented the economy as a topic one might be able to readily bring up on a long car ride with acquaintances or avoid entirely for fear of hearing *everyone's* opinion on the matter. In this way, putting a topic in circulation is one way that a rhetor can produce or constrain social imaginaries, can reduce resistance to an idea (if it seems common or already seen), and can connect and combine otherwise disparate concepts.

In a telling moment where form and content overlap, Casey Boyle ties the concept of the *topos* directly to Fordist production, arguing that "rhetorical *topoi* produce not only an assembly line of places for developing common material upon which we rely for discussing content, but also offer an assemblage of mediations that enact a matter of concern."[7] In this sense, one of the goals of a film like *As Dreams Come True* was to encourage its viewers to see the world through the lens of the Fordist economy and, further, to more readily accept this kind of economic lens in the future.

But an economy isn't just a singular *topos* but a frequently visited site of meaning that is made up of many secondary topics used to describe a wide range of actions, ideas, and objects in economic terms. For late capitalism, the economy is constructed through the definition and combination of topics like futurity, speculation, and capital. In the case of Ford's rhetorical work in the 1920s, however, the company sought to redefine economic relations through the combination of imagined futures, labor, and a combination of value and capital.

Economies, in this sense, have been experienced as *topoi*-driven constructs because they require shared spaces of exchange and shared transformations of value into equivalent terms. Highlighting this point, Gayatri Spivak has articulated a topic-driven framework for approaching the symbolic core of capitalism, providing the following schematic to help depict the need for cohesion between economic *topoi*:

$$\text{Labor} \xrightarrow{\text{representation}} \text{Value} \xrightarrow{\text{representation}} \text{Money} \xrightarrow{\text{transformation}} \text{Capital.}$$ [8]

In this account, it is layered symbolic activity—a matter of varying representations and transformations—that moves individuals through several *topoi* (represented by the concepts of labor on one end and capital on the other) before they get a sense of the functioning economy and their place in it. Individuals, in these models, experience the economy as a network of constellated relations between objects and ideas drawn from the substances in their immediate surroundings that, in turn, get ordered into a set of recognizable economic topics—namely, labor, value, money, capital, and commodity. Spivak's choice to put the work of representation and transformation on the spaces between labor and value or money and capital is particularly significant for understanding the importance of rhetoric in debates over economic reality. It is in these representational and transformational connections that rhetorical economies are formed through appeals that encourage a public to understand interrelated narratives of labor, its value, the role of money, and ultimately the final formation of capital structures.

In this frame, *As Dreams Come True* didn't function by faithfully replicating an existing economy—such a process is largely impossible. Instead, it produced the appearance of a stable configuration out of what William Connolly has defined as "an unstable capitalist 'axiomatic' that consists of knots between capital, labor, and the commodity form." By creating both cohesive and appealing "knots" between these economic *topoi*, Ford rhetorically constructed what appeared to be "axiomatic" and, therefore, was capable of "creat[ing] constraints and possibilities" for economic existence in the minds of the public. For these constraints and possibilities to "function," however, the films needed to wrestle "the stretchability and volatility of elements that both constitute capitalism in some ways and impinge upon it in others" so that "these elements . . . achieve a fair degree of coordination."[9]

Rhetorical economies succeed by producing cohesion among their parts—by skillfully combining those elements traditionally associated with economic relations mapping these elements onto as wide a number of jobs and resources as possible. In this regard, *As Dreams Come True* is also an occasion to examine how the emergence of the cinematic montage—with its ability to condense and combine—enhanced Ford's ability to connect these economic *topoi* to better convince audiences that they understood the economy. Put more simply, montage is a technique that produces perceived wholes; economies are social structures that require such wholeness to exist.

Montage: "A New Filmic Rhetoric"

Like the assembly line, the montage enjoyed a period of important influence during the early decades of the twentieth century. *Montage*, translated, means "to assemble," and like the assembly line's conversion of menial and individual bodily movements into a single unified act of labor, the montage fragments individual images and reconfigures their individual meanings into a new text with the potential to disrupt fixed notions of time and space. In the hands of Ford Motor Company's Motion Picture Laboratory, this cinematic technique was a fortuitous overlap.

On the surface, montage describes a fairly straightforward textual feature—the use of sharp cuts to produce a single sequence from many different shots. However, Sergei Eisenstein, writing in the early twentieth century, argued that the montage was an effective political tool because it could present "undifferentiated wholeness and flow of undifferentiated representations of the stage preceding the stages of consciousness that actively 'makes divisions' at higher stages of development."[10] Working at this "preceding" stage, a stage that theoretically incorporates a spectator before they even have the chance to consider alternatives, Eisenstein concluded that montage could usher in a "new sphere of filmic rhetoric" grounded in "the possibility of bearing an abstract social judgment" through the juxtaposition and disruption of time.

Similarly, drawing on Eisenstein's precognitive account of this technique, Gilles Deleuze argues that, even in the simplest of cinematic gestures (placing two scenes next to one another, progressing through time by cutting out intermediate shots) there is "another way of looking at the cinema, a way in which it would [be] the organ for perfecting new reality."[11] Perfecting a new reality was, as *As Dreams Come True* makes clear, at the heart of the Fordist project.

Elaborating on why this textual feature was capable of such revolutionary modes for meaning-making, Deleuze echoes Eisenstein's claims by suggesting that "[m]ontage is the determination of the whole ... by means of the continuities, cutting and false continuities."[12] In one sense, Deleuze means this literally: the motion picture's simulation of time and motion is dependent on the splicing together of thousands of captured images and, by extension, thousands of fragmented units of time and movement. He also, however, means this as a way of understanding the rhetorical capacities of film. From these accumulated fragments, he argues, comes a cohesive cinematic thought—an understanding of what is real within the particular world captured on-screen (that has profound impacts on what is perceived as real off of the screen). Deleuze suggests, then, that as a physical medium, "[t]he screen, as the frame of frames, gives a common standard of measurement to things which do not have one—long shots of countryside and close-ups of the face, an astronomical system and single drop of water—parts which do not have the same denominator of distance, relief or light."[13] He argues that from disparate concepts the film produces commonality—a sense of a clear, identifiable point that can be seen, understood, and discussed.

More than just making a theoretical point about film's effect on audiences, Deleuze also examined a grammar of the montage as a way of understanding how a set of "relations" can be produced through specific techniques on-screen. Montages, Deleuze argues, can be read through the connections drawn between the frame (a single image), the shot (how this image, when joined with others, "spreads out in space" and "is transformed in duration"), and the movement that occurs as these shots create a "whole." Between these layers of cinematic construction, then, a set of "relations" develop—these can be spatial relations, conceptual relations, or temporal relations—and "through relations, the whole is transformed or changes qualitatively." In this grammar for reading a film, it is not the discrete elements of the images that generate rhetorical force (as was the case with the previous chapter's reading of mise-en-scène) but the interrelation between them.[14] He also, however, notes a number of effects generated by these "relations"—drawing comparisons, condensing time, and overlapping content to create conceptual connections.

As such, montage is an intriguing technology for producing and interlocking *topoi*, generally. However, for an immense company looking to generate a systemic economy in its own image, this formal feature presented a powerful opportunity. Montage-driven films like *As Dreams Come True* made it possible for Ford Motor Company to present a cohesive vision of the economy—what I have called a rhetorical economy—into visual and economic culture in the early 1920s. This rhetorical economy worked to impact its audience's conceptions of what was meant by "the economy" and what the concept could potentially mean in the future. More than this, the film made the economy a familiar, approachable topic by breaking the concept into a set of interrelated *topoi*.

In returning to the film, then, this reading will point out three economic *topoi*—imagined futures, labor, and capital—as they were produced and interconnected on-screen. In turn, I will also treat this as an opportunity to observe these *topoi* more generally as sites that have been written about (and therefore further embedded in what we think when we think "economy" over many years).

Finally, I treat the film as an opportunity to consider how rhetorical features attributed to *topoi*—their ability to limit, to connect and combine, to invent—functioned in one example of economic narration.

Topic One: Imagined Futures

As the title slide of *As Dreams Come True* suggests, Ford grounded its early calls for significant upheaval in the American economy in the biography of its founder. It repeatedly treated this story as a piece of national folklore chronicling, in print and on-screen, the story of Henry Ford as he reimagined the potential for machine-mediated industry to fundamentally shift the very fabric of how the nation lived and worked. This strategy was converted into cinematic form; after the castle, fisherboy, and opening credits of *As Dreams Come True* fade, the audience is introduced to the birthplace of Henry Ford: a moderately sized, unassuming farm home set against the backdrop of rural Michigan and framed by leafless trees.

To see the home exclusively as a humble dwelling, however, would be a mistake, as the image fades into an intertitle that deems it "the birthplace of the dream, the realization of which has increased the opportunities and added to the share of labor." On-screen, this dream is not an abstract, general theme (of the broad "American Dream" ilk) but a specific aptitude—an ability to dream, to imagine, to invent—in short, an economic skill. As a cinematic convention, however, the backdrop of the house serves two purposes: first, it suggests that visionary changes in an economy can come from the most unexpected of sites; and second, the location anchors the film's first use of montage.

As the intertitle identifies, there are two stories being told in this opening sequence, the first a specific story of an extraordinary life that, in turn, materializes the second more abstract notion of an economic dream in the making. All of this is placed, initially, in a brief narration of young Henry Ford's relationship with education. As this film was circulating simultaneously with Ford's many educational films, *As Dreams Come True* both works alongside and adds new frameworks to the educational argument already outlined in chapter 1. These opening scenes also, however, make clear that a number of the cinematic effects made available by the montage—the layering of narratives on top of one another to create new, more complex, meaning and the juxtaposition of separate points in time—would be of particular use to the company's economic narrations.

After establishing this dual setting, the opening shot of the first sequence features an adolescent Henry Ford as he is walking to school when he sees and picks up a discarded machine part while passing the family's barn. He then races off camera, and a sharp cut places him in a medium shot at his desk in the one-room schoolhouse, where, under the cover of a decoy textbook, he is shown working out design blueprints for what would become a steam-powered engine. Eventually, the boy pulls the actual mechanical pieces from his bag and assembles them neatly out of the sight of the teacher, returning finally to the mechanical drawings to record his thoughts.

The audience is invited, in this vignette, to engage in two identifications that were integral to Ford's topical treatment of the imagined future: the "Boy on the Farm" (a moniker attributed periodically to Henry Ford) and the "First Workshop" (what the film dubs school) that produced him. The Boy on the Farm archetype presented a new kind of young man developing into a mechanical visionary from humble beginnings by making his way through an inefficient educational environment. Such identification, on one hand, was a way of making it clear that Henry Ford was no robber baron, as had sometimes been the public perception of tycoons in the Gilded Age.[15] Instead, the scene reiterates a common narrative that Ford had come from the American heartland, had worked his ideas from a common set of circumstances, and was a living, breathing arbiter of change.

On the one hand, this presentation worked to generate discourses of meritocracy—as any industrious figure could become such an archetypal "boy" (where, it implies, traditional academic and industrial structures were elitist in nature). On the other hand, this figure of the "Boy on the Farm" put a human face onto the far more expansive set of arguments about the relationship that was developing between education, "practical" models of knowledge, and the new paradigm of mass mechanical production. Depicting Ford as the model for a new generation of mechanically oriented subjects that simultaneously maintained the traditional values of rural America (self-reliance, persistence, ingenuity) alongside modern mechanized production practices created an important link between the changing economic conditions of the country and traditional values. In turn, the film worked to capture the wholesale shifts in structures of knowledge that were embodied in young Henry Ford, but not in the formal school he was attending.

Reflecting this new subject, the sequence recasts education itself as a concept that ought to be about practical learning and its relationship to modes of production, as the schoolhouse is deemed the "First Workshop." Contrasting with the formal education young Ford is busy ignoring in his rural school, the film then posits that it is outside of school that "the usual arduous tasks did their share to stimulate the mental activities of the 'Boy on the Farm.'" In a montage consisting of scenes located on the farm/"birthplace of a dream," young Ford is shown looking at a farm's water wheel (ostensibly, the impetus for the company's eventual use of hydroelectric power) and watching a boiler-engine tractor in action (the impetus for the diesel engine he was working out in class).

When placed in the historical context surrounding the film's release, the combination of these archetypes appeals to laborers wanting to see their own aptitudes and knowledge sets valued. It also drew on a national mythos that had been closely tied with self-reliance and land ownership as sites of common knowledge rather than with academic achievement as a model for social mobility. This narrative knotting of depictions of the "Boy on the Farm" and the "First Workshop" extended Ford's existing arguments for a more applicable model of education, justified mechanical forms of knowledge as intellectual, redefined what could constitute the successful student, and extended this concept to be available to anyone (in the face of existing models of exclusionary concepts of what intellect is, who has it, and where they ought to apply it). In witnessing the formation of the first "Ford Man," through his relationship with a "hands-on" and informal educational system, *As Dreams Come True*'s opening scenes sought to naturalize machine-oriented production as a form of common knowledge, particularly one drawn from the necessities of a rural landscape.

After this educational vignette, however, the film works to convert this educational system into a sweeping vision of where industrial knowledge comes from and what it is capable of. To do so, the next sequence puts the act of economic imagining on-screen. The sequence opens with a shot composed of a number of medium frames centered on an actor playing a teenage Henry Ford as he transports a wagon of wood slowly using a team of stubborn horses. The film then cuts to a closer shot of young Ford as he halts the horses and looks downward, seemingly lost in deep concentration. In a sharp cut, the film returns to the medium shot; this time the same figure is hauling wood with a tractor at twice the speed. Replicating the abrupt end to his daydream, the film cuts back to the wagon-driving Ford, who forlornly spurs the horses onward at a plodding pace.

Using the same convention, the next scene opens with a shot of young Ford splitting the transported logs clumsily by ax. He then looks off into the distance lost in the daydream once again. The scene then cuts to two older men socializing around a Fordson tractor rigged to split wood while young Ford pulls up on a second tractor to deliver a new batch of lumber—all appear in much better spirits. Once again, the film uses a sharp cut to return to young Ford in his present reality as he clumsily hacks at the wood with an ax. Returning to this identical woodcutting scene in the final third of the film (a section, I argue, that is devoted to addressing the economic topic of "capital"), *As Dreams Come True* drives home this point more overtly.

After an intertitle declaring that "the 'new' relieves and assists the old," this later scene positions the three figures of Ford's youth not only as a dream materialized but as "friends of forty years or more" bound by their production—by their pulling of boilers across farmsteads and ability to chat as a Ford tractor tooled with a function for splitting wood did most of the work. In the later rendition of this scene, the Fordson tractor sits on the left, a belt spans from left to center, and the center of the shot is occupied by a splitter (see figure 10). The two men are pushed to the margins of the shot on the left but look a great deal less belabored than young Ford. Driving home this comparative framework, after several seconds of the two farmers splitting wood using the tractor, an aged Henry Ford hops from his Model T and declares, "Boys, that's a whole lot easier than it used to be." In this moment, the viewer sees the dream of young Ford literally come true and is, in the process, encouraged to understand its significance in terms of both industrial innovation and the humanizing potential of economic advancement in general. The scene, in this sense, is a direct response to circulating claims that Ford's production methods were deeply dehumanizing.

This sequence both functions as an integral step in the construction of the "imagined dream" *topos* and, in Deleuze's terms, is one example of a *"convergent montage*, which alternates the moments of two actions which will come back together again."[16] The frames that make up this sequence feature a stable character and scene—Ford on his farm—but the shots and the movement suggested between them, when juxtaposed, are dialectical in nature. For Deleuze, such a cinematic trick invites an audience to directly compare these juxtaposed points of content to produce "an indirect image of time" or, in the case of Ford's imagination narrative, of two conceptions of time.[17]

Using these two narratives of a single space depicted at two different points in time—the first marked by toil and monotony, the second a dream defined by

10 | Ford Motion Picture Laboratory, stills from *As Dreams Come True*, 1921.

efficiency and social enhancement—the film presents a great deal about Fordism. It projects the importance of finding intersections between innovation and production, it extols the power of machines, it visualizes the social progress made possible by machine's use, and it reframes the idea of "creative destruction" as the boy imagines the supplanting of one form of labor by another as a natural process in the face of human ingenuity.

Of course, the great myth of these scenes is that the economy facilitated by mechanical production would also tolerate three people doing the job one could do and that they could do so at a leisurely pace—but that was precisely the kind of obfuscation the film was designed to produce. This speaks to the power of producing a rhetorical economy. Economic narrations rely, at least in part, on the imagined ideal of an economic system (whether this is of Fordism, of a free market, or of the equal distribution of work and goods) while also offering this idealized vision in comparison to existing economic and social relations.

In this scene, we observe one of Ford's most frequently used topics in economic argument, one that combines ideas of imagination and future to create the conceptual *topos* of the "imagined future." Jens Beckert has argued that "the creation of credible imagined futures . . . is a major accomplishment, necessary for the operation of the capitalist economy" and that scholars studying this economy "must ask why certain imagined futures prevail over others."[18] Indeed, attention to the production of imagined relations is one of the most frequent ways that scholars have defined the economic as deeply rhetorical. For a number of economic theorists, these imagined futures work in two ways. First, individual actors in an economy need to imagine their positions in an otherwise ephemeral construct. Karl Marx, for example, tied this kind of imagining directly to ideas about labor and laboring, arguing that "[a]t the end of every labor-process, we get a result that already existed in the imagination of the laborer at its commencement. He not only effects a change of form in the material on which he works, but he also realizes a purpose of his own."[19]

This ability to position physical production in larger narratives of purpose and progress is what separates "the worst of architects from the best of bees." Second, imagination is positioned as a catalyst—new ideas stem from reimaginings of modes of production, services, or resource acquisition.[20] In contemporary terms, this is often described as innovation. From this perspective, *As Dreams Come True*'s ability to describe the economic as the work of a specific, modeled version of industrial imagination then applied to the work of designing machines to supplant human labor places the concept on squarely rhetorical grounds. For some watching this film, this would presage that mechanical knowledge was the way of the future.

On that note, the economic topic related to "futures" is more or less what it sounds like: economic arguments about identity and innovation grounded in particular accounts of how economies can make for better futures. In seeing the beginnings of mass, mechanically aided production as an extension of an organically conceived "dream," this early vignette makes way for important justifications of new forms of mass-mediated labor.

Through this initial pair of montages, then, *As Dreams Come True* has primed its audiences to see the subsequent appearance of the moving assembly line and its resulting reorientation of labor as part of a much different narrative than just dehumanizing mass production via laborious drudgery. Through narratives like this one, the cinematic story of Henry Ford's ingenuity worked to quell concerns over the potential shocks in labor and production practices as the narrative of the "Boy on the Farm" contriving ways to lessen the backbreaking work of farming functionally naturalized a number of the fundamental tenets of Fordism: a shift from rural to urban economic relations, to divisions of labor, and to machine-augmented labor. These production practices are, instead, positioned as the dynamic outcroppings of both changing and progressive forms of labor as well as new outlets for recognizing proper industrial knowledge and conduct. Attaining this knowledge and maintaining proper conduct, the film eventually argues, were important precursors to achieving the "dream."

In this sense, this montage-driven depiction of an imagined future enacts two rhetorical functions of addressing a topic. First, the scene displays what Richard McKeon has called the "managerial function" of topics that limit the ways in which others can conceive of a social system or invent solutions to immediate problems. Anyone witnessing the film that had previously imagined the chopping of wood or the hauling of lumber as an integral and necessary act of labor is positioned to now see the same tasks as evidence of their slow drift into antiquity as new mechanized forms of labor reshaped the landscape. The woodcutting scene also, however, presents the generative potential of *topoi* as they become "places for the perception, discovery, and explanation of the unknown."[21] Ford has placed elements of both of these principles in this sequence. The company presented one's place in an economic structure as a simultaneously confining practice in terms of production (one couldn't hope to compete without machines) and near endless possibilities for what to do with the acquired capital from these machines. What dreams, it argued, can be conjured within industrial capitalism?

We might also, however, position this as a considerable rhetorical advantage for the economic system. It offered a clear yet flexible network for fulfilling "dreams." One could, in the confines of this collection of *topoi*, shape and direct a life—infuse it with meaning and incentives, share it with others, pass it on to future generations. In drawing on a set of familiar economic *topoi*, Ford reconfigured the radical and disruptive nature of what it was doing to bodies, to the environment, and to conceptions of the local into terms that appeared to be logical extensions of economic development. In this theoretical framework, the rhetorical production of imagined futures is an economic topic of the utmost importance—but also a topic dependent on arguments capable of separating and comparing time frames.

In sum, by examining the various "relations" that created an imagined future on-screen, I argue that the Fordist rhetorical economy relied on an argument that economic development was the domain of a class of farmer/inventor/engineers—at once adept at mechanical knowledge and how to efficiently bring the natural world into accord with human need. Ford's imagined economic realities became credible through their alignment with a version of common knowledge familiar to the audiences it sought to persuade. These realities became "futures" by using this credible knowledge to unsettle its spectators' perceptions of the present. Montage served as an integral feature in each of these processes.

And yet, as convincing as the idyllic scenes of a young Ford developing into a new kind of economic agent would be on their own, economic arguments require a wider network of connections. To ensure the complete structural understanding of "Fordism" as a feasible economic system, *As Dreams Come True* continues to develop these new forms and ideologies of labor via mass production. To do so, the film needed to balance the visual constructions of an otherwise abstract economic "dream" with the more immediately material need in an economy for recognizable forms of "labor."

For many of the moviegoers unsure of industrial production, the depicted principles laid out in the first four minutes of the film needed to align with mass production labor processes beyond the farmstead—a materialization that was carried out next in the film through cinematic depictions of thousands of workers' bodies as labor commodities in an expansive system of production. Taking up this challenge, *As Dreams Come True* follows the story of young Henry Ford's imagined future with a depiction of the modern mass production–oriented corporation and the place of the individual (particularly the individual body) in this process. In this way, the film arrives at a second integral topic in the production of economic imaginaries: labor. What tasks count as work, what separates how valuable particular tasks are, and who gets a say in the pace and configuration of these tasks all rely on narrative, change over time, and make up important elements in the work of presenting labor as an economic topic. Highlighting the rhetorical nature of labor as an economic topic, Karl Marx once observed that "[l]abor seems to be a quite simple category ... when it is economically conceived in this simplicity, 'labor' is a modern category as are the relations which create this simple abstraction."[22] As a "modern category," however, labor is anything but a "simple abstraction." It is, instead, a complex configuration of narrative effects that give meaning to the productive practices that guide economic life.

Observing how the use of labor as a topic has been practiced historically, Hannah Arendt has argued that particular economic rhetors display an ability to generate a cogent system of imagined labor relations by "naturalizing" economic activities. She points out that Marx, in his own right, "had to introduce a natural force, the 'labor power' of the body, to account for labor's productivity and a progressing process of growing wealth" and before that John Locke "had to trace property to a natural origin of appropriation in order to force open those stable, worldly boundaries that 'enclose' each person's privately owned share of the world 'from the common.'"[23] In their particular historical moments and in order to define labor in ways that would fit their larger economic visions, these scholars turned to written texts and the variety of affordances this allowed—figurative language, didactic explanation, and sequential logical reasoning to explain the underlying imagined principles of "labor power" and "appropriation" that applied economic meaning to bodies and spaces. For Marx this meant drawing on the language of dialectical materialism, and for John Locke this meant an extended act of historicization.

Ford too sought to naturalize its mechanized and distributed forms of labor by grounding them in a "dream" (both literal and figural) of a visionary industrialist but also by presenting them as a ubiquitous and neatly planned system. Part and parcel of this argument was the rapid depiction and incorporation of new forms of labor extending out from the River Rouge plant in Detroit. In this next sequence, the film also draws on a second affordance of montage—the rapid condensing of material—to argue for particular understandings of labor as a topic.

Topic Two: Labor as "Links in a Mighty Chain"

After the imaginative core of Fordist economic relations had been established as an act of personal history for Henry Ford, the film pivots on an intertitle that declares that Ford would be "Leaving home at nineteen to work, love and serve the world." It rapidly presents Ford's invention of the basics behind a Model T—"the commercial car on which the company was organized"—and sharply cuts to a frame composed entirely of the Dearborn, Michigan, factory.

Sequences three and four of *As Dreams Come True*, then, turn more directly to the narrative of the existing Fordist production regime itself—a regime, the film argues, that "will endure by faith in your fellowman's service to the World and Justice" (this service, predictably, being composed primarily of that fellowman's labor on the assembly line). The movement across these shots works to capture the full extension of production practices that contribute to the construction of a Model T. The camera first sweeps across a series of panoramic and aerial depictions of Ford's Highland Park production plant: its hulking walls and smokestacks billowing out black smoke contrast with the quick movements of Model Ts on the move and workers smoking outside the factory. The opening frame of this enormous production facility ties together a montage chronicling the many resources and objects that are drawn together to create the automobile—a scene that provides some visual parallels as smoke seems to billow out from all elements of this process—cars, factories, workers.

A single written metaphor binds together this massive network of resources as the film labels materials and laborers that make up its production practices as equal "links in a mighty chain," a metaphor that is supported by a sequence that rattles off scenes of a dammed river used to run a hydroelectric power plant; the mechanical processes involved in the mining, hauling, and refining of trees into panels; the lots of coal stored and shipped for blast furnaces; and the production of raw rubber into a seemingly endless stockyard of tires. These resources are then put into a relationship with human bodies working inside the factory.

For example, the image of young Ford splitting a few branches into logs for a fire serves as context for the next shot of two workers hauling a truckload of timber (at least twenty full tree trunks, stripped of branches) from Michigan's north woods. Juxtaposed with the moving assembly line in Dearborn, this mass foresting is followed by a scene of one worker pulling wooden planks from the assembly line, shearing thinner strips from their trunks, and setting them on the conveyor belt to make up side panels for the Model T.

Consistently, the material labor portions of Ford's films rely on what Deleuze identifies as a "parallel alternate montage" that features "the image of one part succeeding another according to a rhythm."[24] These montages create schematic depictions of complete assembly processes, blurring each unique element in a series into the illusion of a single, consistent act. As we have seen, Ford's films consistently used this kind of rhythmic montage to put hundreds of manufacturing scenes into conversation as they were being brought together in the manufacturing of complex commodities.

While organizational expanse and mass production were the stars of the show for many of these labor vignettes (and, often, entire films), what viewers actually saw, almost unilaterally, were human bodies at work in new and increasingly complex systems of production. Chapter 1 has already examined some of the power of this manufacturing aesthetic to connect and combine at the level of the frame—identifying how color, lighting, and movement were used to celebrate order and interconnectedness. Attending to the role of montage in these production scenes highlights that through this collection of carefully crafted frames, the assembly line developed as a materialized version of montage-reason tasked with incorporating its human figures into a dynamic production process. On film, the specific nature of individualized work is obscured by the dynamism of the montage to highlight individual labor as one integral contribution to the overall product through mechanically aided bodily output.

While the entirety of this process is not captured in most of these labor films (even though a Model T's production-in-full lasted only ten minutes at its height of efficiency, a process shorter than the length of *As Dreams Come True*), the contributions to the construction of the automobile that do receive specific attention on film consist of truncated tasks like pulling a wheel spoke from one machine in the line, turning it 180 degrees, and setting it on a new track for further assembly or inspecting a newly cast part and setting it in a moving bin to be carried to the next point of assembly. These are tasks that require, almost exclusively, a body ready and able to perform repeatedly and without variation. The production of such a body—or, more precisely, producing those willing to occupy a body in such a state—is a matter of particularly intricate incorporational rhetoric.

These tasks, when viewed for longer than the four to five seconds the film devoted to them, would certainly appear menial and repetitive. Yet to mitigate the monotony of Ford work, the individual worker was almost never featured in these labor vignettes. To my knowledge, none of Ford's films features a single camera fixed on a single worker on the assembly line—capturing what ten minutes (let alone eight hours) of turning the same screw or inspecting the same wheel spoke looked like—the fatigue, the monotony, the increasingly shortened bathroom breaks. Instead, montage-reason rules in the rhetorical economy being produced by the film. Organized collections of close-ups and wide panoramic shots were used to present the nature of Fordist production as dynamic and to make many bodies indistinguishable from one another.

More than this, in keeping with the manufacturing aesthetic of the company's educational films, the workers typically occupied the margins of each frame while the mechanical conveyor belt or automotive part takes up the central position. Workers, throughout the film, are often captured in production only in part—as hands, arms, torsos, and faces distended—or as part of a long/wide shot of many workers acting in coordination. As a rhetorical tactic, this kind of shot removes the body part from being a part of the body to instead function only as a part of the production process. As part of the larger process of production, represented by a dynamic movement from one set of bodies in action to the next on film, these menial movements become the new method for producing unprecedented quantities and quality.

In sum, one of the central goals of the many films that captured the assembly line, in their various orientations, was to use the collapsing and condensing made possible by sharp and rapid cuts to generate a narrative of considerable enough scale/scope to allow viewers to accept the value of the menial bodily movement that defined the Fordist laborer as a new form of remarkable value. In the immediate context of the factory, the worker needed to be capable of conceiving the whole of both the production process and the meanings that could be ascribed to it. In a more general sense, the public circulation of these films positioned the assembly line and its new forms of labor as the symbolic center of an idealized American economy. Outside the factory, however, the film gives shifting purpose to the coal miner and the logger, a reason to increase production, and an understanding that their immediate labor is simply another node in a chain.

For the laborer, making sense of these scenes meant coming to understand that the value of one's labor is inextricably linked with the labor of the next worker—the value of each enhanced by the organized fashion in which they are connected. More than this, such a shift to machine-mediated and interrelated labor is not new and threatening but a norm being experienced across regions and professions. For the consumer watching this film, the Ford Model T rolling off the assembly line comes to represent the increased capital invested in the automobile (both social and economic) as these resources and labors accumulate into a single object.

On-screen, this depiction of labor helped to develop an industrial version of what Adorno and Horkheimer have called the "imago of the laborer."[25] The pair argue that through the repeated and overlapping textual depictions of labor—particularly as these depictions get put in the context of larger social constructs—an individual "is persuaded that he does not have to renounce any of his dreams if he eventually becomes an engineer or a shop assistant . . . those dreams which in a class society are already in thrall to the world of things and directed towards the imago of the train driver and the pastry cook."[26] These economic positions have been normalized as systemically recognized and replicable subjectivities, and there is a great deal of safety in that. On-screen, they argue, the individuals who encounter these films will have their sense of economic "[i]magination . . . replaced by a mechanically relentless control mechanism which determines whether the latest imago to be distributed really represents an exact, accurate and reliable reflection of the relevant item of reality."[27] Such an "imago" is one example of what Heinrich Platt has described as "the appeal to *acedia* or mental apathy" that lies at the heart of many topics' rhetorical power. He explains that "[w]hat is already known is the source not of cognition but of re-cognition. It confirms the familiar, offers release from the unexpected. It creates a sense of identification and suppresses any idea of opposition. Recognition of the familiar in imitations and repetitions causes delight, certainly not of the sophisticated sort but rather of a comfortable ease. Empathy may be one of consequence, another a loss of critical distance. The result is at best intellectual stagnation, at worst a total surrender to the dictatorship of commonplaces."[28]

In just under five minutes, then, *As Dreams Come True* has moved its viewer through several valences of economic rhetoric—creating an imagined context that naturalized industrial economic relations as the outcropping of basic observations of the existing agricultural economy and creating a vision of labor dependent on highly organized and distributed divisions of labor. Following Spivak's diagram, *As Dreams Come True* (and the Fordist "rhetorical economy," generally) would require an equally naturalized set of connections order to explain how its structure adds not only value to the economic system but also to the social well-being of those who identify with this structure.

On film, the final and most important element in buttressing the Fordist economic system meant affiliating notions of value and money and then "transforming" them into capital. Less interested in the monetary elements of its production system, however, the work of *As Dreams Come True* balances the production process and its constitutive acts of laboring with symbolic value. The crucial mechanism through which this balancing act takes place is the re-materialization of the body outside of the factory in the form of the consumer, and this makes for the final act of economic rhetoric in this cinematic rhetorical economy. We see one final use for the montage as well.

Topic Three: Capital

A rhetorical account of capital suggests that there isn't an a priori explanation for why individuals imbue particular configurations with exchangeable value. Rather, they are, at least partially, persuaded through arguments about what capital is and how they might benefit from accepting the theory of value at the heart of this concept. The final third of the film, then, addresses the last topic used in producing a Fordist "rhetorical economy" on-screen—the relationship between value and capital.

Perhaps the easiest way to highlight capital's rhetorical nature is to consider the diversity of perspectives within economics, the field most often charged with understanding the concept's nature. For Karl Polanyi, depictions like the one present in the middle chapters of *As Dreams Come True* serve an integral (though dangerous) role in the reification of economic rationality for their ability to present human experience only via its place in a "self-regulating market."[29] Capital, in this sense, names a mechanism through which individuals self-regulate as they both produce and consume. Accounts of the mechanisms guiding this self-regulation thesis include Adam Smith's canonical "self interest" thesis and Thorstein Veblen's "conspicuous consumption" thesis, in which capital is discerned by its relation to the economic actor's "social standing, his social claims, his social assets."[30] Giovanni Arrighi has defined the concept through its relationship to futurity, "as a *means* toward the end of securing an even greater flexibility and freedom of choice at some future point."[31] Like Polyani, Arrighi claims that "the commodity nature of land, labor, and money is purely fictitious" insofar as they can be connected with noneconomic *topoi* like freedom, justice, or prosperity.[32] Peter Murphy and Eduardo de la Fuente suggest that capital gains value because its acquisition allows for "participation in the imaginary collectivity of the people who possess it," adding that "the genius of capitalism has been to supply things or objects or good cheaply in very large quantities that strike a chord with a very large number of people."[33]

Such a social approach to understanding the collapse of value and exchangeable capital suggests that the objects and conceptions of labor created, bought, and sold on the market fundamentally represent an ability to show, hide, cope with, and resolve fears, desires, and relations. In this sense, the process of "transformation" lies somewhere between personal interests and external, rhetorically constructed accounts.

When addressing coal miners and dockworkers of the 1920s, Ford didn't take any chances. Instead, *As Dreams Come True* presented many of these understandings—social standing, freedom of choice, future success, and identification with a large number of people—all as possible forms of value developing out of its production practices. Ford's films, then, prodded the public to understand the economics of car production in frames much more expansive than just matters of time, money, and commodities. In cinematic form, this conglomerated version of capital grounded in a sense of belonging—to a middle class, to a networked economic society, to a generation—was central to *As Dreams Come True*. The montage, as a technique of conglomeration, was particularly useful.

Having moved its viewers from visions of innovation represented by Henry Ford and new ontologies of labor depicted in the expansive material network and place of workers' bodies in the Fordist production process, the final sequences of *As Dreams Come True* begin to shift the discourses of consumption more clearly into socially and personally experienced terms. To do so, *As Dreams Come True* shifts in its final chapters to present the many benefits, both monetary and non-, that developed out of Ford's dream of mass production. The final third of the film, then, is devoted to layering depictions of value and capital.

Once again relying on the affordances of the montage to reorient notions of what forms of value and capital come out of the newly formed structure of labor, "Chapter Five" of *As Dreams Come True* accounts for the company's role in World War I, where "setting aside one's dearest ambitions and releasing a flood of unnatural power to relieve the world in one of its darkest moments." The film depicts a retooled production line as it produces warships en masse to represent this value. In a sharp cut, an overhead shot of a massive ship being built fades into a completed ship speeding into battle and a biplane taking off on its way to war. Though the mention is brief in this particular film, these images take on meanings through intertextual reference. Ford's Motion Picture Laboratory had worked consistently to tie the victory of Allied forces in World War I with their access to superior production methods.

This alignment of manufacturing and staving off fascism would become an integral element of Ford's claims over the next fifty years. Garnering forms of patriotic capital, in this way, the company was able not only to reconfigure the victory in World War I as a victory of industrial capitalism (a theme that emerges again during World War II) but also to argue that labor itself was tantamount to staving off threats to national security. To strike, to demand greater pay, or to slack off on the assembly line was no longer a workplace issue but an ethical and geopolitical decision. In turn, the outcome of the mechanically aided war effort is, for the economy being positioned on-screen, a nation safe for "fellowship and goodwill."

The manifestation of this goodwill sees the film return to the proposed principles of education laid out by the "Boy on the Farm"/"First Workshop" vignette. In this final sequence, then, *As Dreams Come True* presents the Henry Ford Trade School as an integral factor in turning the "founding" of the "Boy on the Farm" into a systematic and cyclical process for producing a particular kind of economic and social subject. The appearance of the trade school is brief, touting the institution as "Giving the boys a chance in the Trade School," and shows students seated in uniform rows while working at sewing machines and then a single student working a piece of machinery under the guidance of a teacher. However, as we have seen, this too was a reference made more rhetorically effective by the many films circulating at the time depicting industrial education as an important site of national pride.

As though ticking off the "dreams" presented in the first sequence of the film, this educational vignette is followed by a quick scene showing Henry Ford driving a train: "another realization to the long list of boyhood dreams." Again, the double nature of this claim comes both from Ford's want to own a train as a boy (apparently) but also from the innovation of a car company buying the train line needed to transport coal to its factories. Following these vignettes, the film turns to images of consumption as they are prefaced by the quote "the greatest pleasure or constructive good that can come to any man anywhere in or out of business is in doing something for another"—a task the film will next work to associate with the act of mass consumption.

On film, the intertitle initiates a montage depicting men and women in overcoats and furs purchasing a variety of prepackaged and mass-produced groceries. Drawing visual parallels between production and consumption, these scenes feature the spaces of consumption at the center of each scene mediating between two embodied figures—buyer and seller—just as the production line mediated the relationship between worker and machine in the production scenes (see figure 11). Ford produces spaces of exchange: where raw material meets with labor power, where finished product meets with consumer.

The film then attempts to rework the large corporate merger as an act of fellowship and goodwill. Outlining the nature of Ford's purchase of Lincoln Motors, the film presents the event as both economic ("a step forward in the automobile world," reads the intertitle) and social ("the making of many steadfast friends"). The images accompanying this merger include the signing of contracts but conclude the transaction with a claim that works to reintegrate the task as a new form of life-affirming friendship. A text-based interlude concludes (as a result of contractual agreement) "old friends are good friends, as in the days of Auld Lang Syne." This, then, is followed by the film's return to the wood-chopping scene, and these vignettes combined present economic activity as a fulfilling form of social interaction. Through these scenes, the film argues that to exchange, to labor, and to invent are important elements of modern social life.

As Dreams Come True, then, rounds out its work by turning to depictions of leisure: Henry Ford is shown in old age surrounded by friends and family, Ford and a prestigious group of friends (Thomas Edison, John Burroughs, Harvey Firestone; a group that named themselves "the vagabonds," though the film simply calls them "playmates") are shown camping, Ford's homes are shown, Ford and his wife go for a drive and then engage in a snowball fight and generally embody the leisure time made available by the film's prior innovations.

The film then concludes where it began—asserting the remarkable potential for new arrangements of labor, capital, and organized action to remake the identities of many across the country. This basic translation, however, is placed in larger narratives aligning this exchange with a variety of social and national visions of capital: fulfilling dreams, gaining respect or a sense of self-worth, advancing civilization, warding off decline. In this sense, *As Dreams Come True* takes the concept of economic "transformation" into capital literally, offering up not one act of transformation but six in rapid succession. To accept the Fordist economy, it argues, is at once to secure democratic, financial, interpersonal,

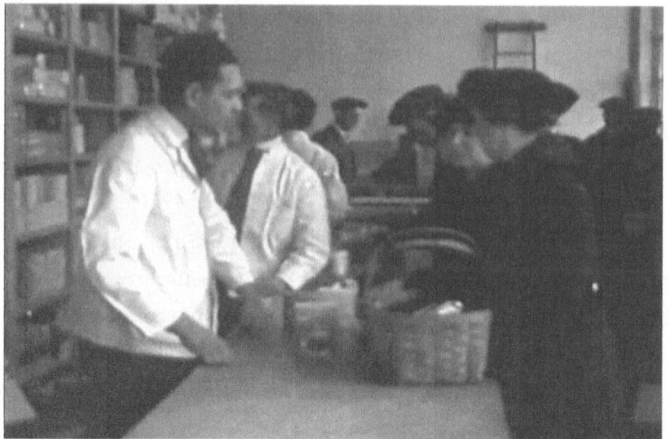

11 | Ford Motion Picture Laboratory, stills from *As Dreams Come True*, 1921.

educational, and familial stability; it is to accept modernity; to ensure that one's family and city remains on the prosperous side of history.

This final act of montage-driven rhetoric functions through compilation. David Bordwell has argued that one way that a cinematic montage can "make rhetorical points" is to produce just such an "assemblage of heterogeneous parts" and through the "juxtaposition of fragments . . . demand for the audience to make conceptual connections."[34] As Spivak's diagram highlights, this kind conceptual connection is the crowning achievement of any capitalist account of economic rhetoric by getting individuals to connect all sorts of value with the act of producing and consuming. In this way, Ford created a complex imagined future predicated on disembodied and collective acts of work. The monotonous work was offset, however, by the argument that such labor would place the laborer in not one but four separate social configurations—a powerful nation, a system of consumers, a class of individuals engaging in contractual (and therefore social) relations, and a generation securing better welfare for the next.

This highlights the potential of a film like *As Dreams Come True* to impact economic reason itself as it invited a variety of "conceptual leaps" between labor, value, and capital. When positioned in the context of a massive company attempting to change the very fabric of economic relations at a given historical moment, the commodity is more than just theoretically "fictitious"; it is the work of carefully crafted fictions, that is, the domain of rhetorical activity.

Conclusion

The final intertitle of the film sets up a shot of Henry and Clara Ford driving away from the camera by declaring "down life's lane together, hand in hand we go." While this functions within the narrative as a version of "happily ever after" cached in a car pun, it also extends to the viewer an invitation to follow Ford in this imagined rendition of a human life. For the logger, the dockworker, and the coal miner, films like *As Dreams Come True* rapidly overlapped economic notions of innovation, mechanically dominated line labor, and social capital grounded in accumulation, national security, and personal fulfillment. In the end, these figures were not offered traditional treatises on theoretical notions of value or the relative relationship between capital and labor but a cohesive set of images—men chopping wood, children going to school, contracts being signed, cars being built—that were, in turn, constructed into a closed system of economic reason—a life of labor balanced by a strong national identity and the promise of leisure and secure family living—that made up the Fordist rhetorical economy.

Using *As Dreams Come True* as an example, this chapter has argued that one way corporate/economic actors have gained power and influence (both inside and outside economic spheres) is by narrating versions of the economy in which they play a central role—depicting, adjusting, and coopting the economic imaginaries of a society, often offering up these imaginaries in historical moments where the public perceives the world as in flux. I have called these "rhetorical economies." The Ford film archive contains a number of montage-driven economic narratives circulating in the 1920s that were used to introduce Fordism. In addition to *As Dreams Come True*, these include *The Power That Thought Built*, *The Ford Age*, and *Building for Quality*.[35] However, this genre of film was also used across decades in films like *Thirty Years of Progress* (1932), *The Ford Year* (1935), *While the City Sleeps* (1940), *The American Road* (1953), and the final film produced for the archive itself titled *Mirror of America* (1963). Watched in succession, these films present a cohesive account of the Fordist economic whole as it shifted over the course of four decades. As I read an example of this genre, however, these films are particularly useful for examining what we might understand as the "rhetorical economy" the company sought to produce.

A film like *As Dreams Come True*, in its varied compiling of "things" and use of industrial progress as a standard of measurement, highlights that economies are, essentially, mental projections mapping a network of values onto material objects and human lives. When paired with the perception that film is an act of nonfiction, the montage becomes a powerful tool of inculcation. The montage's cinematic affordances were particularly amenable to capturing and disseminating a number of economic *topoi*; in particular, Fordist conceptions of imagined futures (by comparing contingent narratives of time), labor (by collapsing distinctions between discrete tasks), and capital accumulation (by overlapping alternative models of value).

Highlighting this collapse of form and function, it is remarkable how much Gilles Deleuze's description of the montage is applicable to the work that an economy does in society. Both, it seems, generate "(1) the sets or closed systems which are defined by discernible objects or distinct parts; (2) the movement of translation which is established between these objects and modifies their respective positions; (3) the duration or the whole, a spiritual reality which constantly changes according to its own relations."[36] In the terms laid out by film theory, then, the Fordist rhetorical economy (or any economy, really) is simply a mental (or perhaps spiritual) existence accepted by enough individuals in a society that can be defined by the same points that make up a montage. This chapter has argued that capturing the dynamism of an economy requires thinking in terms of relationality and circulation between economic *topoi*. It requires thought that much more closely resembles montage reason, and it is for this reason that a film like *As Dreams Come True* was an integral text in Ford Motor Company's ability to construct a successful rhetorical economy.

Economies have long been understood as distributed configurations—webs, rhizomes, networks, etc.—and while these terms highlight that an economy is never fully the domain of any one ideological system, these constructs are also not fully freeform, equally distributed systems of meaning. Rather, as Donna Haraway has argued, tremendous configurations like this ("webs," she calls them) "can have the property of systematicity, even of centrally structured global systems with deep filaments and tenacious tendrils into time, space, and consciousness, the dimensions of world history."[37] This ability to draw out the appearance of a system from an otherwise disorganized or disconnected set is another way of understanding the incorporational.

Highlighting the role that film has played in this process, Steven J. Ross has argued that "by creating a common link between millions of working people who were often divided by ethnicity, religion, race, and gender, movies emerged as a vehicle capable of expressing a new public identity dominated by working class sensibilities."[38] In this context, we might begin to approach films like *As Dreams Come True* and their production of an economy out of a set of familiar topics as traceable manifestations of the "tenacious tendrils" that spread outward from Ford Motor Company into countless communities and industries through a uniform depiction of what the economy looked like. The concept of economic *topoi*, however, serves as a convenient transition to a third visual project enacted by the company in the expression of the economy that will be explored in the next chapter. *Topos* translates to "place," and this etymological link highlights that rhetorical economies—no matter how cleanly constructed as narrative constructs shared among individuals—also must exist somewhere.

3

Ford's Cinematic Production of Economic Space

The first three decades of the twentieth century were a period of intense road building, a time of considerable changes in the living arrangements of millions (first via the press of urbanization, which was followed by decentralization), and a period that saw sharp rises in domestic travel. The physical landscape changed a great deal as trees were felled, roads and neighborhoods were built, and cities expanded outward and upward. The way that individuals were encouraged to understand these physical changes, however, was equally significant, as corporations both advocated for these changes and then used them as evidence that the nation was an economic space—a vast interconnected configuration of production sites, hubs of consumption, and spatial relations dedicated to supporting economic developments.

Spatial relations were one of Ford's most frequent topics across its many public relations for fairly obvious reasons—as a car company, connecting far-off places was simply part of the business model. However, the company's spatial arguments reveal that it was interested in influencing Americans' ideas about spaces well beyond roads. At the outset of a series of published autobiographical interviews titled "My Philosophy of Industry," for example, Henry Ford articulated his own ongoing fascination with changing the spatial practices of all Americans. One of the central tenets of "My Philosophy of Industry" was that, thanks to Ford Motor Company, individuals were liberated to "move about." On a local level, he claimed this would lead to new conceptions of the domestic, declaring that "[h]ome will remain, but homes will greatly change—they always have." Carrying this new mobility outward, Ford then argued that because of efficient production practices (and thus fewer work hours), the availability of cars, and the improving road system, "[p]eople are no longer compelled to stay in the house, but may travel about, economically, and see things." Finally, carrying this vision to its most extreme, Ford imagined that through the homogenizing effects of the mass economy—spread by the airplane, the radio, and the motion picture—"a United States of the World" would "surely come!"[1]

Over the first twenty-five years of its filmmaking, Ford's Motion Picture Laboratory produced films depicting a wide array of spatial entities—parks, roadways, cities, neighborhoods, factories, rivers, farms, homes, and schools. Using these depictions, the company engaged in an extensive rhetorical project to produce an interstitial and economized national landscape by unmaking traditional notions of the local, national, and personal and realigning these concepts more clearly with economic frameworks on-screen. This spatial reconfiguration of the nation carried across decades and featured in a number of genres present in the Ford film collection. To capture this distributed project, this chapter presents three overlapping threads in the company's spatially minded films.

Each thread represents a narrative put forward by Ford and models an approach to cinematic theories of space as they help to explain Ford's production of what will be explored in this chapter as the rhetorical effect of "interstitiality." The first of these threads is represented by the film *Good Roads*, distributed between 1919 and 1921. This film positions roads both as manifestations of a nationalized marketplace and as important parts of a narrative of national progress. The entire Good Roads Movement worked through an extensive act of synecdoche that positioned the quality of roads as synonymous with the quality of society. More specifically, in Ford's films, this argument took up the shape of a historical narrative in which roads served as a particularly rich symbol articulating the boundary between the modern and the antiquated.

The second thread attends to a reemerging fascination with the "village" in the wake of the Great Depression. Ford's cinematic depictions of the many village-industries it built in Michigan and its historical theme park—Greenfield Village—grounded the prominent economic concept of decentralization in material sites that could be observed on screens and, potentially, visited. These sites served as a rhetorical bridge between urban and rural landscapes as well as domestic and industrial spaces. Across a handful of films produced in the 1930s, Ford positioned village-industries as a response to concerns over the "backwardness" of the rural and the blight of the urban. Looking to one of the only examples in the archive exclusively dedicated to these spaces, I argue that these cinematic depictions worked by generating "mental maps" for viewers using what Gilles Deleuze called "movement-images" that highlighted two integral elements of the village-industries—their interconnection and their ideal position between the industrial and the agricultural.

Finally, the third thread is a series of travelogues filmed throughout the 1930s that presented a new form of spatial consumption of nature made possible by the roads that had been built in many of the national parks. Produced by Ford for the Department of the Interior, these films (A Visit to *Yellowstone National Park* and *Fairy Fantasy in Stone: Bryce National Park*, particularly) rely on what John Urry calls the "tourist gaze." For Urry, the actual visual work involved in generating this gaze is relatively simple—one must simply go somewhere out of the ordinary and look. However, the rhetorical power of such a simple act has wide-ranging implications for an economic system. He explains that "[t]ourism is a leisure activity which presupposes its opposite, namely regulated and organized work. It is one manifestation of how work and leisure are organized as separate and regulated spheres of social practice in 'modern' societies. Indeed acting as a tourist is one of the defining characteristics of being 'modern' and is bound up with major transformations in paid work. This has come to be organized within particular places and to occur for regularized periods of time."[2]

The purpose of the National Park films, in this frame, was to provide a spatial counterbalance to the urbanizing and industrializing trends at the heart of Fordism. Setting aside national parks as sites where nature was not reduced to a repository of resources and where workers of any economic persuasion could become part of the recovering configuration of American consumers was integral to the expansion of Fordism. And of course, it didn't hurt that cars were integral to this form of tourism.

Taken together, Ford's spatial project was a multifaceted process of picturing the nation—capturing roads, villages, cities, factories, national parks—in order to crack open codified narratives of social life and insert images of individuals performing industrial and corporate identities. These various films helped redraw the connections between the material and the abstract that constituted both the powerful metaphor of a national landscape and the interstitiality that complicates this metaphor. In each case, Ford's rhetorical strategy was to ground an abstract economic notion (a market, the decentralization of production, affiliations of class and/or consumption) in the material experiences of individuals engaging with a changing landscape. The company's endgame, in overlapping these depictions on screens across the country, was the production of a national landscape amenable to mass production and consumption and reliant on cars for even the most basic of daily activities. A number of scholars have noted that the company succeeded, and car-mediated spatial relations developed into a wholesale cultural shift called automobility, car culture, or autopia.³

Economic Interstitiality

Rhetoricians have long studied how spaces are not only produced, but produced rhetorically as part of more expansive arguments regarding the nature of a society. Attention to the rise of car culture as it appeared on-screen contributes to this conversation in two ways. First, this chapter attends to the rhetorical properties of space in films and second, it examines the specific rhetorical effect of "interstitiality."

There are many ways that film infuses spaces with meaning—through both mundane and extraordinary use of settings to frame its narratives, by giving physical spaces immediate roles in larger narratives, by creating memorable events that populate an audience's memory of a place, by influencing understandings of how to move through existing spaces, by offering up fantastical spaces that viewers might compare to their own surroundings, and by providing perspectives of spaces that might otherwise remain inaccessible. Anne McClintock has argued that "[f]ilms often superimpose illustrative maps over shots of landscapes subliminally asserting a kind of claim over the land, functioning rather like a legal deed to property."⁴ Tom Conley has suggested, similarly, that "a film can be understood in a broad sense to be a 'map' that plots and colonizes the imagination of the public it is said to "invent" and, as a result, to seek control."⁵ Jeff Rice has pointed out that "a filmic space can be placed in relationship to its physical space because of its unique photographic presence" that "forges viewer associations and relationships."⁶

One concept that has received less attention from scholars studying the spatial and the cinematic has been how films can complicate and sometimes fuse the binaries that often define spatial relationships. Working to understand this potential, Ford's many space films repeatedly rely on the idea of interstitiality as both a cinematic and rhetorical effect.

Homi Bhabha has explored this idea, explaining that interstitiality defines spaces in which "private and public, past and present, the psyche and the social develop an interstitial intimacy . . . that questions binary divisions through which . . . spheres of social experience are often spatially opposed."[7] Notably, Bhabha also directly draws out the relationship between the visual and the spatial to understand the twofold nature of the nation as a salient rhetorical entity. On the one hand, Bhabha posits that "the recurrent metaphor of landscape as the inscape of national identity emphasizes the quality of light, the question of social visibility, the power of the eye to naturalize the rhetoric of national affiliation and its forms of collective expression."[8] On the other hand, tempering these homogenizing spatial rhetorics of nationhood is a set of "interstitial, disjunctive spaces and signs crucial for the emergence of the new historical subjects of the transnational phase of late capitalism."[9]

As Henry Ford's sentiments in *My Philosophy of Industry* make clear, in an era before the transnational stage of late capitalism, corporate actors were seeking to create equally disjunctive conceptions of space that could fragment notions of the local, centralized political space of the community and replace it with a set of new decentralized economic spaces understood as extensions of a single national economy. As a technology centrally wrapped up in harnessing what Bhabha has called the "power of the eye," motion pictures served as an ideal medium for executing such a large-scale project in landscape building.

Gregory Flaxman notes that in theories that approach film as fabricated thought (indistinguishable, in theory, from the ideas that naturally spring from the human mind), the medium can function as a primordial meaning-maker because "between one image and another a gap opens, an 'interstice' in which thought experiences its own duration."[10] In this duration, a connection is made between the contents of each scene, often producing messages that blend and blur—never fully landing as part of the former or latter image.

Concrete Metaphors: Roads as the Lifeblood of a Nation

In 1921, the March 1 edition of the *Ford News* declared that "[t]he time is not far distant when each little village, no matter how remote, will have its motion pictures. Then will end journeys to larger towns in such a quest. Pumpkinville will be in touch with the outside world."[11] By 1923, a second *Ford News* article titled "Remote Sections Have Motion Pictures" reveals that the company had taken this process one step further by overlapping the automobile and the motion picture entirely. The article credits "the ingenuity of Lloyd L. King, Ford Dealer in Huntington, California and Sam Remillard, an itinerant entertainer" with building a moving motion picture projector out of the bed of a Ford truck and touring the American Southwest.

These traveling picture shows were an important element of Ford's distribution scheme because they could spread its industrial-cinematic rhetoric into areas where its existing system for the distribution of films could not reach. These articles also reveal much about the spatial imaginary the company was inviting the public to accept. As the "Remote Sections" article makes clear through its title and its tone (the subtitle of the article reads "Isolated Communities Now Go to the Movies," for example), films were being positioned as more than just entertainment; they were a lifeline for rural communities being excluded from new narratives of the Fordist economy.

Throughout the 1920s, getting "Pumpkinville" into the fold of a rapidly urbanizing and industrializing nation was potentially big business for the company, but it first needed the nation—these hamlets included—to invest in roads. This meant convincing rural populations across the country to accept its industrial vision while, at the same time, curbing the rapid urbanization that threatened the potential growth of car-mediated life. For critics, roads were dirty, they were dangerous, they were expensive, and they were threats to the balance of local communities. In short, Ford needed a particularly powerful spatial narrative in which roads and cars would be more than just matters of infrastructure and commerce.

The company had quite a bit of help in this endeavor. For much of the early twentieth century, groups like the National Highway Association and the Good Roads Congress circulated a number of materials and organized a number of events to raise interest in the local and federal funding of roads. One of the central strategies for the Good Roads movement was to position the road as an important symbol in a wide variety of narratives about national progress. Working with these groups, Ford's Motion Picture Laboratory produced a number of films meant to support the Good Roads Movement.

In many of these films, the building of and taking to roads were positioned as a marker of national solidarity and economic progress precisely because these roads were the bastions of a new mass production marketplace. These films also relied heavily one rhetorical strategy for producing space: creating trope-driven affiliations between physical spaces and loftier ideals. One of the best examples of this strategy is evident throughout the 1921 version of a film produced by the company fittingly titled *Good Roads*.

As the title slide of *Good Roads* fades, a second text-based frame replaces it, declaring, "Good Roads? Years before the White Man came, the Red Man came breaking rough trails through the forests" and quickly pans to an actress dressed up as a Native American walking pensively through low brush. Behind her, a male actor—also in mock Native American garb—appears, smiles, waves from his tiptoes, mouths a jovial "hey!," and plants a kiss on her cheek. Moments later the actor grows troubled, points in the distance, plants an enclosed fist over his heart, and then swings his arm in a wide arc as he marches out of the picture. The cause for alarm is a caravan of horses, wagons, and grizzled, gun-bearing men plodding along a trail as an accompanying intertitle declares: "then the pioneer, whose clumsier conveyances demanded wider avenues of traffic . . . travelled 10-15 miles per day." The sequence concludes with a challenge to its audience to maintain such a historical trajectory of progress as the next intertitle declares: "Transportation has wonderfully improved but the highways are lamentably behind the times. In fact, many of them are in identically the same condition when travelled by the pioneer in his oxcart."

This opening sequence of *Good Roads* argued that if modern roads were in better condition than a century before, audiences must be living in a more civilized nation than the seemingly simpler figures who occupied these physical spaces in prior eras. However, if roads were not updated, this narrative of progress would grow stagnant. Through this vignette, the film works to present the road as a crucial bellwether of human development and ties the construction of an extended system of roads to the embedded discourses of Manifest Destiny—charged by racism, colonialism, and cultural superiority—that were integral to national identity at the time. Roads were also, however, positioned as transitional spaces seemingly capable of carrying their users toward social progress.

Having established the idea of the road as a powerful actor within this spatiotemporal narrative of national and social progress, the film works to hit a little closer to home for its rural viewers by applying this spatial logic of performance and progress to more familiar settings. In a call-and-response format, *Good Roads* proceeds through a series of juxtaposed images of pre- and post-automobile/road life to highlight the degree to which the building of roads could potentially transform much of America's landscape as well as its populace. In this patterned manner, the film establishes a clear binary. For pre-road America, the pioneer and Native American are joined by the brooding blacksmith, the frustrated postman, the country churchgoer, and the student attending a rural one-room schoolhouse as vestiges of an outdated and largely backward era. Occupants of these scenes are all muddy, tired, and dressed in outdated clothing. More significantly, these figures are rendered either stagnant or severely slowed by their ineffective roads—in this way fusing literal motion with figurative progress. It is worth noting that this use of the *parallel-alternate* montage was nearly identical in *As Dreams Come True*, also being shown in 1921.

For post-road America, the film depicts a mechanic, an urban cathedral, and a movie theater attended by well-dressed and lively figures as physical manifestations of a new, developing nation. These moviegoers, in contrast to their plodding counterparts, are fast-paced, dressed in luxurious clothing (furs, suits, etc.), and are visibly more content than their road-less counterparts. Moreover, the composition of the pre- and post-scenes differs. For example, the one-room schoolhouse and rural play are represented by caricatured individuals in clearly staged scenes and framed by close shots designed to capture costume and facial expressions, while the modern school and movie theater are presented through wider panning shots of individuals entering buildings framed by bustling urban landscapes. These latter images are live-action, presenting current affairs against the acted-out scenes of rural hamlets. Through this convention, the former scenes highlight the individual while the latter highlight, and are predicated on, vast circulatory systems that shape the very subjects that occupy them.

The underlying argument in this juxtaposition is that progress is contingent upon acts of connection between space and subjectivity. Thus, *Good Roads* posits that the ease with which an individual can arrive and congregate with others defines the very nature of that individual, and this forms a clear historical binary for many of its viewers. Moreover, the film posits that to build new spaces is to build new citizens and therefore to construct a better republic. By presenting the audience with a visualization of the difference between a tattered schoolhouse filled with muddy, worn-out children and a school bus delivering well-dressed, chipper students to a brick schoolhouse (see figure 12) or in considering the plodding work of making a horseshoe against the efficiency of an in-and-out car repair shop, the film has positioned its rural viewers to understand the material outcomes of its final claim that "Good roads make for better homes and better schools for happier and more contented children."

Rhetorically, then, the film's ability to associate considerable potential changes to its audiences' identities (manifested through external appearance) with access to the material spaces of roads is crucial to its final move to explain why roads are capable of creating such considerable transformations: the possibility of a nationalized marketplace. The idea of a national market had been referenced by

12 | Ford Motion Picture Laboratory, stills from *Good Roads*, 1921.

the Good Roads Movement for nearly a decade, though in largely abstract terms.[12] On film, this concept was materialized through the visible changes to a populace made possible by the connections, pace, and movements afforded by roads, and thus the road became a bridge not just between geographical spaces but between one economy and another, between one era and another.

In a series of intertitles, the film next argues that roads allow for "saving time and enlarging the market" by including previously isolated rural populations in wider systems of commerce. Because of these new connections, the film claims, "Cash comes into the house every day as the market shifts to the farmhouse gate" with the all-important caveat "Where the roads are good!" In this way, the film argues that it is through roads that communities come together to build economic relations by gaining access to the new developing (and significantly more interconnected) Fordist marketplace. In turn, aligning with the narrative established in the first half of the film, these communities literally changed into more sophisticated and classed entities as the connection to the market was made.

The images that accompany these claims include a truck picking up a live calf on the roadside to take it to market, a housewife receiving her milk and butter without having to leave the front yard of her home, and finally a roadside stand allowing consumers to come directly to the farm to purchase their products. Once again, a number of cinematic conventions create dynamism for the Fordist system and demonstrate relative stagnation of prior localized marketplaces. Rather than sitting idly, the objects and individuals in these market-driven spaces are in constant movement, and through the use of sharp cuts between scenes of various moments of exchange, these movements reveal the extended network of spaces and individuals that are drawn together through the road that, in turn, serves as arbiter of the vastly extended marketplace.

The film concludes by fusing its economic and its national/historical frames through a final metaphor that highlights this concept of dynamic circulation creating, in the process, the interstitial nature of a market. It suggests that the viewers "not think of a road as meaning merely the distance between two given points or cities. It is one of the arteries through which flows the life blood of the nation," blood that has been positioned as overtly economic in nature. Expanded beyond a bellwether for national and personal progress, on film, roads become a medium for affiliation between individuals in rural communities and play an integral role in making the abstract space of the national marketplace a concrete and performable concept in the public's mind.

Regardless of towns' proximity to other portions of the country, *Good Roads* argued that they could occupy one of two separate kinds of national spaces—a space with access to "car culture" and a space without. Pitching these spaces in terms of both culture and economy, suddenly outlying towns connected to a major urban center by a paved road were being positioned as "closer" to that center than to the other towns nearer but not connected by quality roads. Separated from the "lifeblood" of national identification, spaces and social structures existing beyond the reach of car culture and the road system were, in this way, deeply un-American in nature. More than this, separated from the national marketplace, the figures left outside the road system were living in a premodern society. This act of collapsing notions of personal value, national progress, and expanding markets into a single material manifestation—the road—both paved the way for further economic development and set the scene for a decades-long process of laying an economic map over the top of traditionally national and social scenes using film.

One might imagine the impact of such a film in any number of the "Pumpkinvilles" that a Ford projector rolled into. Suddenly, not investing in roads wasn't just a matter of funding; it was a matter of being on the right side of history and progress. Over the next decade, Ford would release a number of films committed to this way of thinking. Other films in the National Archives collection include *Paving the Way to Success* (1921), the *Are You a Piker?* series (1920–1921), *Fording the Lincoln Highway* (1924), and *Road to Happiness* (1926). Collectively, these films made up a sustained rhetorical project committed to aligning acts of road-mediated circulation with commerce and commerce with a healthier republic.

Guided in part by this rhetorical connection among modernity, roads, and the marketplace, an era of grand national building projects specifically designed to produce a more resolutely interstitial nation envisioned by figures like Ford began with roads, cars, and mass culture at the helm. Translated into material form, in the years following the Depression, the newly formed Works Progress Administration, a branch of the Recovery Act, produced 651,000 miles of highway and 124,000 bridges, while many states and municipalities used aid from the Bureau of Public Roads to construct a more robust network of roads.[13] The Recovery Act was understood, to follow *Good Roads*'s metaphor, as an enormous process of triage to keep the economic "lifeblood of the nation" moving and thus the notion of national progress intact.

As Ford's motion pictures make clear, the immense material project of "roading" America via New Deal initiatives was largely part of an ongoing invitation for the American public to contribute in changing the nature of their own identities—particularly in relation to how they produced and consumed. For a scholar like Michel de Certeau, this fusion of roads, industry, and national identity can be understood in terms of a fundamental rhetorical struggle between the (and this is a fortunate turn of phrase for this book) "incorporation" and "excorporation" that takes place in any space. An institution seeking power, he explains, produces spaces for control through "strategies" that incorporate in order "to distinguish its 'own' place, that is, the place of its own power and will, from an 'environment.'"[14] Individual actors resist these spaces through "tactics" that excorporate and separate them from the dominant spatial narrative. Roads were powerful instruments of incorporation, and having been linked to the national marketplace, their spread from coast to coast was itself a powerful rhetorical act for corporate actors seeking to carve out "power and will" from the environment.

At the same time, these new roads needed to have spaces that they could connect and that their users could occupy through spatial practices like visiting, dwelling, and working. More than this, in film, these embodied tasks could be set amidst Ford's spatial narratives of a planned market made up of a network of economic spaces—warehouses, shops, factories, gas stations, and town centers—as they were being reorganized around another of Ford's rhetorical-spatial projections: "decentralization." This was achieved, in part, through a project that sought to reconfigure the very living arrangements of the American worker and farmer through the construction of "village-industries."

―――――

Village-Industries and Decentralization

From 1918 to 1941, Ford engaged in the practice of opening what it called "village-industries" along the river systems throughout Michigan. This typically involved renovating or building a hydroelectric powered factory in an existing rural community. As the name suggests, at the core of these villages and their on-screen depictions was an attempt to present living spaces as both intermediaries between urban and rural settings (villages) and points of contact between domestic and economic spaces (industries). Before the Great Depression, the general premise behind forming these sites was to find relatively cheap labor in the form of farmers and their families during the non-harvest season, as well as labor that could be isolated from central production factories to discourage the rise of unionization in the 1920s. Perhaps Ford's most obvious motivation for creating these sites was the production of consumers through shifts in spatial infrastructure—living in these villages required cars.[15] In this sense, the village-industries were themselves an act of remarkable materialized spatial rhetoric. Ford wasn't just building industrial sites for production; it was promoting particular visions of how communal life might look in the Fordist economy. While a number of the company's media offerings covered the industries, film could capture the nature of this material/spatial rhetoric in important ways.

Holdings at the National Archives feature nearly an hour of raw footage depicting the village-industries that was used in a variety of company films.[16] Within this collection of uncut material, three primary sequences dominate the subject matter: citizens enjoying leisure in the country, aerial depictions of the villages, and glimpses of small-scale factory production. Collectively, these depictions present a developing project committed to reenvisioning the domestic spaces associated with the village as extensions of mass industrial production/consumption relations while also maintaining a number of the connotations associated with the idea of a village (simplicity, community, traditional craftsmanship).

The clearest iteration of Ford's rhetorical use of these spaces appears in a 1935 film (archived without sound) titled *Village-Industries*. While the lack of sound in the archived copy of *Village-Industries* presents a limited account of the film's rhetorical work in situ, the images provide a wealth of information about the company's larger rhetorical goals. They are also excellent examples for studying the rhetorical potential of film when read as a collection of what Gilles Deleuze has termed "movement-images" that generate interstitiality. Through this term, Deleuze explains some of the ways in which film can disrupt mental configurations of space. One is generating a harmonious sense of a much larger set of spaces. He argues that on-screen "the movement of water, that of a bird in the distance, and that of a person on a boat: they are blended into a single perception, a peaceful whole of humanized nature."[17] Part of the power of film as a space-making text comes from its ability to function "only 'as if' its spectators were experiencing movement through space," and this allows for smoother depictions because "natural perception introduces halts, moorings, fixed points or separated points of view, moving bodies or even distinct vehicles, whilst cinematographic perception works continuously, in a single movement whose very halts are an integral part of it and are only a vibration on to itself."[18] For this reason, on screens, he argues, "the mobile camera is like a *general equivalent* of all the means of locomotion that it shows or that it makes use of—aeroplane, car, boat, bicycle, foot, metro" so that "the essence of the cinematographic movement-image lies in extracting from vehicles or moving bodies the movement which is their common substance, or extracting from movements the mobility which is their essence."[19]

In his theory, the film goes beyond the faithful replication of how space is experienced by humans to produce its own unique conception of space that helps to reconfigure audiences' mental maps once they leave the theater. As a philosophical gesture, his point is that we can scarcely differentiate between the visual experience of walking through a space and watching a film that presents the same space from a tightly edited collection of shots from various vantage points. Both sets of inputs hit our brains as a "thought" about space. While Deleuze's concern is with film as an act of philosophy, the "movement-image" also serves as a useful frame for understanding the rhetorical effect of "interstitiality" required to expand economic space and reveals the deeply rhetorical power of films' on-screen mobility. Offering viewers a smooth, uninterrupted collection of perspectives on the relationship between spaces was a considerable advantage in Ford's quest to decentralize.

Village-Industries accomplishes this goal in part through the perspectives made possible by combining film and airplanes to capture the interconnected nature of various activities taking place in the village-industries. The film consistently transitions between villages by presenting the viewer with a plane-perched shot looking down on the villages from above. Notably, as this footage passes over each of the village-industries, it follows the roads that connect and define these places, depicting the complete spatial logics of road-mediated life. As a visual convention, this overhead view allows the viewer to see not only the ordered fashion of the roads but also the seamless fusion of rural countryside and modern industrial order instated by the roadways that connected one village to the next and all villages to the factory in Dearborn. It was, after all, one thing to read of the interconnections between agriculture, town, and industry in government publications and newspapers about the New Deal; it was quite another to see this physical remaking of the landscape in a single sweeping vision of the new American countryside from several hundred feet in the air. In this sense, while the planes often follow along roads, the film's concern is not the roads themselves but what the roads make possible: the potential for Ford's assembly line to stretch across miles and miles of rural Michigan.

These plane-perched views are part of a larger "movement-image" that sought to place this grand remaking of the landscape with a much more localized remaking of the industrial workplace. The film also captures the interior of the factories at the heart of each village-industry. Consistently, men and women are shown engaging in labor not typically witnessed on the assembly line: hand-crafting smaller automobile parts or tools and making, folding, and packaging linens and uniforms for use at the River Rouge plant. These factory sites are considerably different from the various spaces documented in Ford's other production films. Many of the shots highlight the natural light, the relatively spacious working conditions, and the proximity to nature—for example, as workers exit the factory to picnic for their lunch break (see figure 13).

Having used this perspective to provide a macro-account of the ordered spatial patterns that governed the villages, the film then focuses more directly on the impact such innovative spatial reorientation might have on the daily lives of the village-industries' inhabitants. For example, when passing over the village of Milford, Michigan, the film displays the small riverside factory and then the village's main street, which is lined with orderly parked cars. It then cuts to a camera stationed directly on this main street as a truck drives past. From this vantage point, the audience witnesses a bustling downtown occupied by individuals who have commuted from their homes to the central commercial hub in the town's center by car (see figure 14). The film consistently uses sharp, rapid cuts rather than longer stationary shots that would present the idea of the village as a quintessentially static spatial object.

More than highlighting the tidiness of this car-mediated village center as part of a network of connected commercial hubs within Ford's production, this brief sequence also highlights a space in which going to the grocer and/or pharmacist was as simple as hopping in the car and heading to a centrally located point for consumption. Presenting the interstitiality between communities, the film returns quickly to its aerial view as the camera flies directly above the interstate to arrive at the village-industry site of Hayden Mills, Michigan. Once again cutting away from the aerial view, the film then focuses on a young man as he is riding his bike past the factory. Seemingly, this village has been positioned to capture the social benefits of living and working in an intermediary space between the urban and rural. After several shots of the town, which is neatly organized around a main street, the young man is shown seated with two of his friends as they fish by the river's edge. Using both literal proximity (at times the factory or roads serve as the background for fishing and picnics) and cinematic

13 | Ford Motion Picture Laboratory, stills from *Village-Industries*, 1932.

14 | Ford Motion Picture Laboratory, stills from *Village-Industries*, 1932.

proximity (these activities are blended, through editing, into a "peaceful whole") blurs the distinction between the industrial and the communal and between the urban and the rural.

The film's vision presents decentralization in terms of a relationship between embodied individuals and pristine natural landscape surrounding the villages. In each of these depictions, then, the landscape appears prominently, often enveloping the leisure-seekers and periodically featuring one of the factories in the distance. Through this second sequence, the film depicts vestiges of semi-urban and semi-rural life as both a set of wholesome, leisurely activities and connected spaces made possible by the company's planned and distributed manufacturing processes.

In this way, if interstitiality is understood as the integration of previously binary concepts, decentralization is being positioned as the material counterpart deployed by Ford to break up the traditional binaries between the blight of the urban and the backwardness of the rural—both narratives, notably, that it played a significant role in creating in the first place. Once again highlighting the film's commitment to depicting connectivity and circulation, the camera flies over four more villages to show both their uniformity and relation to one another. The final break from the aerial depictions features images of various moments of transport taking place within the villages that were integral to daily industrial and agricultural relations: first, the film shows a set of farmers loading grains onto a truck and taking the crops to a train. Next, a second truck is shown removing water from a town's water tower and hauling it to the nearby factory.

While *Village-Industries* doesn't produce a "peaceful whole of humanized nature," it does present the largely seamless integration of multiple villages into a vision of decentralized production, peppering within this mapping a set of images that also combine elements of production and modernity with images of rural charm in a single frame. In sum, the film uses the bird's-eye view of an ordered countryside to materialize the internal logic governing a remarkable set of linkages—commerce within individual villages, transit between these villages, and this collective's relation to the grander production scheme of Ford. In this way, Ford's village-industry films worked to take the material spaces it had built into a grand rhetorical object capable of reconciling old and new models of economic activity. This, in turn, allowed for the company to incorporate the very notion of a neighborhood into the wider spatial distribution of the mass-production marketplace.

On the one hand, these sequences suggest that these factories were a far cry from the blast furnaces and bustle of Ford's main production complexes. On the other hand, these scenes of production provide a sense of balance between work and leisure as they juxtapose the two frequently. In this way, boys fishing, men and women walking to church on the roadside in their Sunday best, and a gang of bicycling boys and girls enjoying the open spaces afforded by village life are inseparable from the images of men and women commuting to work, sewing aprons in well-lit work stations, and honing wrenches on a die-cast assembly line within the everyday relations of a village-industry. Through this set of fluid visual associations, the sequence's purpose is made clear: like the domestic spaces being developed between the rural and the urban, work spaces and work itself would evolve into new forms once decentralized.

Through these films, Ford's audiences were presented with visualizations inviting them to exist between the modern and the antiquated, the urban and the rural, the industrial and the domestic, and the public and the private. Mediating all of this were strategic depictions of bodies, fields, rivers, roads, and factories being placed in conversation with one another through the use of perspectives allotted by motion picture technology. As the films narrated the concept, decentralization was not a method of division. Quite to the contrary, it was in excess and overcrowding that isolation and hostility occurred. Reconfigured into villages, individuals could reconnect not only with more natural surroundings but with one another—fishing, playing baseball, and eating lunches on the factory lawns.

Notably, after nearly thirty years in operation, and in spite of Henry Ford's plans to create a national network of village-industries the massive material project never came to fruition. The only system of these incorporated villages constructed directly by the company was the Michigan system, and these factories were sold not long after Henry Ford's death. However, the undergirding spatial argument behind the village-industry—decentralization, with all of its social visions of changing inhabitants—would prove to be a significant rhetorical success. After World War II, for example, a set of advertisements for Ford ran in major periodicals (*Life Magazine*, *The Saturday Evening Post*) as well as Ford's vast media regime (particularly in *The Dearborn Independent*) throughout 1945. These texts argued that interest in suburban living was an extension of innovation at the company—positioning village-industries as the "Famous Ford First [of] decentralization." As the ad tells the story, these villages are home to "nearly 5000 men and women who know the peace and security of having one foot on the soil ... and one in industry."[20]

What the company sought to recover through such an interstitial reconfiguration (in addition to quite a few consumers) was the previously discarded sense of embodied class that could be practiced through occupying particular living arrangements within a wider field of economic and social forces. This meant producing a sense of space that seamlessly integrated urban and rural, natural and industrial, and communal and economic spaces. On film, the various "movements" that fused a nostalgic vision of rural life with the benefits of clean, orderly industrial living helped to accomplish this goal. This attention to reconstructing class relations in the United States is also a point carried over to another genre of spatially oriented films in the archive—the travelogue.

For all of this mapping along the lines of markets and decentralized production sites, it seems that the company recognized the need to celebrate spaces that did not exist as immediate parts of the industrial economy but, rather, as a counterbalance. To create these sites, Ford relied on cinematic tourism— particularly to national parks—to complete its mapping of an economic landscape. Tourism could not only quell concerns over the overwhelming takeover of industrial capitalism, but the idea could also serve as an alternative form of economic production as consuming the natural landscape was recast as an important activity for rebuilding a stable network of car consumers (particularly after the Great Depression).

Throughout the Ford film collection, depictions of the road and the suburb were balanced by depictions of natural spaces like national parks in two ways. First, the company produced a national identity directly fused with car-mediated tourism—to be American was to take to the road to see the nation's grand natural wealth. Second, however, these films worked to reassure the nation that the rampant industrial regime marauding across natural landscapes would not erase these landscapes completely—they were being preserved in special locations and could be visited annually. Freed of this concern, the expansion of economic spaces concerned with drawing resources from the landscape could continue uninhibited.

More than this, however, economic space is constituted through two primary acts in these films—first, reviving notions of leisure (an image buried beneath economic depression) by tying it directly to mobility and second, producing acts of rapid, homogenized, and visually oriented consumption of a national space made available by the automobile and access to space facilitated by roads. The chief rhetorical component of these films was their ability to replicate the visual consumption made available by the road-mediated experience of national parks through a collection of movement-images. However, even this act of looking at nature was a contested place for meaning-making.

Travelogues, Tourism, and the Rhetorical Consumption of Nature

This ability to provide a counterbalance to industrial production explains, in part, why the travelogue is the most prominent genre in the Ford film collection. From the production and screening of *The Columbia River Parkway* in 1917 to *Edsel: West to the Tetons* in 1952, Ford Motor Company served as a prominent figure in the rise of the travelogue as one of the most popular film genres of the early twentieth century. Within this genre, depictions of driving and the many movement-images this practice made possible were particularly significant in redefining the act of tourism, both what it meant to consume and what it meant to be part of an American middle class. Moreover, within the company's ongoing project of presenting the public with an economic map of the United States on-screen, these films were designed to convert a series of natural places into commodified spaces.

Mark Simpson has identified the travelogue as a genre capable of placing its viewer between conflicting spatial concepts; he observes that the films serve as "a method of commodification realized between motion and stasis, mediation and immediacy" made possible as the "celluloid mimicked the materialities of modern travel so as to supplement while capitalizing on its practice."[21] When aligned with the more expansive project of paving and decentralizing America, this practice of spatial capitalization becomes yet another way for Ford Motor Company to foster an economic understanding of nationhood in the post-Depression United States.

On one hand, the draw of these vacations required a fundamental shift in understandings of the relationship between class, consumption, and the natural world. Where many of Ford's pre-Depression manufacturing films developed a physical commodity framework for natural spaces (rivers generate power, ore generates metal, trees generate rubber and paneling, all of that generates the Model T), the travelogue sought to convert place to capital in a less literal fashion via the tourist gaze. Tellingly, these acts of identification functioned through rapid, mechanized consumption made possible by the affordability of cars and the newly built road system.

Some of this is captured in the general style of the films. Unlike the educational travelogues of the 1910 and 1920s, which produced choppy informational jaunts through a locale, Ford's post-Depression travelogues offered up longer shots featuring more dynamic camerawork designed to help the viewer marvel at the world through a windshield. As a form of recognizable consumption on film, the family vacation, the day trip, and the joy ride worked to economize movement through space by generating new forms of spatial consumption as well as a homogenized population of consumers mediated through the subject position of the tourist. Through the consumption of these spatial commodities, James J. Flink has argued that "the automobile outing and the automobile vacation became middle-class American institutions."[22]

The most prominent example of this new form of mobile consumption in Ford's film canon is a series that tied the system of national parks in the United States with the ever-expanding interstitiality of car culture already at work in films like *Good Roads* and *Village-Industries*. The company had already produced a number of films highlighting the national parks, particularly for use as part of the educational film series. Perhaps because of these existing films, Ford Motion Picture Laboratory was asked to produce a series of films highlighting the National Park System and the roads that unlocked the natural wonders therein for the Department of the Interior beginning in 1932. Initially, Ford sent a single cameraman who spent nearly a month in two parks. The resulting films were silent, two-reel productions of *A Visit to Yellowstone National Park* and *Waterton Glacier International Peace Park*, which were produced and distributed by the Department of the Interior and Ford together.

These initial films were relatively simple affairs. For example, the 1932 film focused on the gem of the National Park System—Yellowstone—opens (after title credits noting the collaboration between company and government agency) by depicting the various modes of transportation that can get the viewer to the park. The film first maps the rail lines and then the highways that give the entire country easy access to the once remote region. The film then turns to its primary focus: the Grand Loop Road located inside the park.

Beginning at the entrance at Gardiner, Montana, the film carries the viewer onto the park's car loop through a massive arch brandished with the phrase: "For the Benefit and Enjoyment of the People." Seeking to appropriately frame this imagined visit to the park as an experience tied inextricably with car travel, the film then suggests that "visitors who drive private automobiles will find excellent highways within the park," later explaining that "those who arrive by train or by air will be taken from point to point in comfortable buses with careful drivers." The trajectory of the film then becomes a cinematic replication of the car loop. In sequence, a road sign designating the park's attraction appears and is followed by a rapid shot of cars pulling up to the attraction and, often, the drivers get out to see the object, pose for a picture or two, and then return to the road (for example, figure 15 displays a car cutting through a valley, and figure 16 shows park attendees watching the Old Faithful Geyser without leaving their cars).

Notably, the nature of the park is set up primarily for consumption, as the film strikes a balance between depicting convenience and depicting pristine natural wonder as the two points that constituted value. In this way, the films function for the Department of the Interior to celebrate the American landscape as a place for Americans to come and see their own greatness. The more immediate goal, however, was to get more visitors to the park.

Seemingly, this pitch worked to spur the stationary moviegoer to become the mobile tourist. Between 1933 and 1934, trips to national forests and parks rose dramatically; a sixty-six percent rise in attendance was experienced at Yellowstone, for example.[23] Due to the popularity of both the parks and the initial films, the decision was made independently, by both the Department of the Interior

15 | Ford Motion Picture Laboratory, still from *A Visit to Yellowstone National Park*, 1922.

16 | Ford Motion Picture Laboratory, still from *A Visit to Yellowstone National Park*, 1922.

and Ford Motor Company, to produce additional films set in the national parks. On June 14 1937, M. F. Leopold of the Department of the Interior wrote to C. C. Cheadle of Ford's General Sales Department explaining that "[t]he Yellowstone and Glacier films are certainly receiving a Nation-wide distribution and we are receiving many most favorable comments." He also requested two new films in Bryce Canyon and Zion National Parks. In a handwritten note on the bottom of the page, Leopold suggests, by way of motivation, that "if we could produce these fresh films in color it would be a lunch-out for Ford Motor Co."²⁴

Here, however, Ford's archives reveal a point of rhetorical contestation about the nature of these spaces. Ford had already thought of this opportunity and produced sound versions of the films for specific use in its dealerships. The Department of the Interior did not care for this decision, recognizing, it seems, that it might lose the ability to influence the rhetorical inscription of the depicted landscape. Correspondence from Fanning Hearon of the Department of the Interior suggests that two options were discussed: sharing the created sound films or letting Randal White come to Dearborn "at [Ford's] expense to re-edit the two-reel [silent] films" so that they reflected the interests of the Department of the Interior. A. M. Krausman, of Ford offered the following account of the affair: "Summing up the whole thing; inasmuch as the Ford

Motor Company produced their sound pictures, without the supervision and approval of the Department of the Interior, and the fact that the Department of the Interior failed to notify the Ford Motor Company of their desire to change from silent productions to sound pictures, it is understood that the Ford Motor Company ought to waive a point and co-operate with the Department of the Interior in producing and providing them with the next best, even if it is the producing of silent films."[25] While the issue was resolved, the separate circulating versions of the films highlight that the idea of the tourist and meaning of a visit to national parks were both contested points that various entities were seeking to use film to project to the public.

Reflecting the more specific audience for the sound films Ford had produced on its own, a new set of narrative frames were applied to the material. In these newer films, the importance of the family vacation in the economic life of many Americans moved from undertone to stated purpose of both the automobile and the park system. Thus, during this second wave of national park travelogues, these depictions of spatial practice became as much about producing the subject position of the consumer as about the visual and natural commodity being consumed.

This shift, while consistent throughout the re-released travelogues, is particularly clear in the 1937 film titled *Fairy Fantasy in Stone: Bryce National Park*. The film works its way through the many transportation methods for moving throughout the park, beginning with the declaration that "walking, man's oldest form of locomotion, is a popular sport here." Other patrons "take advantage of the fine supply of horses in the park," and finally the film arrives (almost inevitably) at the car as the dominant medium for consumption in the park. The point of this setup is to highlight the value of ease provided by roads.

Not surprisingly, in many of Ford's travelogues, the central perspective through which viewers come to see the parks is via the roads that pass through them. To achieve this balance, the most dominant feature of the new national parks film series is the use of a car's-eye view of the scenery made available for rapid and mass consumption. This entailed mounting the camera on the hood of a car so that as viewers watch the footage, they look down the hood as they might have looked from within a car while passing through the park. The combined effect of this is to first display the speed with which individuals could take in nature and to feature the roads themselves as a sign of civilized passage through untamed wilderness. As such, these early national park travelogues served to narrate a series of spatial practices through which individuals could embody their class status and fulfill the promises about roads bringing modernity made during the "Good Roads" movement. As these travelogues accumulated, however, they became a medium through which American middle-class tourists could also recognize themselves as spatial consumers on-screen.

Placing greater focus on the homogenizing potential for this kind of spatial consumption, the film then focuses on the tourist. In a particularly deliberate scene, the camera collects close-up shots of license plates from Utah, California, Missouri, Washington, Texas, Hawaii, New York, and Michigan as the narrator claims that "every state in the Union is represented among the license plates each summer . . . and people from all over the world are represented." Immediately following this depiction of a homogenized national identity represented by the license plates, the film turns toward what brings these many figures together: their ability to consume nationalized natural spaces. On film, this principle is carried nearly to the point of farce.

As the narrator quips that "some of the visitors have their own special ideas of how to utilize this newest, most convenient way of modern travel. One enthusiastic visitor is determined not to miss a single thing . . . ," a man is shown strapping himself to the hood of an automobile and, moments later, being whisked down the road "with nothing to interfere with his view of mountain and scenery" (see figure 17). This whimsical scene is the culmination of a narrative about increasingly easy forms of consumption of the national landscape—both on screens and from behind windshields.

In this way, these cinematic depictions of roadways rendered national parks as sites where individuals could exist in a deeply interstitial space constructed to reify their occupants, at once, as nationalized citizens experiencing a purely American landscape and, at the same time, as members of a reemerging middle class plugged in to a wider network of identities created through acts of consumption. Blurring the lines between natural, national, and economic space, consuming national parks visually becomes an act of taking part in national identity—heading West (echoes of Manifest Destiny), affirming the return of a healthy economy, and seeing and being seen by fellow classed travelers.

The symbolic work of such a film allowed for nature to become re-inscribed as a visual commodity through its interaction with the road and echoed the notion that roads represent collective national progress as they make available a set of consumable nationalized spaces that constitute a collective based in class and leisure. Ultimately, then, the travelogue served as yet another genre of film that worked to produce an interstitial economic space between the mythos of a nationalized set of natural spaces and a collection of consumable tourist spaces. This third spatial narrative completes the production of an abstracted economic map in which road building produces market-oriented modernity,

118 RHETORIC, INC.

17 | Ford Motion Picture Laboratory, stills from *Fairy Fantasy in Stone: Bryce National Park*, 1937.

village-industries represent decentralized economic space, and national parks serve as commodities consumed through movement and gaze. The films were very popular, and the silent versions were sent for "distribution to schools universities, etc. while more than 300 copies of the sound versions were released ... to all of our Domestic, European, South American, and Asiatic branches."[26] Moreover, copies of the films were reportedly booked six months in advance.[27]

As texts concerned with establishing habitual identifications that presented natural places as economic and classed spaces, these films argued that roads could provide the tourist with cultural capital within more expansive visual narratives about freedom and class based largely on the idea of seeing and being seen. We might, alternatively, understand Ford's later national park films as part of a second rhetorical project being conducted by the company after the Great Depression devoted to reconstituting a public made up of spectators for the industrial economy.

Conclusion: Economic Space on Film

Roads, villages, and national parks may not immediately conjure economic relations in American cultural imaginaries (particularly in the context of a company's film work that so frequently displayed factories, quarries, mills, and sales floors on-screen). Instead, these sites have been more readily positioned as spaces of freedom, escape, and grandeur. However, as this chapter has shown, Ford Motor Company consistently worked to reposition a series of "lived" spaces (Main Street, Nankin Mills, Michigan, Yellowstone) as manifestations of abstracted economic collectives (markets, classes, and consumers) by projecting a series of part-to-whole relationships across the production of physical, political, and economic ways of life. These relationships were facilitated by three affordances offered by the motion picture: a set of visual tropes outlining two separate spaces (the modern and the antiquated) defined by their relationship to roads, the ability for the "movement-image" to collapse distinctions between the urban and the rural to present village-industries as a spatial argument for decentralization, and the mobility of the camera to produce alternative understandings of movement through space (both national and economic) through car-mediated tourism. Once captured and disseminated on film, these fragmentations and reconnections helped naturalize material neighborhoods, parks, roadways, and residential areas within a larger vision of economic existence in the United States.

The significance of this case is twofold. On one hand, Ford's motion picture work contributed centrally to a period of political and cultural change in the United States whose legacy is still experienced daily by the vast majority of its citizens as they are encouraged to experience the rise of industrial capitalism as a set of spatial practices: building roads, moving to the suburbs, and engaging in road-mediated tourism. Indeed, a number of prominent spatial practices of the twentieth century—suburbanization, segregation, city planning, and car culture—developed significantly during the reconstruction period after the stock market crash. As the company developed particular narratives about mobility and class, its films also highlighted that space was not always exclusively perceived as a social or geographical entity.

The relationship forged between Ford Motor Company and the National Park System—particularly parks located in the Rocky Mountains—has remained. For Ford's centennial celebrations, the company refurbished the buses in Glacier National Park and produced a number of educational materials for schools and tours. In 1998, the Motor Cities National Heritage area was formed to produce a recognized corridor of industrial spaces in Michigan that tell "the story of how tinkerers became titans and how auto and labor helped build the middle class while transforming manufacturing worldwide."[28]

On the other hand, these films draw our attention to the way that spatial arguments take place both in individual texts and across coordinated sets of texts. Studying three narratives as they worked together is one way to better attend to "the interlocked relation" between spatial nodes as they "fold into and spin across one another, working together to accomplish the production of space."[29] This chapter, then, is also a challenge to reconsider one of the frames I used as a transition in the introduction of this work. There, I suggested that Fordism appeared in the greater Detroit area, spread to the American Midwest, and then branched out to appear in different nations. While materially true, to describe this physical spread of the company as its "spatial" footprint is to oversimplify the complexities and pluralities of the spatial arguments being made by the company as well as the nature of the regions. In this sense, the ideas of rhetoric, film, and space explored in this chapter are also an argument for greater attention to postmodern theories of space in order to better understand the nature of contemporary capitalism.

Henri LeFebvre theorized that what we experience as space is really an overlapping network made up of the material places we encounter and ideas about what those places mean.[30] Edward Soja, in his interpretation of LeFebvre's work, complicated this binary by asking questions of the spaces where "the concrete materiality of spatial forms" and "thoughtful re-presentations of human spatiality" could not be so easily contrasted. He called these "real-and-imagined" spaces or "thirdspaces."[31] Capitalism, particularly industrial capitalism, creates these thirdspaces as part of its need for increasingly complex networks of exchange and accumulation. As Soja put it, through capitalist narratives of space, "the everyday world was *everywhere* being colonized, infiltrated, by a technological rationality that was extending its effects well beyond the market and the workplace into the family, the home, the school, the street, the local community into the private spaces of consumption, reproduction, leisure and entertainment."[32] In short, space was yet another conduit through which Fordism was working to spread its influence by "substituting everyday life for the workplace as the primary locus of exploitation, domination, and struggle."[33] Throughout this chapter, we have seen a set of "real-and-imagined" spaces produced, in part, by the company's films. The "real" in these spaces is composed of roads, villages, and national parks; the "imagined" are notions of the market, decentralization, and spatial consumption. For film scholars, this attention to Ford's films encourages pressing the study of motion in films from philosophizing about film to answering questions about historical conceptions of space that film has worked to produce. In the case of Ford's interwar spatial films, this means attending to what Homi Bhabha has called the "cultural construction of nation-ness as a form of social and textual affiliation," made possible by rhetorical work seeking to produce interstitiality.[34]

The culture taking shape around the tourist gaze serves as a poignant transition to the next chapter. At the same time that Ford's treatment of the National Park System evolved from 1932 to 1937 to more readily highlight car-mediated consumption, the company was staging a series of immense events positioning the American public as tourists of economic development as well. At these exhibitions, both roads and village-industries were incorporated into a larger argument about how individuals might comport themselves in relation to corporate-industrial capitalism. In short, the company simultaneously argued that Fordism could move humans physically but also move people emotionally. It is to these immense acts of corporate spectacle that I turn next.

4

Spectacle and Spectatorship in Ford's World's Fair Films

We have thus far observed Ford Motor Company's films working in three areas to engage in incorporation: the intellectual (incorporating education), the ideological (incorporating the economy), and the spatial (incorporating the national landscape). In combining these constructs, the company's work throughout the second half of the 1910s and all of the 1920s sought to produce a number of powerful rhetorical constructs: an industrial aesthetic perceived as integral national knowledge; a set of interconnected ideas about futures, labor, and value that added up to a knowable Fordist economy; and a set of symbolically significant roads, village-industries, and national parks. In addressing each of these areas, the role of Ford's films was to connect and, ultimately, combine first, industrial reason and public education, then human livelihoods and industrial society, and finally national spaces and acts of production and consumption. We have, finally, considered a number of rhetorical principles along the way (similitude, *topoi*, interstitiality) and film elements (aesthetics, montage, movement-images) that explain how these films conjoined these disparate objects and ideas.

After nearly two decades, this industrially minded rhetoric had, it seems, successfully convinced many Americans to associate education, spatial use, and their own livelihoods with mass production. They learned, I have argued, to look to the economy for answers to foundational questions in their lives—for purpose, for knowledge, for comfort. When the stock market crashed in 1929, this carefully constructed narrative of mass culture, incorporation, and the inherent wisdom of economic reason all teetered on the brink of collapse. The shock of this event created a moment in which many realized that the economy had so completely enveloped their lives. As Bruce Lenthall has argued, "[f]or many Americans, the 1930s brought the twentieth century's mass culture home. The crisis of the Depression was not only a sudden economic jolt, but the climax of disorienting cultural changes long in rising. Nothing, of course, made clear to millions of Americans that they belonged to an interconnected and national economy like the devastating economic crisis."¹ In Davis Houck's study of rhetoric at the time, he argues that during the years following the Depression, "Capitalism as a viable economic system came under serious questioning" and so, it seems, did capitalist ways of seeing.² Reflecting this skepticism, visual culture in the Depression Era was torn between arguments about what the public should do with the realization that mass culture had been fused with a national, corporate economy. On one side, a markedly anti-industrial aesthetic developed that used photographs, films, and graphic descriptions to document the carnage caused by corporate culture; on the other emerged an increasingly bombastic set of corporation-driven spectacles designed to convince the public to stay the course and revive industrial capitalism as it was.

Sometimes called the "documentary decade," the Depression Era featured many visual projects deeply critical of the Fordist vision of economic relations. The Film and Photo League (formerly the Workers' Film and Photo League) produced *Winter, Hunger,* and *Bonus March* in the early 1930s. Starting in 1935, a set of New Deal films (*The Plow That Broke the Plains, The River, Power and the Land*) was sponsored by various government agencies and argued in favor of government intervention in regulating industry.³ These films worked "to demonstrate in concrete terms, how this redistribution of power worked in a particular setting involving real people."⁴ The Farm Security Administration also sponsored a photography series that presented an evolving and complex "rhetoric of poverty" that captured an impoverished rural America to justify government intervention, to engender pity, and to produce images that evoked visceral pleasure.⁵ Each of these projects worked to warn viewers of the human cost of rampant economization (the overproduction of agriculture in the Midwest, the overdependence on finance, the sharp divides in income inequality). These projects also turned many of the cinematic/rhetorical strategies observed thus far against industrial capitalism by generating visual narratives of education, economy, and space that proposed the redistribution of power to the government or to workers. They sought, using these strategies, to mobilize a critical public where Ford had worked for decades to produce a reliably pliable, economized public.

In the face of these challenges, Ford (and corporate culture, generally) didn't change the nature of its economic structure but encouraged, instead, a new understanding of the relationship the public should have with corporations. Rather than drawing on realist depictions working to illustrate an interconnected economy, companies sought to remind the public of the immense and seemingly unnatural powers unleashed by industrial accumulation, of the visceral pleasures surrounding them on account of mass production, and of the tremendous power that could still be mustered by an economy in spite of the downturn. As William Bird Jr. describes the period, "[a] shift from the rhetorical to the dramatic occurred as America's largest industrial corporations entered the entertainment business—and entered to stay, as the most expeditious way of asserting their social and political leadership. The dramatization of the personal meaning of corporate enterprise . . . propelled to new heights a popular culture of sponsored films, exhibits, and fairs."[6]

Reflecting this shift, the contents of the Ford film archive after 1929 display a sharp stylistic contrast from the relatively simple, straightforward films produced pre-Depression. Part of this change can be attributed to different production practices as the Ford Motion Picture Laboratory was closed in 1932 and company films were instead produced, many with sound, by professional public relations firms like Scientific Films, Inc.

In this period, Ford-sponsored films presented a variety of spectacles—the second run of national park films of the previous chapter, feature-length motion pictures, a collection of films associated with World's Fairs, and footage of stops in more than thirty cities from a publicity stunt in which the company had its twenty-millionth produced car tour the country in 1931. These films engaged in more than just entertainment, however. They animated (sometimes literally) the changing nature of economic rhetoric during a period in which capitalism shifted from, in Paul Crowther's terms, a system concerned with creating the "worker at the machine" to creating the "man in the crowd" as its defining subject.[7] This chapter, then, is about audience—about the place of audience in rhetorical readings and the use of audiences as content in cinematic texts—but also works to answer a question that has puzzled observers for some time: How did corporate capitalism manage to not just survive the Depression era but emerge from it more influential than ever?

One answer to this question is that corporations actively worked in the period to shift the very nature of the economy itself. Where the film *As Dreams Come True* sought to make the Fordist economy knowable through visions of labor, ideas of income distribution, and relationships between production and consumption in 1921, corporate actors used fair and film to press economic relations into the realm of the sublime as a response to economic recession throughout the 1930s. That is, to they suggested that the economy is less a knowable, personal entity than a timeless defining feature of civilization. However, where

Bird Jr. draws a distinction between the dramatic and the rhetorical, rhetoricians have long asked questions about how the dramatic can function as a deeply rhetorical practice—particularly in the service of producing senses of affiliation and connectedness. Tracing Ford's use of these dramatic elements through the World's Fair films, this chapter turns to three rhetorical concepts that further unpack the specific iterations of spectacle taking place at the time: *theoros*, *amplitude*, and *megethos*.

World's Fairs, the Sublime, and Spectacular Rhetoric

Taking up the theme "A Century of Progress," the 1934 World's Fair in Chicago, Illinois, sought to both summarize the previous century's accomplishments and forecast the next century's prospects. Described as "the great drama of man's struggle to lift himself in his weakness to the stars," the fair was promoted as an event featuring no less than "all the manifestations of man's restless energies—the patient laborious researches of the cloistered scientist, exploration, adventure, war, [and] the vast works of industry" resulting in a narrative chronicling "the slow climb from the naked caveman to his descendant of today."[8]

The fair functioned as a vast and thinly veiled pageant looking to sell one vision of industrial capitalism. In the wake of economic catastrophe, then, it served as an extensive argument that civilization itself would only continue to progress if its citizenry recommitted to accepting and supporting the mass production–oriented corporation as their defining institution. As Cheryl R. Ganz has pointed out, "Fair organizers' futuristic plans for what came to be called 'A Century of Progress' championed corporate capitalism, the very culprit that many Americans blamed for their economic woes."[9] Of the exhibitors listed in the fair's official program, 224 appear with "Company," "Corporation," or "Incorporated" in their titles. By comparison, all other institutions (nations, charitable groups, labor organizations) comprised 128 exhibitors (and six of these were general federations representing industries).[10]

For the first year of the fair, Ford did not participate—outraged that General Motors had been given the right to build a moving assembly as part of its presentation. The company, instead, staged its own exposition in Detroit—to middling success. After the success of the World's Fair's first year, however, the company moved its own exposition to a lavish new site in Chicago. With the addition of Ford during the second year of the fair, automobile manufacturers rose, both literally and figuratively, above all other exhibitors. The scale of these expositions and their rhetorical goals was staggering.

Three of the largest expositions at the fair were hosted by Ford, General Motors, and Chrysler. The Ford Exposition Hall alone was more than four acres in size, featured live reenactments of car production, and was adorned by two-story-tall murals painted by Diego Rivera depicting the industrial age.[11] Outside the building were another seven acres of designed material including a reconstruction of roads from around the world that visitors could drive through, a fully industrialized farm, and a bandstand where evening performances would take place.

Summarizing the cumulative rhetorical goal of these various elements, a company brochure explained that the exposition's central purpose was to grab the attention of "the masses of humanity [who] think of an automobile merely as a powered vehicle for use in transportation" and convince them, instead, that "it is infinitely more than that, it is a tremendous Social Factor . . . one of the bases on which all Modern Civilization is founded!"[12] Using a coordinated network of bodies, objects, spaces, and texts, the fair sought to persuade audiences that an ideal society was grounded in mass production and defined by its relationship to the automobile. Amid the throngs of visitors, the clangs and whirs of production, the ultra-vaulted ceilings, and the modern lighting, the company flexed its communicative muscle, hoping, it seems, to recast the American economy, once and for all, as a corporate economy.

The production of this kind of display was certainly a risk. During some of the worst years of the Great Depression (unemployment peaked in 1933 at nearly 25 percent), companies were spending thousands of dollars to construct and publicize these enormous events and were asking the public to spend money to travel to and attend them. More than this, the overall tone of outsized adoration for industrial capitalism certainly could have struck the wrong tone with the public. However, the World's Fair was a considerable success, and Ford's Exposition was such a hit (more than 39 million people attended) that producing a similarly scaled industrial spectacle became a regular affair at sites around the country. In 1935, the concept was taken to San Francisco for the Pacific International Exhibition; it was then reconstructed for the Texas Centennial Exposition in 1936 and the California-Pacific International Exposition in San Diego in 1939–1940, and finally a second and more expansive exposition was designed for the World's Fair held in New York City in 1940. Offering a more permanent site for this spectacle, the centerpiece of the 1934 Exposition, the Ford rotunda, was replicated at Ford's River Rouge factory in Detroit and could be toured by visitors throughout the period.

For the second half of the 1930s, then, corporate actors maintained a nearly constant material site dedicated to producing the corporate sublime. David E. Nye suggests why this turn to the spectacular was an effective response at the time, explaining that "[o]ne of the most powerful human emotions, when experienced in large groups the sublime can weld society together. In moments of sublimity, human beings temporarily disregard divisions among elements of the community."[13] In particular, Nye notes that "World's Fairs exploited every form of the man-made sublime" and sought to display "that private corporations could solve the economic crisis and create a better world."[14]

The sublime, broadly construed, is a word that accounts for something that we know happens but aren't entirely sure why (hence all of the philosophizing about it). To achieve the sublime is to lift an audience from immediate time and space through the artful choice of images, sounds, and words; through moments of bombast; and sometimes through careful displays of restraint. When swept up in successful acts of sublimity, the audience encounters and contemplates a sense of self or any number of emotions (love, hatred, jealousy, empathy) or reflections (existential crisis, communion with a larger purpose). Once achieved, the sublime allows for texts to expand, to challenge, and to adjust subjectivity in ways few other concepts can quite capture. In this frame, World's Fairs submitted to the public a vision of society in which production practices could carry humanity to its greatest heights, and the corporation was the mechanism for this process.

The irrepressible nature of this sensation and the profound nature of its theorized effects explain why, in the wide world of textual effects mapped by rhetoric, few are afforded the power of the sublime. Scholars have long studied such power as well. Longinus, Edmund Burke, and Immanuel Kant each theorized what to make of arguments that sought less to engage with audiences and more to wow them into a state of disengaged cooperation. World's Fairs like the one in Chicago, however, brought about additional questions about the sublime as some have asked, "What if this power could be faked?" What if the same principles that govern sublimation could be applied to produce systems of power, domination, and ideology where enlightenment should be? What if, like cars rolling off of an assembly line, the sublime could be mass-produced?

Walter Benjamin, writing contemporaneously with the World's Fairs, sought to identify their contributions to a "reifying representation of civilization" that functioned at the heart of shifting capitalist reason—a representation called *phantasmagoria* (a name he drew from ghoulish puppet shows that used lantern projections to summon terrors). The world, in Benjamin's account, was becoming increasingly dependent on a version of capitalism that brings about the "atrophy of experience" as individuals were carried away by the projections produced by capitalism. Chief among these projections, he explains, were commodities, and "World exhibitions are places of pilgrimage to the commodity fetish . . . They open a phantasmagoria which a person enters in order to be distracted."[15] He elaborates that "[w]ithin these divertissements, to which the individual abandons himself in the framework of the entertainment industry, he remains always an element of a compact mass . . . in an attitude that is pure reaction. It is thus led to that state of subjection which propaganda, industrial as well as political, relies on. —The enthronement of the commodity, with its glitter of distractions."[16] Some have taken this concept a step further, suggesting that the whole of a society would eventually be structured around these acts of "divertissement." Writing in 1967, Guy Debord named the outcome of *phantasmagoria* "The Society of Spectacle," explaining that "[t]he society which rests on modern industry is not accidentally or superficially spectacular, it is fundamentally *spectaclist*. In the spectacle, which is the image of the ruling economy, the goal is nothing, development is all."[17] Industrial capitalism's ability to jump from an economically circumscribed set of relations to an all-encompassing "social relation among people mediated by images" was a tremendous victory for companies like Ford. The spectacle has moved the purpose of a human life from "being" to "having" to "appearing" so that the apex of capitalism shifts past consumption and into the distractions created by projections of consumption. This process was integral, then, to the "concrete manufacture of alienation."[18]

In such a theory, it is the rhetoric of the sublime—but falsely applied—that constitutes the most fundamental of economic rhetorics in a period of development that has lasted, arguably, to this day. In this frame, corporate rhetoric sought to convince individuals not simply to tolerate work and to accept the use of commodities but to see some fundamental elements of their humanity as wrapped up in both. In shifting the nature of the rhetorical economy, massive industrial actors shifted from producing worker-citizens who were willing to build cars (or anything, really) to a rhetorical project in which consumers of capitalism become an important (perhaps the most important) by-product.

At the same time, these early critiques were largely theoretical and presented little in the way of specific evidence connecting the broad social changes and the particular textual features of the images in question. As Douglas Kellner has pointed out, "Debord presents a rather generalized and abstract notion of spectacle."[19] Less generously phrased, Kevin Gotham and Daniel Krier point out that "spectacle" is a concept that has been hampered by its original theorists' (the Situationist school) "tendency toward hyperbole and exaggeration, their orthodox and naïve faith in the revolutionary agency of the proletariat, and their lack of attention to the crisis tendencies and sources of opposition and resistance that affect capitalist societies."[20]

Put differently, contemporary theories of the spectacular have been less prone to present what figures like Longinus, Edmund Burke, and Immanuel Kant did in centuries past: a systematic treatment of what particular elements led to the effects being claimed.

Thomas Farrell, for example, has pointed out that "very little of substance has been written on the multifarious ways in which largesse, degree, quantity, and priority are themselves composed and nuanced." He suggests, then, that "we will need to ponder the way 'big events' have come to capture, and then overwhelm, and then exhaust public imagination" because "a series of 'big events'—a worldwide depression, a world war, a machine age, a nuclear and then a terrorist age—has forged a kind of grim rhetoric of accommodation (literally, 'an adapting of the eyes to view objects at varying distances')."[21]

Since that time, scholars have worked to place some clearer parameters around "the vaguely defined aesthetic conventions associated with 'spectacular entertainment.'"[22] Megan Sutherland points toward "the distinctly visual and spectatorial conditions of excess" as one place to examine these developments.[23] Similarly, Gotham and Krier argue that scholars attend less to spectacle and more to the process of *"spectacularization"* or "a conflictual and contested process by which the major institutions of society are adopting the logic and principles of entertainment and spectacle to their basic operations and organization."[24] In attending to Ford's contributions to World's Fairs in the interwar period, this chapter further explores the specific textual features that contributed to the production of *phantasmagoria*/spectacle.

These theories, while certainly broadly conceived, do present a number of signposts for where the rhetorical intersects with entertainment. First, much of Benjamin's language points to the material nature of the *phantasmagoria* as a place that one goes that is, in turn, occupied by crowds. One wanders, feels a part of, and is enveloped by spectacle. Film spectatorship is, in this sense, one way to approximate this sensation. Second, both Benjamin and Debord point to the idea that capitalism works in part by simply overwhelming its audiences in two ways—first, by producing (and sometimes synthesizing) a variety of emotional responses and, second, by simply outsizing its competitors. Rhetoric has a name for each of these tactics—*theoros, amplitude,* and *megethos.* The remainder of this chapter examines these rhetorical principles as they appear in a collection of Ford's films associated with World's Fairs taking place in the Depression era.

Ford and a Century of Progress: The 1934 Fair On-Screen

For Walter Benjamin, amassing crowds was one of the most important elements of producing phantasmagoria. He explained that "the crowd is the veil through which the familiar city is transformed for the flaneur into phantasmagoria."[25] In this moment, he presents two figures as important to capitalism's spectacle: the crowd itself transformed into a living conglomerated setting and a subject position that bears witness to this crowd that he calls the *"flaneur."* Kenneth Michael Panfilio argues that the *flaneur* isn't just about presence but the comportment of the figure looking on. The *flaneur*, he explains, is "a nomadic wanderer within the architecture of capitalism unable to muster a free intellect capable of threading together an image of the self across time." As a spectator, then, the *flaneur* is a person "whose existential condition is one of ephemerally engaging with the grand artifacts of capitalism merely through the senses."[26] This idea points to a more fundamental rhetorical tactic, however. Gathering spectators and ordering them into crowds can have important rhetorical power.

Rhetoric has long theorized about this ability to produce figures like the *flaneur*. Aristotle, for example, examined three ideas of spectatorship in his treatise *Rhetoric—krites,* the audience positioned to engage and judge; the *phronemos,* the audience positioned to learn and improve; and the *theoros,* the audience positioned to observe.[27] The *flaneur* is of the third type—a viewer positioned to observe and viscerally appreciate the economy. At the same time, where Benjamin and Panfilio highlight the hapless nature of this position, for classical Greek thought, bearing witness had important cultural impacts that largely redeemed any loss of critical thinking in the process.

As Aristotle used this term, however, he drew on a custom in ancient Greek culture that recognized that there is more to being openly receptive to a social system than just mindless wandering. The *theoroi* were venerated individuals who would travel from one city-state to another to oversee the preparations for festivals or Panhellenic games. The term was also used generally to describe the many travelers who would travel to attend religious, cultural, and athletic events. These events were integral to suturing together various groups into some functioning understanding of Greek culture as an affiliation of city-states. The place of the *theoroi* was particularly important because the events that they attended were considered important enough to suspend war, create spaces for intercultural exchange, and uphold the social values of hospitality. As a set of privileged individuals, the *theoroi* represent a willing suspension of existing tensions to sustain focus on a particular kind of spectacle—religious, athletic, or political. In the case of massive events or points of cultural exchange, an audience is a witness who has set aside other matters to attend to the spectacle of a culture. For a city-state, sending a *theoroi* was an act of honoring and being honored, and for the host site, the work of articulating cultural values and impressing these delegates was an important part of achieving political prestige.[28]

This term *theoros* is particularly useful in explaining corporations' work to shape visual culture in the 1930s but also in considerations of audience as a point of analysis in rhetorical study. It becomes particularly important, then, that the World's Fairs staged and invited the public to arrive, to commune, and to convene with one another. Mobilizing these immediate publics at the fair, the company sought to also produce spectators of the fair—and, by extension, industrial capitalism—around the country. In this sense, perhaps the most important affordance that the motion picture offered to the company's spectacular project was mobility—where a select few could be true *theoroi* in ancient Greece, film allowed for the masses to occupy such a position.

For example, a much wider audience was given access to the World's Fairs—and Ford's goal of repositioning the corporation as a foundational institution in post-Depression reconstruction—through the films that sought to replicate the spectacular nature of the original events. The archive contains a number of these films: *Ford and a Century of Progress* in 1934, *Fair in the West* in 1935, *A Visit to the California Pacific International Exposition* in 1935, *Trip to the San Diego Fair* in 1936, and *Scenes from the World of Tomorrow* in 1940.

Ford, then, generated many films that were about spectatorship—about throngs of spectators and tremendous acts of witnessing. Replicating the fairs on-screen, these films consistently rely on two conventions. First, the films consistently generated views as if the audience were a part of the crowd. Second,

18 | Ford Motion Picture Laboratory, still from *Ford and a Century of Progress*, 1934.

19 | Ford Motion Picture Laboratory, still from *Ford and a Century of Progress*, 1934.

they drew on a number of shots specifically designed to highlight and celebrate the masses of bodies pressing through the exposition. This second tactic was described in the first chapter as a film's elasticity, the rapid combination of many perspectives of the fair (ultra-close-ups, extremely wide shots, shots taken from ceilings and from floors) cut into sleek montages. Using this technique, these films offer enhanced vision, allowing for theatergoers to see both extremely long and extremely close shots of exhibits unavailable to fairgoers, to move between elements of the fair faster than possible in person, and to frame these elements with running commentary.

The 1934 version of this genre, *Ford and a Century of Progress*, includes spectators in nearly all of its scenes but also positions the viewer often as an embodied fair attendee. Filmgoers peek over the shoulders of fairgoers, they share seats and stare out windows with them, and they get lost amid scenes made up exclusively of crowds (see figures 18 and 19). The result of these cinematic pairings is twofold; on one hand, these cinematic spectators take on the same overwhelming experience as the fairgoer, but they also are positioned as consumers of the idealized economy on display.

In the "Foreword" to the film, a slide declares that "[a] permanent product of the 1934 Century of Progress is the renewed confidence and vision which it inspired in the millions of people from all parts of the world that attended it" as an orchestral rendition of "Chicago, Chicago" plays in the background. Onscreen, the film converts one medium—the public exposition—into another—a cinematic narrative of economic reality grounded in spectatorship. At the fair, the company's enormous exposition hall functioned as a series of manufactured reenactments of labor, international roads, and resource harvesting aligned spatially into a comprehensive vision of an economy but one that could be wandered through, touched, and shared with others. In the film, montage allows for these examples to be piled on top of one another with the kind of speed that allowed for slippages and blurring, for an institutional whole to take shape, for a uniform narrative of economic reality.

The establishing shot for the film begins with a slow zoom onto the enormous rotating globe that served as the centerpiece for the exposition. The zoom is timed so that the city of Chicago rotates into view on the surface of the Earth just as the camera arrives. In one dynamic editing practice, the screen splits into three shifting patterns (first diagonal columns, then symmetrical pentagrams, and a finally a collection of random shapes), each containing crowds bustling about the fair's grounds. While this dynamic depiction of the fair's many visitors is taking place, the narrator declares the fair to be "the greatest show on Earth" and the "focal point of a nation" and finally "this is America, America on parade!"

At this point, a long (nearly fifteen-minute) narrated montage of spectacles unfolds: a dance troupe performing a minuet outside a replica of George Washington's Mount Vernon home, the world's biggest thermometer, the Latin Quarter of Paris, a "colorful bit" of old Madrid, views from on board the Goodyear Blimp, animatronic dinosaurs (which are described in particularly Fordist terms: "Mother Nature discovered they use too much fuel, so she discontinued the models some time ago"), the "veritable fairyland of light and color" that is the fair after dark. All of this, however, serves as a precursor for the film's climactic feature: the appearance of the Ford Motor Company Exposition. As a temporal experience of cinematic spectatorship, then, the many kitsch depictions of national identifications build up to the seemingly superior and sleekly designed modernity of the automobile pavilions.

Some of this contrast is captured in the establishing shots that introduce the Ford Pavilion section first featuring the overlapping neon-lit "Ford Signs" and then a blimp-mounted view of the Ford grounds during the day (see figure 20). Highlighting the immensity of the exposition captured in these shots, the narrator declares for the former that "on the Ford building alone, there is more lighting used than illuminated the entirety of the World's Fair of 1893"; for the latter image, the narrator compounds the scale of the image by framing the fair itself as a "galaxy of huge structures and grand ideas." At this point, over a montage of fairgoers interacting with the grounds, the narrator outlines the specifications of the exposition's size, highlighting that there was simply more than could possibly be captured in a single film taking place at the fair. Nevertheless making an attempt, the second half of the thirty-minute film is composed of a series of montages capturing the diverse set of concepts brought together by the exposition: the advance of automobiles over the years; the "basic operations of mine, farm, and factory"; "the vast extent of the Ford World" captured on a three-dimensional map marking where materials come from and where automobiles go; a selection of the "15,000 separate parts" or "byproducts" required to produce the car (aluminum, cold steel, spark plugs, and wires are each briefly featured).

In a broad celebration of fair attendees, a montage captures fairgoers at a snack bar, a Henry Ford Trade School student indexing a gear head and workers hammering materials in a reenactment of the assembly line in front of a lineup of fairgoers, fairgoers looking at Ford's new line of cars, industrial murals painted by Diego Rivera poised above a crowded hall, a worker hammering a

20 | Ford Motion Picture Laboratory, stills from *Ford and a Century of Progress*, 1934.

rod on an anvil, fairgoers leisurely chatting under umbrellas, soybeans growing in a field, workers assembling a V8 engine, a packed exposition hall, and more workers working with machinery. In this sequence, the montage works through repeated juxtapositions alternating images of mechanical displays with images of spectators enjoying the displays. The movement here is dialectical in nature, and through this back and forth, the film presents the most basic of economic production practices as an act of remarkable spectacle—as content that millions would pay to witness.

At one point, in the middle of this scattered configuration of disparate ideas and objects, however, the film begins to take a clearer shape around the act of attending the fair in a more sequential order. This shift is marked by a montage that works to replicate the experience of moving through the main hall of the exposition. During this portion, more than five minutes of the film is dedicated to establishing the idea that Ford Motor Company is a corporation made up of other corporations, that its ability to produce the car is, in itself, an industry made up of the incorporation of many industries including, for example, "The United States Rubber Corporation," "The American Brass Company," "The Aluminum Company of America," and "Essex Wire Corporation."

Each of these contractors is presented first by a written sign and then a five- to ten-second clip of the combined labor of man and machine that comprises the corporations' contribution to the assembly of a car. (This section of the film functions much like the early Yellowstone film in this regard.) After this visual parade of the contributing corporations, the film presents the production of a Ford V8 engine in less than ten minutes—as a physical journey through the hall, this construction is the literal endpoint of an immense network of resources, labors, and institutions.

Each of these objects is placed in several frames that produced a collective notion of outsized scale (notably, two of which were unavailable to those in attendance at the fair): a long frame capturing the place of the object in the wider exposition, a medium frame featuring exposition patrons viewing the object, and a close-up featuring the object itself. The three images that make up figure 21 capture this set of frames as it applied to the film's depiction of "L.A. Young Spring and Wire Corporation."

The ultimate use of these variously scaled shots is to present the audience with both an immediate sense of what the exposition contained as well as how these contained elements fit together. As a set of frames, however, the scenes moved the viewer from seeing the scale of the exposition to humans interacting

21 | Ford Motion Picture Laboratory, stills from *Ford and a Century of Progress*, 1934.

with machines to a focus directly on the machine itself as the location for innovative labor. In this sense, they make a basic explanatory point about production itself as it was becoming increasingly automated. However, when this same structure is compiled into more than a dozen different iterations of this automated labor, the explanation begins to take a more argumentative form.

After detailing the manufacturing processes that make up the company, the film next turns to more expansive arguments about the implications of this conglomeration to history and culture. The scenes in this sequence include a narrative of Henry Ford's invention of the Fordist production method; a set of village-industries where America develops with "one foot in the soil and one foot in industry"; and a set of "roads of the world" where, returning to the exposition's theme, the narrator declares that "the auto makes roads, and roads make commerce and civilization." Each of these declarations is accompanied by a set of rapidly shifting camera shots capturing fairgoers witnessing Ford workers assembling engines, farmers using industrial methods to harvest soybeans, and patrons riding in cars on the simulated roads and taking in the immense rotating display of the materials that go into a Ford automobile.

Capping this longer montage-driven narrative, the film concludes with a summative, and far more rapid, montage capturing fragments of each of the previous scenes as the narrator declares that "[i]t has been a memorable day, this one, at the Ford exposition. Here we have [caught a glimpse] of the humble machinery and the throb of busy activity from the greatest of all industrial plants. Here, we have been able to sense something of its high purpose and its vast significance. The Ford Exposition is at once the fulfillment of a prophecy, and the realization of a dream. It is an indication of the future, a reassuring prophecy of another century of progress!" The company's plan is made clear in this conclusion; at a moment in time where this very prophecy of American exceptionalism was in question due to high unemployment and general social malaise, audiences across the country would leave theaters comforted not only by such a "reassuring prophecy" but by the material evidence that has given the "something" of the integral role the mass-production corporation could play in a return to prosperity.

More than this, the film concludes by including the audience in the throngs of fairgoers who have come together to witness the event, at once marking them as figures capable of appreciating the sublime delights of the fair itself as well as the economic culture capable of delivering up these sensational features. These films worked to frame the rest of the enormous exposition in wider social contexts and continued to circulate for years after the fair ended—narrating again and again a salient moment where a vision of corporate America materialized.

Understood as a modern iteration of the *theoros*—an audience positioned to embody social cohesion through their shared attention—these films allowed for thousands of Americans to perform and witness cultural uniformity in a time of tremendous upheaval. But the role of film in the World's Fairs' rhetorical power was not limited to replicating the proceedings on screen.

In addition to nationally circulated films presenting the World's Fair to distant publics, films were integral parts of the expositions as well. The Ford Pavilion in 1934 featured two rotating films each dedicated to summarizing the nature of the Fordist economy in truncated form. Ford wasn't alone in its automotive/exposition/cinematic combination. Rather, the fair was replete with utility films. In one of the fair's most unique features, the world's largest car at the time (an eighty-foot-tall Studebaker) was built and converted into a theater in which "films are shown telling the story of motor car manufacturing"; Chevrolet produced *Triumph of America* in 1933—a film that also relies on the rapid-cut vignette structure to disrupt narratives of time and progress.[29] These films draw on a number of traditional rhetorical features—*amplitude, hyperbole,* and *megethos*, namely—enacted through a set cinematic affordances offered by the motion picture—multimodality, pacing, and perspective. The purpose of these rhetorical maneuvers was to further shape an economic *theoros* by simply overpowering audiences with cinematic content.

Rhapsody in Steel: Amplitude, Nonsense, and Escape

In the first century, Longinus explained that one mark of the sublime was when an audience "is assailed, not by one emotion, but by a tumult of different emotions." This, classically, is the device *amplitude*, which describes "when a writer or pleader, whose theme admits of many successive starting-points and pauses, brings on one impressive point after another in a continuous and ascending scale."[30] The result of these rhetorical strategies is a text that draws on "conflicting emotions: fear and awe, horror and fascination. It sweeps the public off its feet in an overwhelming experience of beauty mixed with terror and admiration."[31]

A concept like *amplitude* is a particularly useful way of thinking about Ford's use of multiple modes not only in the films it produced for the World's Fairs but also for the events themselves. Nothing, pseudo-Longinus argued in the first century, "is so conducive to energy as a combination of different figures, when two or three uniting their resources mutually contribute to the vigor, the cogency, and the beauty of a speech."[32] Film provides two features particularly useful for generating cinematic amplitude: speed and multimodality. As Dennis Dake has put it, the films rely on the basic fact that "Words can only speak one thing at a time, but images arrive holistically, everything present simultaneously. Visual logic must be understood as a wordless way of speculating, considering, and eventually knowing."[33] Seymour Benjamin Chatman similarly points out that "[f]ilm gives us plenitude without specifics" in contrast to written accounts that must limit attention and information.[34] The motion picture's ability to draw on various modes—speech, writing, bodily movement, music, images—opens it to particularly vivid accounts of this cacophonous version of the sublime. What has been less clearly outlined is the ways in which this capability has been put to specifically rhetorical ends.

In 1934, the Ford Exposition featured two rotating films—*The Human Ford* and *Rhapsody in Steel*—each dedicated to summarizing the nature of the Fordist economy in truncated form but with very different stylistic perspectives. By many accounts, *Rhapsody in Steel* was a marvel. It combined traditional documentary film practices with stop-motion animation, drawn animation, and a riling symphonic score to produce a text that purposefully used the multimodal to create spectacle.

While the film was impressive for its layering of different cinematic modes, it was also, from the perspective of traditional film and rhetorical analysis, a symphony of nonsense: a disjointed narrative defined by two distinct sections accompanied by an originally composed symphony for the film. The first half of the film is a standard production film that takes full advantage of the perfect rhythm of the production process to work in near-perfect sync with the music. The result is an oddly soothing iteration of the production film. The unexpected pairing of high culture (a symphony) and low culture (the factory floor) worked to elevate the latter.

The first half of the film, then, focuses on some of the more spectacular elements of the production processes—much of the early footage is of enormous blast furnaces as sparks fly as glowing pools and bars of steel move from one end of the screen to the other; these bars of molten steel are then stamped into parts through the power of perfectly timed machines and the precision of careful workers. These glowing parts were a visual boon for the film and for the fair's larger goal to elevate industrial manufacturing beyond its purely economic state.

In this sense, the first half of the film relies on the company's longstanding celebration of the machine aesthetic, but positions production as an arresting, if not beautiful, collection of remarkable visual spectacles. However, the film does not end with a peaceful symphonic juxtaposition between orchestral composition and industrial production. Rather, it jumps the tracks of this standard narrative to present flights of fancy. The second half of the film is centered around a cartoon sprite leading a parade in which each (non-animated) part of a Ford V8 assembled itself into the 5000th car to roll off of an assembly line in a given day. The sprite, then, serves as the hero by allowing the factory to meet its quota.

After the rhythmic, sensory experience of traditional production, the film pivots via a sequence in which an engineer—jaw clenched—stares up at a board that reads "Production Schedule for To-day: 5000. Completed: 4999." Distressed by this failure to meet production goals, the nameless worker scratches his head and walks out of the scene. The next shot shows his figure asleep in a chair, his visage fades out as the grill of a Ford V8 fades in, and the logo becomes animated. Literally, the V8 logo morphs into an animated sprite, who hops from the grill of the car and looks up at the board. Unlike his human counterpart, however, the sprite envisions the 5,000th car in a thought cloud above his head and flies (literally) into action.

Using stop-motion animation, the film shows the figure setting into motion the many material elements of the V8 as tires roll into place, struts slide along the floor of the factory, and the engine waddles across the screen. In succession, these many parts are shown aligning into the various parts of the V8 like a marching band developing formations. The images that make up this parade seem to have little reasonable connection to one another or to the subject of the film. The assembly begins as a marching band and then turns to what looks like the pillared hall of a palace as a group of stirrup-shaped parts engage in a square dance while a grandstand of shock absorbers bounce in approval (figure 22). Later, the hood of the car enters, flapping like a pair of wings as it is flanked by animated birds. In what might be the climax of the movie—though it is very hard to be sure—at one point the car's gear shifter becomes a dragon, which the sprite must vanquish to complete the car (figure 23). All of this hits the viewer with the added force of a riling symphony blaring in the background.

This nonsense, however, may just have been the point. For fair attendees, after months of reading bad news in newspapers, of worrying about the potential for lost jobs and further economic downturn, and of rumblings about totalitarianism in Europe, there may have been little more satisfying than pure, unmoored cinematic nonsense. These effects would be compounded, one might

22 | Ford Motion Picture Laboratory, still from *Rhapsody in Steel*, 1934.

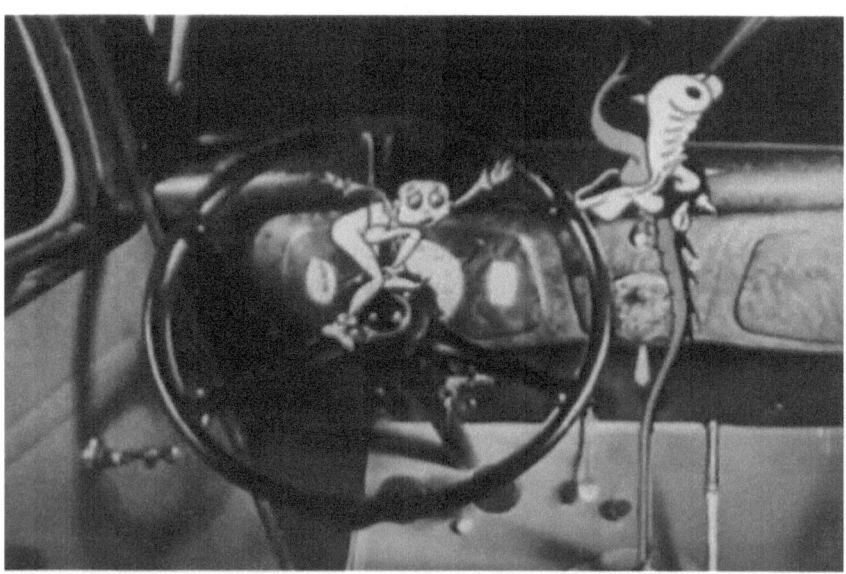

23 | Ford Motion Picture Laboratory, still from *Rhapsody in Steel*, 1934.

imagine, when entering and exiting the theater meant entering into an equally fantastic set of spaces. The film was being viewed by 10,000 daily just at the exposition—more, it seems, were viewing the film across the country.[35]

As this makes clear, *Rhapsody in Steel*'s montages make no attempt at conceptual cohesion. Their purpose is not to disrupt time or establish cause and effect or draw comparison. Its plot is to build a car (the same plot the company had been pushing for decades), but this plot takes an oddly non-sequential form with non-intersecting plotlines. Instead, the film offers up an overwhelming cacophony of concepts. In this sense, *Rhapsody in Steel* toes a difficult line. If the film were any more ridiculous it would lose its referent to become an inconsequential cartoon—by recasting production as a sensorium of impressive feats the film reminds viewers of just how remarkable the building of a new automobile is. If the film tilted too far the other way—becoming a straightforward production film—it would remind the audience too clearly of economic conditions, becoming an all-too-apparent piece of crass propaganda. By tempering the real with the fanciful and mashing this all into a hyper-condensed animated feature, the company managed to entertain, potentially confuse, and largely dazzle fair attendees. The film's ability to toe this line is further highlighted by its symphonic nature—as a visualized rhapsody devoid of explicit narration, the film relies on not just animated plot but music to draw its viewers into a state of escape. In material form, this is one of the underlying assumptions behind the World's Fair as an event—to collect an otherwise impossible menagerie of miscellany in one place. Film would prove a useful medium in enhancing this experience of the fantastical layering of objects, ideas, and (perhaps most importantly for the present study) modes.

Witnessing firsthand the "bread and circuses" that supported Roman imperial might, Longinus wrote of the power that could be produced in generating narratives that disorient audiences by keeping them off-balance through shifts in tone, emotional appeal, and intensity. *Rhapsody* revived these strategies for the machine age using a variety of film's affordances. These strategies included the overlapping of high and low culture via the mismatched genres of a symphony and an industrial film. It also alternated production's remarkable scale—from the sheer power and beauty of tons of glowing liquid alloys and titanic machines to the intricate workings of the smallest of mechanized parts. Finally, the film's two acts paired the hyper-rational, orderly sequencing of production with the ridiculous fanfare of an industrial cartoon. The whole film appears on the surface to be a haphazard affair. However, the concept of *amplitude* suggests otherwise.

There are a few ways we might think about this elevated form of cacophony as an immediately rhetorical act at the World's Fair. The first is that the film functioned as a palate cleanser; if one of the goals was to sweep fairgoers away, this film—with its ambient work to lull the viewer followed by its nonsensical animated visual overture—would have certainly set the tone to simply let go of any particular attempts to stay grounded in the world beyond the fair's gates. However, the film was seen by even more people outside the context of the fair. In this second context, blatantly drawing on the multimodal potential of film over sequential plot lines—animation, stop-motion, layered sound—the company sought to reduce manufacturing down to its visceral nature—the beauty of exploding coal coke, the intricacy of combined parts in an engine, the intensity of a line worker's lined face.

More than just a single-use strategy, however, the rhetorical work of the 1934 World's Fair would become a template for the company over the latter half of the century. Within this template, films based in amplitude were never working in isolation. Rather, the World's Fair films worked in tandem, pairing the fanciful nonsensical whimsy of symphony films with a second genre of film that worked in more expository form to argue that the sheer size of industrial production was evidence of its inherent superiority. Once again, rhetoric has a name for this kind of appeal: megethos. To observe this appeal in action, however, we must move away from 1934 and "A Century of Progress" and toward its rhetorical legacy as it can be observed at the 1940 World's Fair.

Drawing on the success of the World's Fair in 1934, Ford Motor Company once again developed an intricate exhibition, putting this on display in the films. Not one to meddle with success, the company stuck with the cinematic strategy of the earlier fair as well, producing *Symphony in F, Harvest of the Years,* and *Scenes from the World of Tomorrow,* "a six-minute pictorial whirl over, around and through the New York World's Fair."[36] *Symphony in F* featured "doll-like figures which animate the Ford Cycle of Production exhibit at the New York Fair . . . The farmer, chemist, lumberjack, miner, cotton picker, rubber man and transportation worker all dramatize—in song and action—their parts in pouring raw materials from all points of the compass into the River Rouge plant, the world's greatest industrial unit."[37] By many accounts *Symphony in F* was as celebrated as its predecessor, though not necessarily within the company.[38] The 1940 exhibition's attendance averaged more than 6,000,000 people per week, and these movies were shown to more than 1,700,000 people at the exposition alone.[39]

At the same time that the World's Fair and its films functioned through the overwhelming overlap of multiple sensory experiences coordinated through their own spectacular features, the fairs also produced arguments that aligned size with quality and effectiveness. To better understand this second element of Ford's World's Fair films, *megethos*, I turn to the 1940 film *Harvest of the Years*.

Harvest of the Years: Pacing, *Megethos*, and Hyperbole

Harvest of the Years, in particular, serves as an example of cinematic *megethos* that mirrored the rhetorical strategy of the wider World's Fair. Jenny Rice defines *megethos* as "an aesthetic inflection of a quantitative mass that gives a *sense* of weightiness, a sense that sustains the epistemic without relying on epistemology to structure it." Jonathan Mark Balzotti and Richard Benjamin Crosby have similarly claimed "*megethos* establishes the subject's superiority by virtue of the way it outsizes other subjects." In sum, *megethos* is understood as both an effect—the argument that bigger is better—and a set of textual features that produce the experience of magnitude. Examples of the rhetorical impact of *megethos* offer a wide berth for its use: reorienting public memory (Balzotti and Crosby), framing national identity (Olson), and suturing the tremendous ruptures in established systems of meaning (Rice).[40]

Harvest of the Years is made up of vignettes ranging from thirty seconds to two minutes grafted together with abrupt cuts. With the film's consistent focus on displaying efficiency (and repeatedly declaring that this value is being passed on to the buyer), the purpose of this film, as explained in an internal company memo, was to "emphasize the Ford Motor Company's unique position in the industrial world and in industrial history," adding that "[i]f the right facts are presented, and presented in the right way, a lasting impression can be made which will be extremely favorable to the Ford Motor Company and to the sale of Ford products." The "right way," it seems, was to present the entirety of the company's actions at a breakneck pace.

We have already seen, in chapter 2, the importance of montage to industrial rhetoric for its ability to replicate the piece-by-piece nature of production and for capturing the interrelated nature of the Fordist economy. *Harvest of the Years* takes this capability to the extreme. The twenty-two-minute film features just shy of 250 distinct shots separated by a variety of fade-ins/outs. These shots are organized, further, into five broadly themed montages focused on spectatorship, extended production practices, recycling and efficiency efforts, and a bit on labor relations propaganda. There are three kinds of cinematic appeal that enact the company's *megethos*-driven work: pace, naming of quantities, and hyperbolic narration. The film opens with a frame that combines all three of these appeals, declaring that "[f]rom small beginnings sometimes come abundant harvests. From this tiny workshop came the vision that built a thousand highways. From this rude bench and lathe and drill have spring the tools for 80,000 men. From this small shop has grown a city of work and opportunity an industrial city covering a thousand acres a city drawing visitors from all the world who come to wonder and to learn." What is clear from this narration is the focus these World's Fair films had on size and compilation. The first of these extols the ongoing value of spectatorship, highlighting that the remnants of the 1934 World's Fair have been on display in Dearborn for the past six years. The narrator explains that "from all over the world and from all over America come visitors by the thousands daily. Some are everyday citizens as you and I, some are industrialists, scientists, students, business leaders, some are eminent engineers. Why does this one industrial city attract so many visitors . . . what is there here that is unique in the entire automotive industry?" The answer to these questions is cinematic *megethos* at its finest. The pace of this section picks up considerably as shots are shortened from an average of six seconds to four seconds. Part of this shortened average comes from extremely rapid sequences of one- and two-second clips of manufacturing.

Harvest of the Years deploys an extended metaphor/montage pairing that moves beyond the immediate physical site of the assembly line and is captured in multiple montages to establish the line as just one in a much more extensive set of contributing types of labor, using the metaphor of the "city" to make sense of it. This section is particularly useful for observing another rhetorical strategy deployed by the company's *megethos*-driven films: the excessive list. Take, for example, the narrator's description of the first answer to the framed questions— the "city of transportation" composed of the sum of Ford's production practices: "[T]his is a city of transportation, where carriers of materials and things lighten and lessen the task of building carriers of men and burdens . . . to bring materials and things to forge to lathe, to bench, to the busy hands of men. For the city of transportation is a complete city, a city founded upon an idea, a different idea, a city whose every source and resource bring here the means, find here the methods, join here the opportunities, to work, to tend, to spin, to weave, to form, and transform so that from within this city great advances in transportation are made available to the world." It sounds, here, like he might faint for lack of air in trying to compile all of the elements the film is presenting to the viewer. Visually, this section of the film set up by this narrative framework is composed of four montages. After the assembly line, a second labor montage appears, this time of the engineering department. A third montage returns to the resources, which are listed out by quantity while brief scenes of each farm and farmer amid production make up the background. A fourth montage outlining the design department takes center focus as a drawing melts into the material, built car—the narrator noting that "nothing is approved, until it is proved."

The film presents a frame narrative of the manufacturing regime springing from Ford's original workshop and works its way through Ford and Lincoln plant workers in action, Ford Engineers inventing and testing new materials and ideas, the raw materials from around the world harvested to create the Ford automobile, an economic explanation of mass industry as "a give and take," village-industries and the production of soybeans, the work of the design department, a series of testing practices, the vertical integration of industry, the scope of factories producing materials for the car, the company's recycling of materials, steps taken for "saving men from burden," and finally a return to the frame narrative presenting the process as an extension of Henry Ford's vision. With its consistent focus on displaying efficiency (and repeatedly declaring that this value is being passed on to the buyer) this overwhelming montage of features repositions the industrial corporation as a much needed value creator.

Visually, all of these sections share basic features—the use of short, rapidly interspersed snippets of laborers engaging in otherwise stationary or menial work to generate dynamism—but extend the idea of both labor and production out to the careful coordination of engineers, laboratory technicians, chemists, and quality control employees. From the industrial sensibility, a layered understanding of labor manufacturing, technical, agricultural, each come into conversation under the evolving Fordist regime, "spreading work and wealth to every corner of the nation."

The business within these scenes is equally muddled by the variety of shots being used. Quick panoramas of harbors are juxtaposed with tightly shot hands flinging bolts from one side of the screen to another. In this sense, the films work to specifically highlight size as a virtue made possible by the industrial corporation. But the attention to size is further enhanced by a second feature of the film: hyperbole. If the visual elements of the film highlight sheer accumulation, the narrator supplements these images with over-the-top language.

For example, the film also works through a variety of quantitative appeals. In explaining the importance of industry to agriculture in America, the narrator explains that "[f]or every million cars produced there is an annual purchase of 3.2 million pounds of wool, 1.5 million square feet of leather, beeswax from millions of honeybees . . . 69 million pounds of cotton, 500,000 bushels of corn, 2.4 million pounds of linseed oil, 2.5 million gallons of molasses, 2 million pounds of turpentine, and 69 million pounds of rubber . . . these together with other purchases from more than 7,000 suppliers total hundreds of millions of dollars, spreading work and wealth into every state of the union." This use of pacing also allowed for emphasis. Standing in significant contrast to the extensive visual pile of materials working across the screen to this point, the longest sustained shot in the film (it lasts for just over a minute) features a series of parts emerging from the River Rouge plant and ascending (as a halo of light surrounds the factory) to the heavens while a steam ship floats by (see figure 24).

In this moment, the filmmakers have used pacing to shift attention away from the steady stream of visual images sutured together to generate focus on the verbally delivered point. This happens three times throughout the film, two to conclude montage-driven sections and once in the final summative announcement of the film's purpose. After the brief break, the film pivots as the narrator asks (once again, rhetorically) what sets Ford apart from its competitors. Combining hyperbole and quantity, he explains that it is "an idea, so mighty as an ideal, that within half a man's lifetime a tiny workshop has grown into the world's largest industrial development" before the film turns to a final montage designed to explain how all of this size leads not to dehumanizing labor but to a reduction in toil, a rise in "expertise," and a revolution in new white collar jobs. "[S]hortcuts and savings, here, are made with machines and materials, not with men; it is this efficiency which makes the work go faster, not the men; an efficiency that produces higher quality and less cost, and at high wages . . . it is the conveyor that makes to work easier, the burden lighter and thus enables men to produce more, earn more; not as day laborers, but as specialists on their line." The purpose of this last montage is to celebrate efficiency, as the narrator argues that of all the products generated by Ford's assembly practices, time is the most important. It is the saving of seconds at each point of production, he argues, that produces "minutes" for the workers to take breaks, to enjoy leisure, and to consider quality.

24 | Ford Motion Picture Laboratory, still from *Harvest of the Years*, 1940.

The film concludes by directing the viewer to the home of this overwhelming spectacle, the River Rouge Plant and its now several-year-old rotunda from the 1934 World's Fair. The narrator declares:

> It is the combination of all these that explains why thousands of people from around America and from all around this world visit this plant each day. They know that here is a fountainhead of industrial and technological progress that has raised standards of production methods around the world. They see that the more anyone has success, the more everyone can have. And leaving, each carries this thought: "this is the only plant of this kind in the world, and only from this plant can these cars come at these prices. And so this is the time of the Harvest, a harvest of the years, a harvest founded upon an idea, an idea from the mind of a man for whom it is always early morning in America.

The focus of the film's conclusion is not the act of production or the marvel of the car but the impetus for thousands of individuals to witness these processes—to bask in the feeling of economic recovery. As an argument, the film presents *megethos* in cinematic form through the combined force of a hyperbolic script, the continuous reference to quantitative mass, and the use of montage to produce a generally overwhelming pace of images punctuated by vistas of summative points extolling mass production.

Conclusion: On the Importance of Spectatorship

This examination of the World's Fair films suggests that, often, the most rhetorically powerful arguments are the ones that work to put the world back together in fractious times, and this includes narratives that offer escape. One way to do this is to create overpowering acts of spectacle. As Dana B. Polan has argued, when corporations entertain in this way, "[w]hat we find is an 'entertainment' in its virtually etymological sense—a *holding-in-place*, a ... strategy of containment against any depth of involvement with that world."[41]

I have argued here that we might understand one line in this "strategy of containment" in a number of ways—by producing a narrative in which spectatorship was itself a point of important social cohesion, by producing a nonsensical narrative through the interplay of various modes, and by using film to highlight the sheer size and scale of corporate production. These various cacophonous texts produce a narrative that can be seen and experienced, but not really sensed, and one whose overwhelming layering of disjointed plot points and lurching shifts in visual materials leads to a complete abandonment of being sensible, of trying to hold what one is viewing up to a logical framework. Through these events and the films that related to them, Ford's compilation of overblown narratives engaged in a struggle over how the public was being positioned as spectators of capitalism and how they were being encouraged not just to see but to understand the reflexive relationship between their ability to see and their position in a larger social system.

The World's Fairs and their films served as staged events designed to first arrest national discourses and then redirect these discourses into new, alternative frameworks. More generally, however, the fairs' films functioned to produce a long rhetorical tail, remaining in circulation for years after their initial appearance. Eventually, under the brief leadership of Edsel Ford, motion pictures would become much more dedicated tools in the implementation of "mass selling," rather than general education, aimed at bending the whole of American culture toward Fordist practices. In a letter to domestic and foreign branches, the Edsel Ford's office advised that "[m]ass selling must be made a more definite part of our sales activities, and should be built primarily around our motion picture releases . . . following this, arrangements should be made to provide a regular film service to schools, high schools, colleges, technical schools, service clubs, social clubs, business clubs, employees clubs, fraternal organizations, church groups, veterans organizations, etc."[42] By 1940, Ford was distributing a number of films to its dealerships meant to highlight a nation steeped in car culture. The World's Fair films were central to this collection (they were joined by the national park films examined in the previous chapter).[43] Nationally, reports suggested that nearly ten million individuals viewed this collection of films in 1940, and as they gained popularity from January to March 1941, 5,901,626 individuals attended screenings of these films at various branch locations around the country.[44]

This chapter has also worked to revive a much older conception of the relationship among systems of power, texts, and audiences. David Blakesly, for example, has argued that rhetoric can provide "a revision of spectatorship to include the ways that film language works rhetorically to reconstitute the subject."[45] However, presenting a rhetorical take on spectatorship enters into a contested landscape over a term that already struggles with having too many meanings. Particularly since the arrival of empirical study of film, claims to "spectatorship" have been positioned as a murky coverall that allows for critics to make meanings out of texts by positing audience response without there being any inherent connection to actual spectators.[46]

For some film scholars, critical scholarship has acted "as if" spectators function according to psychoanalytic or Marxist principles of meaning without clear explanations as to why. These studies, then, are positioned as more about the critic and the thought processes of the discipline than an actual reading for texts and effects. Carl Plantinga, in responding to this charge, suggests paying greater attention to the "grounds of response," which are "rooted in the relationship between the human psyche, textual characteristics, and viewing context" can result in greater understandings of how spectatorship and affect are related (while also avoiding broad claims about spectator response).[47] Affect, then, has also been mapped out of what has traditionally been studied as rhetorical. These kinds of affective responses are integral, however, for incorporational arguments about what structural network will continue to guide a society. In this framework, Catherine Chaput has argued that "the market is an affective force that influences rhetorical action by linking bodily receptivities to economic persuasion."[48]

Drawing out from Plantinga, I have explored another way to position spectatorship and rhetoric that sidesteps critiques of the jumps made from screen content to identification to subjectivity. By placing competing uses of spectatorship (that is, attending to how particular actors positioned the "grounds of response") in the context of larger historical projects, we might better heed criticism of analyses that posit how audiences should or would respond. Rather, this model for approaching spectatorship works by considering how the cinematic rhetor actively contends over the place and purpose of spectators in a given space and given time. In this way, a rhetorical account of the concept draws on the plurality of theories that have sought to account for the relationship between texts and "the audience" as an analytical framework.

Thus, a rhetorical approach to spectatorship in rhetorical studies of film—drawn out in part by this connection to the *theoros*—might function by considering the appropriateness not just of general formations of an idealized spectator or assumptions about how individuals respond but of questions of why appeals to spectatorship are important in particular historical contexts. In this sense, holding World's Fairs was a deeply felt rhetorical act of inviting individuals to experience the best economic culture had to offer, and films allowed for the figures who attended to fairs to function much as ancient *theoroi* did—as representatives observing the events, suspending other pressing material concerns, and drawing out notions of cultural cohesion.

For rhetoricians, publics amenable to the spectacular are not just sociological subjects or *ex post facto* social groups to be observed; they are the result of rhetorical attunements that accrue over time and serve important roles in articulating societal value. More than this, claims about size, scope, and sensory overload present opportunities to inquire into the gradations that make up terms like scale or excess. Further still, attending to the rhetorical capacities of size and scope is particularly important in the study of corporate actors for two reasons: first, size offers up important rhetorical advantages in the public sphere and, second, achieving these remarkable proportions serves, arguably, as the very purpose of contemporary impulses toward incorporation.

5

War, Industrial Globalization, and the Managerial Gaze

On December 29, 1940, just months after the conclusion of the 1940 World's Fair, President Franklin D. Roosevelt addressed the American public looking to garner support for the Allied forces in World War II. In a fireside chat, he asked for the nation to mobilize not for military intervention or in a call to engage in political diplomacy. Instead, Roosevelt's speech drew straight from the World's Fairs' spectacular playbook. He declared that "American industrial genius, unmatched throughout all the world in the solutions to production problems has been called upon to bring its resources and talents into action" to turn the tides of the war. If unwilling to engage through military force, he explained, the nation must instead "be the Arsenal of Democracy" by devoting much of its energy to building war machines and funding credit lines to those democratic nations that needed them.[1]

Aligning production directly with discourses of national sovereignty, Roosevelt further argued that to ensure the "preservation of American independence, and all of the things that American independence means to you and to me and to ours," the nation needed to produce en masse to outmuscle encroaching fascist regimes. In this way, his speech posited that the continued sovereignty of the nation (understood as the right to continued "independence") would come down to the decisions by individuals to consume less and labor more. Notably, Roosevelt took this a step further by directing the speech to a series of economic subjects, calling on "the workmen in the mills, the mines, and the factories, the girl behind the counter, the small shopkeeper, the farmer doing his Spring plowing, the widows, and the old men wondering about their life's savings" rather than to nationalized, militarized, or politicized subject positions (insofar as any of these individual positions can be separated).

This is a classic example of what Louis Althusser has described as a "hailing," a sitting American president taking to the radio airwaves to call the sum of a nation to answer its sovereign as economic subjects (and, in the process, to recognize and accept this subject position). In response to the acceptance of these roles, Roosevelt also recast the nation itself as an economic entity, promising that "the strength of [the United States] shall not be diluted by the failure of the government to protect the economic well-being of its citizens" as it entered into wartime production.

Arguments like Roosevelt's turned World War II into a rhetorically powerful occasion that could bring to fruition many projects; his vision of nationalized industry was articulated by the New Deal, for example, but it also opened the way for the American corporation to continue to generate fully incorporated economic populace. Charles Sorenson, a chief executive at Ford during the period, spoke of the struggle that would ensue for the meaning of such an arsenal: "Orators, columnists, professors, preachers, and propagandists performed magnificently with the theme that World War II was a war between two ideologies. But whatever inflamed people's minds in warring countries, victory was on the side of the heaviest-armed battalions. The conflict became one of two systems of production."[2] This final chapter inquires into what was unleashed by the military-industrial system represented by the "Arsenal of Democracy," or, rather, it inquires into what visual configuration could possibly have incorporated this global vision for American power. The short answer is managerial capitalism. Justified by this industrial framework, postwar development was largely an unfettered system of Fordism working in conjunction with new globally minded financial mechanisms.

The longer answer, however, is an extension of work by Dana D. Nelson to understand the pervasive nature of "professional manhood" that lay at the heart of this industrial regime. She argues that the rise of "[p]rofessional manhood diversified and formally articulated national manhood's investment in management logic on behalf of its own gender, racial, and class advantage." Ford's films, then, had always worked to train "men, as part of their civic, fraternal grant, to internalize national imperatives for 'unity' and 'sameness' but also understand the manifestation of this sameness to be dedicated workers."[3] In this analysis, many of the films in the Ford collection embody a system where the masculine and the economic serve as a potent combination for producing particular configurations of hegemony.

Observed in visual culture, this system of homogenizing masculinity (in the service of homogenizing a workforce) has been explored through another concept in spectator studies in film that has developed around the idea of the "gaze."

In this chapter, I seek to trace how a particular "managerial gaze" shifted from influencing national interpretations of the "Arsenal of Democracy" to asserting an economic world system governed by Fordist principles. In Ford's vision for the arsenal, newly hailed economic subjects like those called on in Roosevelt's speech would need to be managed to ensure the most effective results. (First, this meant the defense of democracy, but this quickly converted into the spread of free markets.) This managerial gaze, in many ways, incorporated other gazes—particularly the male and the colonial gaze—and repackaged them into another way of acquiring and maintaining power under the premise of economic expansion.

Rather than a general analytical concept, however, Ford's films highlight that the "managerial gaze" was, in part, a trained capacity. Both during and after the war, cinematic materials (propaganda during the war and training films after) spurred a visual network that tied global capitalism to the normative structures already in power prior to the war. More germane to the trajectory of this book, the idea of the "gaze" names what happens when a system of incorporational rhetoric succeeds. Claiming the formation of a Fordist "managerial gaze" then suggests Fordism's near completion as a hegemonic structure and its ascent to gaze-like influence on its workforce's visual field.

Gaze theory is an approach to analyzing visual materials that attends to the power dynamics that are inherently wrapped up in the act of looking. The questions that gaze theory asks include "Who gets to look?" "Who gets to interpret the meaning of what is being looked at?" and "What are the effects of this on the figures who are positioned as objects of signification?" In the original psychoanalytic version of this theory, it is desire that drives how we see, and as a result there is no general vision even within individuals. Seeing, rather, is as fleeting as desire. If gaze theory began in the deep libidinal recesses of a Freudian theory of desire and lack, however, the concept has expanded to name a framework for understanding the role of the visual in the production of hegemony.

In this sense, gaze theory names the outcome of a variety of fully implemented incorporational rhetorics. Certain apparatuses (gender, citizenship, whiteness) are so thoroughly shot through with ideology and so completely supported institutionally that they can shape—like desire or lack in Freud—the very act of seeing. Put differently, from a rhetorical perspective, the gaze names instances where hegemony has been internalized to the point that the world can no longer be conceived through terms outside the hegemonic system.

Capitalism, then, can generate a deeply felt system of need, of power, and of longing organized around the "managerial gaze." Internalized by spectators, this gaze suggests that one must adhere to managerial control or bureaucracy. One way of reading the cumulative effects of Ford's films, then, is to consider the contribution that this Fordist way of seeing played in other structures of power, namely "the interpellation of the film spectator into a hegemonic viewing position in which the Western, white, male identity is normative."[4]

Gaze theory informs the hypothesis, forwarded here, that the generation emerging from World War II had been weaned on Fordist Educational films, convinced of economized living by Ford's rhetorical economy, and enthralled by its World's Fair exhibitions and were utterly sure of the righteousness of its order and the need for its expansion. To draw out a metaphor, this was a churning hive of middle managers ready to pollinate the world with industrial capitalism—all they needed was to know where to look and how. The "Arsenal of Democracy" set them loose.

Having a sitting American president draw out this connection between economic subjectivity and industrial production would become a cinematic boon, as well. Across wartime propaganda films, as workers were shown toiling and tanks rolled out of factories, narrators punctuated footage of assembly lines with praise-oriented claims like "here is the Arsenal of Democracy" or "this is mass production, as only American engineers know how" (direct quotes from the 1942 newsreel *U.S. Reveals Armed Might for Churchill* produced by the Office for Emergency Management, News and Features Bureau). The final installment of Frank Capra's widely circulated *Why We Fight* series (sponsored by the Department of War) was titled *War Comes to America* and featured a riling ten-minute montage celebrating "the blood and sweat of men from around the world that built America" that showed the mass production of industrial workers as well as tanks and planes. Unsurprisingly, the opening lines of the film's central production montage declared that "we are first and foremost, a working people."

Industrial corporations were also quick to take up the opportunity afforded by the connections made by the "Arsenal" to generate narratives placing corporate institutional structures at the heart of an American model of sovereignty guaranteed by an "economic army."[5] Kimberly-Clark (Kleenex's parent company) produced *These Are the People*, the story of Lakeview, Wisconsin, mobilizing for war; the Frigidaire division of General Motors dedicated *These People* in 1944 to celebrating "free Americans working in free enterprise"; DuPont screened *Soldiers of the Soil*, a lengthier feature film celebrating the contributions of farmers to the war efforts; and Firestone produced *All Out for Victory*, a general account of the ongoing conversion of a regular economy into a war economy.

Ford's wartime offerings were incorporated, along with these other firms' films, into larger national initiatives orchestrated by the Office of War Information (OWI) and a collection of fellow corporate actors. Notably, Ford's films weren't particularly distinguishable from the more general offerings being coordinated by the OWI; there were, however, comparatively fewer of them. David L. Lewis posits two explanations for this: first, Henry Ford's "lifelong aversion to boastful advertising" in the face of dire circumstances, and, second, a decision by the public relations department to focus, instead, on radio.[6] The exception to this, however, was the company's use of its newly built Willow Run plant and, more specifically, the female workforce employed there. Using this factory as the locus for a number of films, Ford's specific take on the wartime propaganda film worked to assure viewers that industrial production could produce far more than guns and tanks but also a patriotic army of domestic workers attuned to the cause of defending democracy. The company would consistently present Willow Run as the symbolic centerpiece for industrial patriotism, first in the repeated cinematic narration of female workers and later in the production of a global workforce.

This chapter will analyze two films that represent Ford's wartime and postwar rhetoric as it worked to train individuals to see management as an important feature in mobilizing and managing economic systems but also to argue for who should manage and who should be managed. The first film was a 1943 piece of war propaganda called *Women on the Warpath*. I read the film as a different kind of hailing—one that functioned to temporarily extend the power of the industrial regime to women through their ability to be properly managed. The second film was produced after the war for a series of Ford management meetings held nationally (and at some international branches) throughout the 1950s. This film is an excellent example of how the managerial gaze overlapped and at times relied on existing masculine and colonial gazes. It also provides an opportunity to study how late-stage editing (used to omit certain figures) can be used as a rhetorical strategy.

Women on the Warpath: Hailing Subjects, Engendering Difference

The film *Women on the Warpath* opens with a vignette featuring panning depictions of factories and production practices (accompanied by a rousing rendition of the song "America the Beautiful"), dedicating itself "to American women everywhere, whose valor on the industrial front has sped the day of victory." The film then engages in a narrative that, alongside moments of overt condescension, works to extend a degree of authority to a population systematically stripped of such inclusion in other formats and economic settings prior to the war. The film regularly reminds the viewer of women's adequacy and, at times, superiority as industrial workers but only as substitutes for their male counterparts and, often, as a shocking feat facilitated by the surge of patriotism and remarkable organizational clarity of the Ford production process. Significantly, the film presents its female subjects not as inherently powerful as political agents but as being suddenly imbued by the power of the nation through the mechanism of mass production–mediated labor.

Placing particular emphasis on the voluntary nature of joining this "industrial front," the film then depicts four women as they turn away from activities of leisure and domesticity to instead take up positions on the assembly line. As the sequence progresses, the film portrays this conversion from the classed figures of the post-Depression era to wartime figures of national power through a narrative in which the women are "hailed" by a set of war planes flying overhead. Four women are shown individually: one shopping, one golfing, one swimming, and one hanging laundry. These figures, however, are immediately shamed as the narrator suggests that in the face of patriotic duty, "some still window shopped, not hearing the first call. Others played golf, [and] idled golden hours away when every moment was precious."

Suddenly, in the same sequence, a set of airborne bombers flies overhead as the narrator declares, "Wake up Miss America! Wake up Mrs. America" (see figure 25). As the camera zooms in on the face of each woman, the scene chronicles the repeated act of gazing up (rather than turning 180 degrees) through which, Louis Althusser would argue, these figures become "the subject" by recognizing their place and responsibility within wartime production. This scene highlights film's ability to replicate one kind of gaze.

On screens across the country, the roar of the bombers' engines was positioned as the equivalent of the "call" to subjectivity, and the sequence closes with a close-up shot of each subject in the very moment of being hailed. In his

25 | Ford Motion Picture Laboratory, stills from *Women on the Warpath*, 1943.

reading of such production of power, Althusser argues that sovereignty takes place through the production of an archetypal identity ("the Subject") as it gets mapped onto the identity of individuals ("the subject") through hailings like this. As *Women on the Warpath* makes apparent, in the hands of industrial corporations like Ford Motor Company, this process was taking place on wartime cinematic screens as a powerful vision designed to create a very particular kind of democratic "Subject"—the industrial laborer—from a relatively unexpected (at least within the film's narrative) "subject"—American women.[7]

In addition to hailing these individuals, one of the primary goals of *Women on the Warpath* is to present how they might perform the structure of industrial power that had just hailed them. It is particularly significant that the structure that welcomed these individuals on film is a complex of production practices, national defense systems, and social support structures mediated through the economic organization of Ford Motor Company. It is, in short, a fulfillment of the promises made a decade before about the potential for recommitting to the industrial corporation.

The film argues (seemingly directing this argument to any husbands angry that their wives were working) that during war "labor became a patriotic privilege" and develops a narrative of new forms of political agency as the hailed women take to the assembly line in response to a "call for help" represented by the planes overhead. In this new phase of the film, the previously hailed women are then shown arriving at the bomber factory in Willow Run, Michigan, and the film claims that a complete transformation of these subjects takes place once they enter this space.

The narrator declares that, through her involvement with the Willow Run plant, "the lady of the clothesline became an expert of the hydraulics line" (in figure 26, the actress who was hailed by the plane while hanging her laundry is now pictured examining the bomber's hydraulic tubing), and through the smallest of associative leaps, the film claims that Ford's Willow Run factory could turn "beauty operator to crane operator" and "sewing machine operator" into "jigsaw operator." These films generate power for the company not only by affiliating mass production with militaristic power and military power with democracy but by grounding this power in the ability for the mass production system to discipline subjects into such a system.

In this moment, the other ideological shoe drops in the company's narrative. To become an industrial citizen is to submit oneself to the managerial gaze, and in such a narrative it is in management, not individual sacrifice, that the power

26 | Ford Motion Picture Laboratory, still from *Women on the Warpath*, 1943.

of the arsenal lives. Femininity, itself constructed in the first half of the film as frivolous, is briefly suspended through the exceptional status of war. At the same time, however, femininity becomes an obstacle for the manager to overcome or to find innovative ways to utilize on the assembly line.

Jordynn Jack has argued of the importance of paying "more attention to gendered rhetorics of bodies, clothing, space, and time *together* in order to construct more thorough accounts of the rhetorical practices that sustain gender." In the depictions of wartime female laborers, she argues, these overlapping registers presented an argument grounded in three elements: "delicacy, appearance, and domesticity." Beneath the apparent feminist sheen of a Rosie the Riveter narrative, then, Jack argues that "the rhetorical and material shifts that permitted women to enter into the workplace on a broader scale never really challenged the notion that women were different than men—weaker, more domestic, and more fully invested in the frivolities of beauty and appearance."[8] Film not only allows for a more seamless integration of these overlapping gendered rhetorics but highlights the dual nature of the gaze wrapped up in these rhetorics of difference.

The film concludes having depicted a complete process of interpellation and performed national sovereignty, with a scene more directly pointed at the audience. The shadow of the bomber returns, this time overlaid on top of a sea of uniformed women saluting and singing "Glory, Glory Hallelujah" (see figure 27). The combined symbolic thrust of this final set of images is a direct call to those still abstaining from joining the "Arsenal of Democracy." The audience is now hailed by the already initiated and by the cinematic roaring of bomber engines to similarly "perform" the structures of national sovereignty that are being extended to them through mass production. If, it suggests, the assembly line and its varying social ramifications can "turn" housewives into the very substance of global power, it can surely be the mechanism through which anyone can become productive members of the "Arsenal of Democracy."

When filtered through gaze theory, a film like *Women on the Warpath* highlights two different gazes being produced by wartime films: first, the internalization of a need to be vigilant in recognizing one's responsibilities in a national-economic nexus of power and, second, the right to look at and manage particular bodies. For the former, Ford Motor Company reifies an *a priori*

27 | Ford Motion Picture Laboratory, still from *Women on the Warpath*, 1943.

subject that will—when the "call" (threats to American sovereignty) appears—also make the important turn to laboring within a system of industrial production and broadcast it across the country. Moreover, it establishes metaphorically that such a "turn" is also the very instantiation of American power and managerial power, but a power only temporarily extended to individuals on the line—especially women. In this sense, *Women on the Warpath* is an interesting example for observing the masculine gaze at work.

While on the surface *Women on the Warpath* troubles traditional iterations of the gaze in which "men act and women appear," the women on film are certainly acting. However, as stand-ins, this ability to act is only ever borrowed. This gaze is a matter of management—the responsible delegation of masculine power for a short, exceptional period of time by the always-in-power industrial regime.

The film replicates a variety of visual practices designed to position and direct its audience to recognize how they should see their own patriotic responsibilities and for how they should submit to the organizing gazes of managerial capitalism in order to better fulfill these responsibilities. The result of such a gaze is the articulation of corporate power at its most disciplinary—its ability to produce, and disseminate power to anyone (and, eventually, to remove this power)—without disrupting existing networks of power and production. When placed in longer trajectories of the company's rhetoric, however, this ability to hail American citizens as economic subjects into an Arsenal of Democracy would lay the groundwork for global expansion along Fordist lines as well. It only stood to reason, in the logic of these films, that if Fordism could incorporate with American women (long symbols of economic inferiority) it could certainly rebuild a global workforce.

Accounting for the success of the company in pressing this ability to manage, Robert G. Ferguson has argued that through the "rhetoric of mass production," Ford Motor Company outpaced its competitors for resignification of the emerging national collective organizing around the war effort, thereby "stealing the rhetorical high ground from General Motors and [President] Roosevelt" so that it was Ford's production practices, its workers, and its industrial expertise that quickly became the "pre-eminent symbol[s] of the Arsenal of Democracy."[9] Having achieved this high ground, convincing the public of the inherent wisdom in industrialism was largely unnecessary after the war. Rather, the ceding of global reconstruction to the industrial was a given as it had been won by securing freedom for the nations' citizens. Having won this dominion domestically, the company next worked to produce the Fordist global empire along the same lines.

What Ford developed during wartime production, then, was both a reification of the ongoing arguments about the centrality of industry to national health and labor as both a form of patriotism and an extension of its own constitutive abilities. The war, in this frame, is a unique rhetorical transition period both in the film archive and in the economic and symbolic registers that had been accumulating since the stock market crash. If, prior to World War II, the United States had isolationist tendencies, a celebration of economic individualism (within corporate structures, of course), and a cultural imaginary grounded in the venerable farmer and line worker, the postwar world expanded before American viewers in ways previously unimagined. While these elements would certainly stay intact, Ford's postwar films highlight the extent to which global expansion, honorable toil in the name of capitalism (particularly in the face of communist encroachment), and the figure of the manager would become the symbolic core of the postwar economy.

Where much attention has been paid to the "subject" as he/she is called on to become the "Subject," less attention has been paid to the figure doing the hailing (so, attention to FDR as a figure with the right to call a nation or the nameless police officer who calls out in Althusser's hypothetical account). Some scholars, however, have paid attention to the inculcation of these figures that feel the right to hail as an important actor in the process of materializing and reproducing power. These figures argue that it is in the gaze of the person doing the hailing, their act of looking first, and then hailing in response that power disseminates.

In examining this concept, Max Weber articulated the idea of "rationalization," a critical term for understanding the performance of governance, that relies on a "conceptual simplification and ordering of the contents of the law" by privileged classes of individuals who embody the values upheld in a particular ideological system (visibility in feudalism, divinity in theocracy, deliberation in democracy). After a long period in history where the divine rights of royalty were secured through a fiefdom, he posits that Christian asceticism anchored itself in the figure of the monk and German pietism in the missionary, and carrying this logic into modern structures of political governance, he argues that "the specialist official [is] the cornerstone of the modern state and of the modern economy in the West."[10] In the global rhetorical economy placed on-screen by Ford Motor Company, it is an army of middle managers that takes up the position of the new clerisy for a global economic age, and it is these figures who the company actively sought to utilize as hailing agents. First, however, the company would need to encourage them to see the world in particular ways.

This is reflected, in archival form, through the presence of management training films after World War II. These management films say much about the shape of a corporate society in the second half of the twentieth century. First, the company was using the mobility of film to create cohesion between branches, ensuring that particular managerial quirks were, in themselves, being managed directly from Dearborn. Second, the company returned to film as an educational and training medium. The archive contains a number of these films, including "Steering with Standards," which introduces the Industry Standards program; "Big and Basic," which explains the operations of the Basic Products Group at the company; and "Meet Tom Gordon," a "how to be an executive" piece.

Some of the films are in-house affairs narrated by a generally uncomfortable-looking Henry Ford II or another of the executives at the company; others are sleekly produced affairs where Ford's renewed Motion Picture Laboratory collaborated with an outside commercial firm (Wilding Picture Productions and MPO Productions in particular). Regardless of the producer, the films generally featured a preface and conclusion featuring an executive welcoming the group. The program ran for a number of years. As a general genre of texts, then, these films replicate the same managerial gaze present in *Women on the Warpath*, one that trains its viewer on ways to see workers as produced figures. However, one film, in particular, captures the global ambitions for the company to extend the "Arsenal of Democracy" to a planetary scale.

―――

Around the World with Ford Motor Company: Global Bureaucracy and the Managerial Gaze

As was the case for much of the world, 1945 was a year of monumental change for Ford Motor Company. The company would need to reconstruct itself in the wake of immense conflict (not, however, because it had been adversely effected but because it had so unilaterally remade itself into an agent of mechanized warfare and now the world needed cars and commerce again). At the conclusion of the war, the metaphorical "Arsenal of Democracy" shifted from defense to offense, now devoting its energy to developing and expanding Westernized democracy through the development of a global marketplace. As it did so, the movement also changed weaponry, trading in the production of tanks, ships, and planes for more abstract economic arrangements grounded in credit and global production structures: 1945 saw the formation of the International Monetary Fund, the General Agreement on Tariffs and Trade, and increasingly complex supply chains under the Marshall Plan. These policies would, in turn, form new markets to ensure the feasible extension of mass production and new forms of intellectual labor based on quantitative reasoning and product planning.

Working in concert with these developments and under the new leadership of Henry Ford II, the company would change its approach to international commerce. In the notes to the archival records titled *Reconsolidation of Foreign Operations Records*, the postwar period is described this way: "After the war, Henry Ford II made a tour of Ford's European operations to get a firsthand understanding of the company's situation. In order to address the financial and administrative challenges of the post-war world economy, Ford initiated a reorganization of the corporation including the foreign operations. Beginning in 1948, Ford began negotiating with the Canadian, English, and French Ford companies to purchase and consolidate all Ford operations worldwide in Dearborn, Michigan."[111] In turn, these branches would become hubs through which Ford products shipped out from a series of central mass manufacturing points (Dearborn, Michigan; Dagenham, England; Windsor, Canada; and Poissy, France).

Mirroring this ambitious project, the film department began to place much greater emphasis on depicting the spaces of this global marketplace while also using films to communicate with its expanding management structures. In 1948, the company began documenting its many global factories to articulate this wider plan. Over this period, the company drew on thirty-six international film crews to capture the reach of the Fordist manufacturing and commercial empire—seeking new economic agents as the conduits for its expansion. This film is a rare opportunity to see the Fordist "world picture" begin to take shape, particularly as it can be filtered through the managerial gaze.

It is also an opportunity to study the managerial gaze in four ways. First, it produces a way of seeing that privileges the seamless movement of capital and commodities over social systems. Second, it partitions a center and periphery of workers, both in terms of who can be a manager and how particular populations should be managed. Third, it produces a "world picture" that expanded the dominion of managerial power across national boundaries to envision a global market organized along production lines. Finally, the managerial gaze is dependent on selective visibility or, in the case of the film, on active omission of images that do not fit with the larger narratives outlined in a particular gaze. To best capture the work of the managerial gaze in this film, then, the reading that follows lays out the film in full and then analyzes its content using many of the frames developed throughout this book. On this point, *Around the World with Ford Motor Company* is a blend of the previous four chapters' formal features—presenting at once aesthetic, montage-driven, spatially minded acts of spectacle to its executives. At the same time, a number of telling omissions and framings occur that sought to produce a world picture that reified particularly gendered, racial, and global North/global South relations.

In the opening scene of the film, an unidentified executive stands at a podium, hair cropped, suit pressed. His introduction to the film offers much of its context. He explains that "[i]t seemed to us that a word description, without an eye picture of Ford International, was somehow a bit inadequate; hence, the motion picture. This is, essentially, a homemade movie produced by the overseas family. If you will just imagine thirty-six Ford men, scattered all about the globe, going around with their Eastman motion picture cameras taking shots of their organizations then you will have an idea of what you are about to see." At this point, the executive pantomimes a cameraman waving a camera around wildly and then composes himself and continues: "The idea of the picture occurred to us only six weeks ago, so you will appreciate the amount of time available to prepare and send cables to all of our companies, getting the job done around the world, and then contending with the delays of customs. For instance, because of a lack of export permits, the Italians, a very resourceful bunch, sent their film by plane—inside a fruitcake! Believe it or not, we got it. Unfortunately, the film was a bit overexposed. Hence, you will see the inside of the fruitcake instead of our Italian operations." He then goes on to thank the many employees who had a hand in producing the film so quickly and cues the managerial audience one last time that "you are now about to have the quickest trip you've ever made around the world."

In sharp contrast to the somber, faux-meeting introduction, the produced film opens with a bit of bombast. A trombone blares and a rousing orchestral score strikes up as the phrase "FORD International Company presents" is superimposed over the top of a spinning globe. The film then officially opens at the company's new international headquarters in New York City, featuring only footage of the building, before moving to the Highland Park plant in Dearborn "where all export orders are received and processed." It is here that one of the first unifying images appears: a wooden crate. This first crate is stamped with the Ford logo and "MADE IN U.S.A." as it is being loaded onto a ship. The crate will serve as one of several transitional objects designed to produce a sense of globality to Ford's production practices—it is joined by a spinning globe and Mercator maps that appear when moving the viewer from one geographical site to another (see figure 28).

In many ways, these crates make up the central protagonist in this journey—their appearance often signals a new branch, and the movement within a number of scenes works by having the crate leave a production site and, via a hard cut, arrive at an assembly or distribution site on the other side of the world. Through this feature, the company argued that what connects the world into a unified market is the movement of cars and parts in a massive network of production, distribution, and sales. The film further argued that to let the crates, a talismanic object representing global production, stop moving is the ultimate failure. As a cinematic technique, however, focalizing the film on the crate also grounds the viewer's understanding of space and movement in the film as distant cities become seamless parts of a single economic space. While this first pictured crate does not go anywhere in particular, it sets the tone for these later depictions.

Having pictured the headquarters of global Fordism, the world tour begins with a "trip across the border" to Ford Canada. Using a Mercator map and basic highlighting, the "territory" of Ford Canada includes Sub-Saharan Africa, India, and Australia. This is followed by a series of shots focusing on buildings—the powerhouse, the foundry, and the assembly plant. The film then shows the corresponding shop floors for each of these sites. A shipping crate becomes the transitional point as it is shown moving by crane to a truck, and in a hard cut, a second truck with the same crate reappears on "The Park Avenue of Bombay" as it carries the parts to a production site.

At this site, the film then explains that "human labor in India is cheaper than mechanized equipment, and it certainly is more easily obtained" as a team of men drags the crate onto the assembly floor and builds the car "with the aid of very little special equipment." And that's it; the India section of the film offers up no indication of sales practices, of a budding industrial hierarchy, or of concern over the quality of workers' lives. All Ford's presence in India presents is a

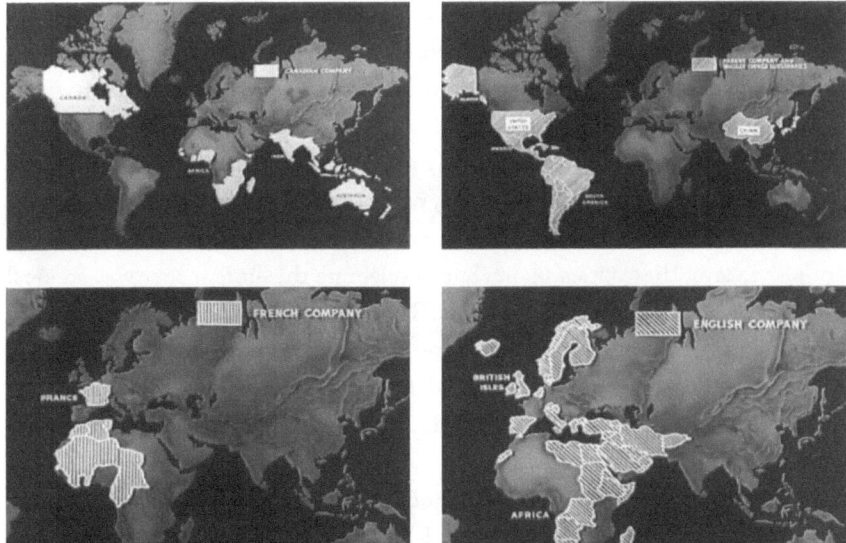

28 | Ford Motion Picture Laboratory, stills from *Around the World with Ford Motor Company*, 1948. Four separate depictions of the "territories" captured by Ford: Canada (top left), United States (top right), France (bottom left), and England (bottom right).

gesture to Western influence ("the Park Avenue") and an argument to its executives that human bodies remain cheap and easily obtained machines in global production. As we will see, cinematic moments like this laid a visual imaginary over the world that argued that there are some places where capitalism is experienced in full and some places where global capitalism is a matter of manual labor, of cheap and readily accessible bodies for work.

Highlighting this, the film then fades to a shot of the spinning globe and takes its viewers to Wellington, New Zealand, as a panoramic shot of "one of the most beautiful harbors in the world" frames the next section of the film. Contrasting with India's street-level depiction, the film uses sweeping panoramas taken from airplanes to produce a sense of grandeur to the Australian operation. This sequence is among the most visually dynamic in the film, using a wide variety of movement-images—planes capturing cities, car-mounted shots as the vehicle pulls up to a factory, slow panning shots moving alongside a car on the assembly line, and wobbly handheld shots of Fordson tractors mowing over the Australian countryside.

Through these images, Ford Australia is presented as a uniform entity bringing together the whole of a continent—the narrator noting that "here, as throughout the world, our general designs follow a more or less standard plant design." It is made up of five primary locations—Melbourne, Sydney, Brisbane, Perth, and Adelaide—for each of which the film provides the same cinematic treatment as for Wellington: shot one, panorama of the city; shot two, factory front; shot three, assembly line. As an act of visual consonance, this functions not just to level these cities' plants but to celebrate this homogeneity as an ideal example of Ford's overseas operations. The narrator concludes this section by explaining that the next phase for these factories is to move from assembly via imported materials to a fully independent production process drawing on the resources of the continent and Southeast Asia. On that note, the film moves the viewer north to "Singapore, Malaya."

Singapore is given a significant amount of screen time in part because its purpose is to communicate the "typical Ford plant in a true Oriental setting." (What a false Oriental setting might look like is unclear.) The opening sequence features a panoramic view of government buildings, the financial district, and the Chinese quarter; then the factory is shown with all of the modern amenities of a typical Ford plant but scaled down to a smaller size. Once again, the social and managerial elements of Singapore are not pictured. The city is instead positioned as, first, a site worth visiting and, second, a place where workers build cars.

The film uses the spinning globe again to transition viewers to a new region: Port Elizabeth, South Africa, where a new plant was completed in 1947. Beginning with a series of street-level shots in the city, the film quickly turns to a panning shot of an open field filled with Ford crates, filmed from the factory's roof. This top-down panorama is used again to depict the factory floor and service dock, before a set of medium shots captures the remainder of the moving assembly line–driven production practices. At this point, the film presents the same general cinematic process associated with production practices—tight close-ups of hands maneuvering machines and workers standing alongside assembly lines. One notable addition is the recognition of a manager responsible for particularly orderly results, a theme that will run throughout the film. The section concludes with a shot outside of the plant with six separate Ford models parked beneath a massive neon Ford logo perched atop the South Africa plant. Over the top of this last shot, the narrator explains that "the pictures you have just seen tangibly demonstrate what a fine job Ford Canada has done over the years in pioneering Ford throughout the commonwealth."

At this point, the Mercator map transition returns to show viewers the American domain—a region made up of the United States, the whole of South America, and China. Where the sequences depicting Ford Canada focused primarily on material elements of the assembly line, the "America" portion of the film displays an expanded sense of the economic chains that generate the corporation and vice versa. This portion of the film works to make clear that it is the executive and not the line worker who exists as the beating heart of the multinational corporation. Presenting a second managerial figure in the film's developing capitalist-hero narrative, the manufacturing sequence is interrupted by a shot that features Fred Sigler, "who should be given credit for pioneering this [boxing] operation thirty years ago."

The viewer then learns of the crate itself through a montage of manufacturing scenes building the crates that are also interspersed with shots of overwhelming stacks of the crates waiting in shipping yards to head overseas. The narrator, highlighting the intricacy of this integrated system of work designed by Sigler, suggests that "[t]he mechanization has developed to such a point that the boxes never touch the ground." In a sharp cut from production, the film next shows four suited executives puzzling over a stack of paperwork in the office of the Edgewater, New York, plant manager—a "Mr. Harris."

In a montage of office scenes, executives are shown puzzling over, signing, and filing stacks of paperwork as the narrator makes clear that "[t]he cooperation of Edgewater is a testimonial to the 'Ford scheme of things.'" In a sequence harkening back to the education films capturing production in the 1920s, the film uses a variety of close- and medium-range shots of many interrelated tasks to capture "the way they have hand-tailored operations to meet export peculiarities and specifications. Notice the amount of paperwork which is necessary to all overseas transactions."

Opening the American global "territory" in this way highlights two important features. First, these scenes depict to rooms full of executives around the country that labor in America is becoming increasingly abstracted through the movement of information and the processing of quantitative data. Moreover, it claims that the design and upkeep of extended statistical reason, quality control, and apparatuses of accounting are every bit as important to the idea of manufacturing as the making of cars. Second, these early management scenes allowed for the company to communicate that, while integrated production has gone global, true management lives in America (and just who can be a manager is made clear by the consistency with which this work is conducted by white men in starched shirts, guzzling coffee and discussing paperwork in wood-paneled offices). The section concludes with a transitional scene that pictures the Edgewater plant from the Hudson River, followed by the spinning globe. The next destination is Mexico City.

The establishing shot for this portion of the film features a long shot of Mexico City's central square as the camera tilts upward. The bustling square is flanked by cathedrals to the rear and traffic to the front. After a short montage featuring traffic-riddled streets, the viewer arrives at a cluttered factory where the narrator notes that the plant suffers from a "problem of congestion" because of high demand and a lack of proper space. Creating direct contrast with the orderly American offices, a rapid montage shows materials strewn about much of the factory while workers toil away in cramped quarters. These workers, it explains, are putting in extra time to prepare damaged materials (due to poor storage) before they engage in proper assembly. The plant is the picture of disorder.

The congestion has gotten so bad, the narrator points out, that the branch now uses its lobby for office space. The shot depicting this congestion is an important contributor to the running theme of paperwork and desk jobs. In a long shot, the lobby of the Mexico City branch reveals dozens of desks and workers, the latter hunched over papers. The sequence finishes with a standard overview of the production process at the branch, and then the film moves on to São Paulo, Brazil, where the depiction is very similar.

The film first sharply cuts to a panning shot of São Paulo's modern skyline as the narrator declares that "these pictures will be an eye opener to most Americans who think of Brazil as still a jungle." He adds that "São Paulo is often called the Chicago of South America." Once again, the narrative is one of struggle to replicate American equivalents to production and presents a cluttered factory floor and cramped office spaces where "the boys operate under very difficult conditions." Next is Buenos Aires, Argentina, which is "often called the Paris of South America" and is represented by a series of city shots. Notably, the narrator again offers an equivalency to give the viewer some sense of identifiable civilization. Highlighting these small asides as contributors to the budding world picture of a globalizing Western economic structure, the narrator never states, for example, that Copenhagen is the "Buenos Aires of Denmark." These comparisons are, it seems, a one-way street.

The narrator next notes that "the Argentine used to be—and someday may again be—one of the richest markets." The film, however, shows an empty factory that had been built in 1919 to produce the Model T and explains that the company is waiting to rebuild (as it still owns the land) once bans on foreign products are lifted. The section concludes with distribution sites in Montevideo, Uruguay, and Santiago, Chile. Both are given brief overviews that make two points: first, the cities are beautiful tourist destinations and, second, the plants need to be bigger and modernized. In a telling interlude, Ford's Yokohama, Japan, plant is shown only in photographs as the narrator notes "we hope this branch will be activated within a year or two," and the film next turns to its European branches.

Ford's European distribution plants are divided into the French and English branches working out of Poissy, France, and Dagenham, England. However, the German subsidiary—which had separated from the company (though there is some considerable debate over this)—is given attention outside the larger global territories being presented. For Germany, the film is tellingly brief on details regarding its operations, choosing instead to highlight the quality of footage sent to the company. In this case, the city tour features only "[t]he cathedral, the ruins, and our plant" captured in three succinct shots. The film then presents a collection of tightly framed close-ups of manufacturing in action.

In stark contrast to the films in South America, the European films highlight quality of working conditions rather than the need for quality control and capacity building—in Finland, the footage touts bright lighting and on-site showers; in Copenhagen, a clean, orderly campus for its workers; in Amsterdam, workers are shown eating meals at cafeteria tables with tablecloths (the managers sit separately at a large round table). After such careful concern for the male body's ability to labor in Finland, the company provides a telling depiction of the female body in Stockholm.

In a jarring reminder that *Women on the Warpath* was a temporary narrative, after a similar depiction of rising quality of life for workers, the film displays two women sunbathing as the narrator quips "telephone numbers at request." That's all from Sweden (quite literally, that's the only scene), and the film moves on to provide the sense that managing European plants is a distinctly different project than managing non-Western branches, one that consists of maintaining worker morale rather than organizing disorganized labor.

Antwerp serves as one exception to this narrative of cleanliness and pleasant production as this plant features the same problems as Mexico City—it is too small and has too much volume coming in. However, this problem is not because of mismanagement but because "Belgium is one of the few countries where American cars can be imported, and can pay for them." The film then presents

Ireland (where European Fordson tractors are made), Portugal, and Spain (where the civil war severely reduced production of cars) very briefly and with little worth noting. At last, however, the audience is shown the promised Italian fruitcake, and the European continental tour is complete.

For the penultimate factory featured in the film, viewers are shown one of Ford's global successes: Ford Egypt. Perhaps because of its success, this branch is given more attention than other non-Western branches. The footage taken in Egypt opens with a Ford coupe pulling up in front of the pyramids and its occupants leisurely stepping out to take a look at the wonders. The film then cuts to an overhead shot of the Ford Motor Company plant set amid a modern Alexandria. As the plane circles, the clear grids of tree-lined streets surround what appears to be a complex of factories, apartment buildings, and distribution hubs. A second rapid jump cut positions the audience just outside a car dealership attached to the factory, and the familiar block letters "FORD" are now joined by Arabic counterparts. From 1,000 feet above, the organized industrial park has the visual effect of creating a seemingly nation-less economic zone.

The film enters the factory just as a crate of parts (ostensibly designed in Detroit and produced in Dagenham, England) is being transported by a conveyor to the shop floor. Notably, the production of cars assembled in the Egypt plant at the time of the film did not use Ford's standard moving assembly line. Instead, raised on platforms, the cars are assembled by teams of workers methodically piecing them together through craft labor. In a notable shift, however, rather than just attending to the labor potential of non-Western bodies, the Egypt footage also credits the plant's production as an important contributor to Britain's success in the region in World War II and then focuses on finance and consumption as the economic center of a postwar "Arsenal of Democracy."

Once inside the building, the film begins to capture the consumption side of the Fordist global process. A woman enters the attached dealership wearing a black dress, high heels, and a striped headscarf (the only sign of difference from a woman entering a Ford dealership in Perth or Poissy or Topeka). She speaks to a similarly homogenized suited businessman who directs her to the show floor. Briefly, the film dwells on the automobiles themselves as the viewer is positioned directly as the consumer who inspects a line of new Ford and Lincoln models. The camera-as-consumer focuses in on the new hood, wheels, and steering console of an automobile.

The film then quickly cuts away from the cars and focuses on a room full of underwriters as the customer's credit request is given to one of the underwriters in the center of the room. In a sharp cut, the salesman is shown waving goodbye as the woman pulls away in her new car. In one sense, the Egypt portion of the film reveals the globally oriented extension of a wholly different kind of assembly line concerned with marketing and financing. In another sense, the film focuses on the spaces and mechanisms that would make consumption possible in markets where the democratic influence of nations could not immediately intervene.

One explanation for this extended attention to the Egypt branch was its importance to the company's global strategy. Henry Ford II had been placed on the board of directors, and almost immediately, construction of a new Alexandria factory designed for production rather than just assembly began. Notably, this new factory was also deeply rhetorical in nature. At the structure's groundbreaking ceremony, booklets were handed out that declared, among other messages, that *"today Ford Motor Company (Egypt) S.A.E. has the sole right in thirty-one separate countries or distinct territorial units to trade in Ford products. This is the Empire of Ford Egypt."*[12]

Further evidence of such an economic/juridical/spatial model of expansion appears in a June 11, 1947, wire report from Belgrade, Yugoslavia, that ran in the *New York Times*. The report explains that Ford Motor Company of Egypt obtained a "contract for approximately $500,000" that would allow the company to sell cars and parts in the country despite its fraught position between the democratic West and Communist East.[13] This, then, was the model for a vision of the company organized around a set of international production hubs. While the term was not used in the film, American managers were similarly being presented with the "Empire of Ford."

Finally, the viewer arrives at Ford's largest and most successful overseas plant: Dagenham, England. This portion of the film uses only production and shipping images, outside of a note that "a new statue of Henry Ford was built, recently"— another clear nod to the role Ford Motor Company played in winning the war. After a montage capturing the production site, the narrator abruptly declares, "[T]his concludes your tour around the world," and the film ends.

Using the frameworks developed throughout this book, *Around the World with Ford Motor Company* uses a number of the aesthetic features of its earliest films, but to depict the homogeneous network of "management" practices rather than "manufacturing." In this sense, the company draws on mise-en-scène to create a dynamic and interlocking vision of the technocratic and hierarchical application of quantitative data, innovation, and one-way flows of communication that would become global Fordism. While there is no shortage of machinery pictured in the film, its system of similitudes works outward from a vision of infrastructure, paperwork, and executives that align to create a cohesive picture of what guides the global postwar "rhetorical" economy.

Producing visual consonance, most of the film fragments follow a uniform format: they open with a depiction of local landmarks to situate their viewers and then follow with a sequential depiction of the relationship between consumption and production in the new global setting, ending by highlighting the degree to which Fordism has extended access to the global marketplace for individuals around the world. Similarly, these introductory tropes worked to redraw the simulacra of global economic spaces through their most recognizable features.

Alternatively, the film generates a cohesive link between three economic *topoi* in order to produce a new iteration of the postwar Fordist economy. The film's "imagined future" is captured by the theme of global expansion. Factories in Singapore, Malaya; Port Elizabeth, South Africa; Poissy, France; and Copenhagen, Denmark, are presented as newly built models for spreading American influence. The planned factory in Alexandria, Egypt, is presented as the cornerstone of a new "Empire of Ford" in the region. More than this, the whole of Australia is presented as a possible new domain for the complete production of parts and cars, while each of the South and Central American sites is presented as in need of new facilities. The concept of "labor," as an extension of this expansion, is recast through dispersed, global chains of manufacturing, shipping, and managerial oversight. Finally, the construction of "capital" in this film is more elusive. There are no overt claims to company power or empire or personal gain in the film; it simply explains company plans. This, in itself, speaks to the changing dynamics of corporate culture as it suggests that the postwar managerial class simply needed to understand what the company wanted them to do. There was no need, then, to explain the value of this project; rather, the film assumes a totally incorporated sense of capital accumulation.

In many ways, the most important work of the film is spatial, as *Around the World* works to stage the planet as an economized space much in the way the company's interwar films approached economizing the American national landscape. By producing a series of central hubs that could define particular transnational territories and then, within these territories, offering up a set of interconnected spatial practices—the movement of ships, the transport via trucks, the mobility of paperwork—the company worked to produce in the minds of its executives the idea of a global market interconnected by manufacturing. More than this, the repeated use of plane-perched shots emphasized that Ford complexes in Belgium, Australia, and Egypt each looked the same—homogeneous square buildings surrounded by a grid of tree-lined streets.

Moreover, the company used the visual convention of following a single object—the wooden Ford crate—to draw immediate connections (that is, to produce movement-images) among production hubs, assembly plants, and distribution centers but also spatial cohesion among all of the global sites. We have already seen the rhetorical power of producing economized space by reconfiguring local and national spaces into an abstract collection of nodes and linkages that work between commodities and source materials. In this sense, *Around the World with Ford Motor Company* presents the same mental map for its executives that it once applied to the village-industries in eastern Michigan, wherein there are a handful of centralized global cities (generally one per country or region) and these cities then reconfigure work outward to generate a collection of manufacturing empires. It also, however, presents a number of the cities as worthy of visiting (though it is hard to know if this is a nod to the "tourist gaze" or a ploy to get managers to accept being sent to these locations).

The concept of spectatorship for the film, then, generates a broad celebration of and identification with the executive. Throughout the film, important images constituting the global assembly line take the form of suited men staring at paperwork, gesticulating toward factory floors, and informing other suited figures of what to do. However, these scenes are bifurcated as many of the branches in the Western world are positioned as orderly and ready to worry about the welfare of their workforce. For the plants in South and East Asia and South and Central America, executives are framed in chaotic terms, and plants are either shut down or overcrowded. The workers are presented not as valuable bodies to be preserved with lunches and showers but masses of human force capable of assembling cars until Western management can bring machines to help. When taken collectively, the various cinematic and rhetorical elements on display in *Around the World with Ford Motor Company* produce a particular kind of normative gaze that was, in many ways, the most important byproduct of managerial training. But the film also reveals a rhetorical tactic not yet explored in this text.

This gaze-driven production of spectatorship is further apparent by attending to what has been left on the cutting-room floor in this film. In previous chapters, this work has explored the incorporational through notions of combination, coordination, and accumulation. *Around the World*'s archived state allows for another approach—one that supplements the power of "skillful combination" with the equally powerful act of willful omission. That is, where previous chapters have attended to where the camera has been pointed and how films have been circulated, this chapter ends by taking up an opportunity offered by the Ford Motor Archives' preservation of the source texts from which this final version was cut.

Totality by Omission: The Rhetoric on the Cutting-Room Floor

Around the World with Ford Motor Company is a different kind of archival occasion than other films in the archive. The raw footage produced by the many branches has been preserved in the archive and presents, in itself, a remarkable act of corporate textual production. Rather than the province of any one cinematic unit, this film represents more than thirty archived films each set in a different country. This footage, while never cut for public circulation, was produced with inherent narrative patterns—like silent films, their sequences reveal not only the rhetorical resources available to the "overseas family" but also how these figures saw their branches as significant to the larger project of producing global Fordism.

The nature of the source films varies considerably. The Port Elizabeth film from South Africa is a disjointed collection of shots featuring buildings and manufacturing. The film produced from Antwerp, Belgium, on the other hand, featured a stylized opening and directorial credits. This film has title slides and a clear sequential argument about the orderliness of the factory. The São Paulo section is also highly produced and appeared with only light reconstruction by the parent company.

There are, however, a number of telling choices made between receiving these various branch depictions and the final film shown to executives. For example, the remarkably brief accounts of Ford India were not the result of a lack of source material. Rather, Ford India sent along more than six minutes of footage containing the same managerial narrative as many of the other branches. Figure 29, for example, is one of the shots that central management had at its disposal but did not use. The scene, wherein a spacious and orderly room of tie-wearing workers pore over paperwork, is part of a larger montage of scenes presenting India's management and finance features. Clearly, Ford India offered up similar orderly accounts of managers, offices, and paperwork as well as an orderly shop floor. However, in the management meetings where the film was finally shown, this branch is reduced to a backward operation free of machinery and composed of grunt labor.

In Singapore, there are three significant scenes that did not make the final film. The first depicts a worker being tended to in an onsite first aid station, the second depicts a kitchen where food is being prepared, and last is a scene where the all-British managerial team was shown seated (very uncomfortably) at a large wooden table. Once again, however, in the final cut, the film reduces the site to a typecast of "oriental" operations that represents another global node made up entirely of laboring bodies.

In the Egypt footage, in spite of its extended coverage, there is another telling omission. Between the scene on the sales floor and the scene in the back room full of underwriters, the film has a scene that would have maintained the theme of moving paperwork but features a set of workers who would have disrupted the films' gendered tone. In the original film, the sales scene cuts to a close shot of a

29 | Ford Motion Picture Laboratory, still from *Ford Bombay, India*, 1948.

typewriter processing the order and then tilts upward to reveal the operator of this typewriter: a young woman in a business suit. More than this, she is sitting, along with a dozen equally Westernized others (also identified by business suits), behind a glass partition in a clean, well-lit room (see figure 30). In spite of its brevity, logical transition between scenes, and thematic appropriateness, this focus on the female worker is cut and the produced film only shows this white-collar female worker in the process of carrying the document to her male counterpart.

When presented to rooms filled with American executives, then, these omissions created a world picture in which Europe needed to be reconstructed while the rest of the world needed pseudo-colonial management through the spread of new factories and quality executive oversight. Where men act and women buy or suntan. Whether an unintentional manifestation of dominant ideologies, a matter of haphazard editing with such a short time frame, or the deliberate spread of the "managerial gaze," the final edit of the film produced a clear center-periphery narrative in which differing quality of life for workers, different conceptions of managerial ability, and differing gender narratives (neither unobjectionable, as in European plants women are objectified, but in non-European plants, women are minimized if not erased altogether) place the white, male, Western executive as a figure that the world needs.

30 | Ford Motion Picture Laboratory, still from *Ford Alexandria, Egypt*, 1948.

While creating apparent wholes by simply excluding rather than assimilating aberrant features is a basic rhetorical tactic, for film production it raises the question of late-stage editing as a form of rhetorical action, and this has not been studied enough. Studying what gets left on the cutting floor, however, is a challenge to any analytical project precisely because it requires locating often lost source material. Archival research has the opportunity to better inform this element of film composition. Even when it is possible to locate film, the rhetorical process of simply erasing an element from the potential narrative hardly warrants much theorization. Nevertheless, attention to final editing in film can offer important insights into the ideological positions being taken by a filmmaker—these editing decisions inform us of what a rhetor-editor finds worthy of seeing and offer up further concepts to rhetorical analyses of film like pacing and proportion.

―――――――

Conclusion: Managers Gazing on Six Continents

A decade after the conclusion of World War II, the image of Ford Motor Company as a force of global political good was fully integrated into the company's rhetorically constructed identity circulating publicly as well. One of the company's many promotional films from 1955 opens with a visual depiction of the "Fordist Empire" spreading from one side of the planet to the other. As a map of the world scrolls across the screen, every nation is highlighted in yellow (seemingly representing "Fordist" territory directly) except Eastern Europe and the Soviet Union as the narrator declares, "The Ford mass production idea spread all around the world, creating new jobs, and now there are Ford People at work on every continent."

Driving this point home visually, the film then turns to six identical scenes: a Ford worker introducing himself while screwing in the rim surrounding the front headlight on various 1955 Ford models. The significance of this repeated scene comes from the fact that each worker represents a different arena of Ford's international production: Norman Florcheck from Dearborn, Michigan; Dennis Weatherhill from Dagenham, England; Hugo Swaggenbach (speaking German) from Belgium; Joaquin Verlin (speaking Portuguese) in São Paulo, Brazil; and Keith Dawson in the Australian Ford assembly plant.

To mirror their worker counterparts, the film then shows the British, German, and American car models joyriding in their respective spaces before launching into a "product planning" narrative—this time narrating the three-year process that went into the reemergence of the Lincoln Continental. Positioned in the historical context of this chapter, this film is a victory lap of sorts. Ten years after the conclusion of World War II and forty years after Ford first showed interest in producing a global Fordism, the company was presenting a unified vision of a globalized company and a marketplace linked by the labor of Fordist workers around the world meeting consumer needs on six continents. These performances and their recursive relationship with discourses about an "Arsenal of Democracy" and "managerial gaze" play an integral role not only in the rise of economic power in the second half of the twentieth century but in understanding what rhetorical work aided this rise in the process.

To summarize, this chapter has examined the production of the managerial gaze as it developed during World War II and its aftermath. As the concluding chapter in a book that has outlined the role of cinematic rhetoric in the growing influence of corporatism in society, the staging of this gaze is a culmination, of sorts. Film scholarship has long used gaze theory as a way of understanding the intersections of power and vision—a gaze occurs when a system of power or desire saturates identity so thoroughly that it changes the way that a subject sees the world. Ford's films throughout the 1940s and 1950s suggest that this is a twofold process in which publics are encouraged to see themselves as part of larger structures of economic power and a privileged class of individuals is trained to enact these systems of power through particular ways of looking.

The chapter has considered, then, both sides of the gaze as an analytical principle. In a film like *Women on the Warpath*, film replicates a series of vision-based arguments that rely on seeing and being seen. The film is about internalizing threats to national sovereignty and, in turn, submitting to the disciplinary gaze of managerial capitalism in order to better ward off these threats. This system also required managers to engage in such a disciplinary process. Once again, Ford used films produced for a management meeting series to train its managerial class in how to observe the world. Unsurprisingly, both of these arguments reified existing structures of masculine, Western power while also embedding them in expanding structures of capitalist development.

It is, in many ways, fitting that the final chapter of this work takes up Ford's process of incorporating the world itself through such a gaze. The system has sought to expand both capitalism and corporate influence to the very ends of the Earth and draw the planet itself into a networked articulation of corporate and economic reason—at first in search of raw materials and workers, then markets and consumers, and finally investment opportunities and tax shelters. The reason for this final aim is that once an ideological construct like the economy manages to cover the whole world, it can stand in for reason itself. Jean-Luc Nancy notes, for example, that this concept of globality has come into much sharper focus over the past century and has been a matter of establishing a "totality grasped as a whole."[14] The role of visuality in this process is well noted.

For visual rhetoricians, these films are strikingly ripe texts for responding to W. J. T. Mitchell's call for greater attention to "[i]mages of the world and the global as such ... the metaphors, figures, and pictures that constitute discourses of globalization, ancient, modern, and postmodern."[15] While Mitchell argued that post–World War II conflicts were over the "world pictures" that divided East and West, capitalist and Communist, democratic and socialist society, the grounds on which even these conceptions of the global were made had already been saturated with images of global Fordism's masculine gaze. For Ford Motor Company, reconfiguring the globe as a knowable object functioned through the work of a collection of homogeneous middle managers and the technological/ material work of accounting and numerical reason.

By the mid-1950s, the formalized construct of managerial capitalism was ingrained into the fabric of American economic life. Texts like William H. Whyte's *The Organization Man*, Alan Trachtenberg's *The Incorporation of America Today*, and J. K. Galbraith's running column *The Industrial Hour* were designed to make sense of the cultural shifts in economic relations after the war. For Galbraith, the collective thrust of the many changes in the company are evidence of "a new shift in the industrial enterprise, this time from capital to organized intelligence" taking the claim a step further to argue that "this shift would be reflected in the deployment of power in the society at large."

Affirming the claim being held in this chapter, such a shift in power, he argues, must take place through "the association of men of diverse technical knowledge, experience, or other talent which modern industrial technology and planning require." Galbraith then termed "this new locus of power in the business enterprise and in the society," which consists of "all who participate in group decision-making or the organization which they form" as "the technostructure" in which statistical knowledge becomes the locus of decision-making and an integral portion of a wider nexus of power.[16] Training these figures to see in particular ways, Ford produced a cinematic trace of what Michael Hardt and Antonio Negri would identify decades later as "the long transition from the sovereign right of nation states to the first postmodern global figures of imperial right."[17] They argue that the postwar political environment witnessed "(1) the process of decolonization that gradually recomposed the world market along hierarchical lines branching out from the United States; (2) the gradual decentralization of production; and (3) the construction of a framework of international relations that spread across the globe the disciplinary productive regime and disciplinary society in its successive evolutions."[18] Tellingly, they pinpoint the capitalist utopia imagined by this process as "a global factory-society and a global Fordism." The notion of "global Fordism," in this context, was the culmination of decades of cinematic work striking at a moment of tremendous rupture in the geopolitical order. At this point in the book, the next sentence may be a predictable one. Hardt and Negri's invocation of Ford at this moment is the consequence of the company (and many companies like it) engaging in an active and powerful rhetorical project during and after the war to position a world picture in which the corporation was the defining institution in a new phase of global development.

The long-term effects of this Fordist world-picture extend beyond the symbolic, however. Alain Lipietz provided an in-depth critique of global Fordism, concluding that the system leads to "hegemonic crisis," which, as I have positioned it here, is really an extended form of rhetorical crisis brought on by acts of incorporation. He argues that one result of this crisis is that "it is difficult to represent the interests of those groups who benefit from peripheral Fordism as coinciding with the 'interests of people as a whole' for any length of time." Long term, he explains, the relationship breaks down: "Chaos of social relations, which both democracies and dictatorships find difficult to manage, is probably the major obstacle to the transition of which the apologists of capitalist development dream: an economic sequence of 'primitive Taylorization . . . peripheral Fordism . . . autonomous Fordism . . . leading quite naturally to the sequence dictatorship . . . liberalization . . . (social-) democratization.'"[19] Nevertheless, this chapter has worked to chronicle where this dream and this want to speak for the "interests of people as a whole" have been a central part of larger processes of incorporation.

As the closing moments captured by the archive, it is hard to ignore the cleanliness of the circle created by this film. From a melting pot ceremony in which immigrants in Michigan were paraded in front of "throngs" of interested community members and businesspersons to a film in which these same figures were being encouraged to view global locales as sites, bodies, and resources ripe for managing, incorporation has been a guiding principle for Ford Motor Company, and Ford is still, as that observer in 1937 noted, "a corporation like other corporations."

Conclusion

Let's finish where we began. When the CEOs of the three largest car companies in America sat before a congressional panel and testified that the livelihoods of millions relied on the survival of their corporations, they weren't really embellishing the point. The bailout hearings were never really about rational debate or persuasive appeals—they were an argument to the nation about what was holding society together. This book has shown that, in this regard, most of the rhetorical work required of these executives had already been done for them. Across decades, the corporations they headed had gradually woven together a vast network of connections and coordinations that could be presented on that afternoon as the "fabric of countless communities."

In this sense, for all of the hand-wringing that surrounded the idea of "too big to fail" from an economic perspective, I see this moment as one of rhetorical crisis, a point of clear evidence that hegemony has been achieved by corporations and that they can often work to subvert or reshape what we traditionally consider rhetorical action. As the introduction put it, they have succeeded in pressing past the need for persuasion or even identification by producing an interconnected system in which the terms of many debates have already been set. This, in one sense, is the very nature of hegemony. However, as the chapters in this book have worked to clarify, to claim hegemony is not to simply point at power but to analyze the tangled bundle of discourses, norms, and materials that have been arranged ("skillfully combined" as Gramsci described it) by powerful corporations.

Using rhetoric as an analytical framework to understand one of these hegemonic bundles and Ford Motor Company's motion pictures as a textual substrate making this bundle visible, I have examined how corporations can function as powerful rhetorical actors capable of both constructing large, interconnected arguments about the structure of social life and circulating these messages widely. These arguments carry across many texts and, at times, over the time frame of one or more generations. I have called this the study of "incorporational" rhetoric. To review the main claims that make up this idea, I return to the questions first raised by the hearings.

CONCLUSION

How did corporations take on such an integral role in American society?

Answering this question through "a rhetorical history of events," I have tried to show that corporations, Ford specifically, rose by drawing together larger and larger configurations of objects, ideas, and people into their institutional confines. Within just one sample from one branch of one company's media work, we have seen how such incorporation significantly impacted national systems of education, changed conceptions of the economy, produced an economized sense of the national landscape, raised industrial economies to the level of the sublime (that is, as a place the public could turn for questions of meaning and direction), and trained a generation of men to see their right and responsibility to manage.

All of these narratives were, in turn, compiled into a simultaneous configuration of overlapping arguments that spread relentlessly. Because Ford's films ranged so widely, scholars interested in Progressive Era education, the National Park System, or World's Fairs will (hopefully) find Ford's narratives an interesting and often-overlooked contributor to these ideas but will also consider how these seemingly disparate ideas were also connected by the company.

In sum, the narratives on display in Ford's films are a textbook case of incorporation in action. We can recall Raymond Williams's point that the "process of incorporation" takes place when "the processes of education; the processes of much wider social training within institutions like the family; the practical definitions and organizations of work; the selective tradition at an intellectual and theoretical level ... are involved in a continual making and remaking of an effective dominant culture." This dominant culture, I have argued, has been guided by the corporate and the economic. This has meant studying, in Michel Foucault's terms, how a "general domain" developed over time composed of "a very coherent and very well-stratified layer that comprises and contains, like so many partial objects, the notions of value, price, trade, circulation, income interest."[1] This leads to the second question asked at the outset of this work.

How were these CEOs able to position their companies as central to the economy and, in turn, the economy as the defining feature of the nation?

Working to answer this question has meant trying to explain what, exactly, an economy is and how it might work rhetorically. The second chapter is most useful in this regard, as it explored how economies can be approached as a set of commonplaces—or topics—like labor, value, and capital as they can be used to organize much of social life. I have argued that, acting as a grand lens for understanding the relationship that many have with the world, economies effectively produced economic ways of seeing.

As a rhetorical construct, economies are experienced in part via the narratives that frame daily actions as a part of this larger economic reality. As such, changes in the communicative landscape can have profound effects on the nature of the economy (and mark an important but less readily studied framework for understanding economies). By aligning as many disparate material entities and ideas into a single institutional structure and then cutting these into hyper-condensed narratives of corporate expanse on-screen, Ford presented itself repeatedly not just as an integral part of social life but as the defining institutional structure and ideological construct through which social life takes shape. The motion picture, then, gave the company a remarkable advantage in wider histories of economic persuasion.

In this frame, we might consider the economy a cumulative set of stories we are, at some point, told and eventually tell ourselves that map a set of explanatory principles onto the orientation of objects and individuals. In the case of "capitalism," in its various iterations, these discourses define our willingness to take part in an economy defined by capital exchanges, to accept the centrality of corporations in this configuration, and to believe in the curious myths of value wrapped up in money, exchange, and speculation. When "the economy" was on the line, the Big Three rolled out a narrative of economic existence we saw seventy-five years before in the film *As Dreams Come True*. My answer to this question, then, is that Ford has consistently generated powerful and cohesive economic stories.

On this point, I align this work with rhetorical scholarship that has long studied economic rhetoric as a set of manufactured "realities" presented to the public. This scholarship has suggested that rhetorical activity has contributed to the broad rise of the bourgeoisie in the eighteenth century (Longaker), that shifting notions of the finance economy were enhanced by realist novels in the nineteenth century (Kornbluh), that presidential economic rhetoric across the twentieth century fundamentally contributed to the rise of "late capitalism" (Houck), and that contemporary defenses of free-market capitalism have relied on a wide variety of rhetorical appeals (McCloskey and Klamer, separately).[2]

I also, however, hope this work is of use to a number of other fields, from anthropology to economics, that have been working to develop similar approaches to the economic through ideas of "capitalist realism," "economic sublime," "economic persuasions" (Gudeman), and "aesthetic capitalism."[3] Punctuating this turn, Nobel Prize–winning economist Robert Shiller recently published a book calling for a new field of economics: "narrative economics."[4]

As a general concept inserted into this conversation, incorporational rhetoric invites anyone studying sweeping narratives of economic existence—such as Fordism, post-Fordism, Keynesianism, neoliberalism, the information economy—to do so not as a set of uniform economic monoliths but as an ongoing and cumulative series of rhetorical narratives. These narratives cope with historical challenges, advocate for the incorporation of more social and material capital into structures of the corporation, and adjust the terms by which we understand economic relations to account for new institutional structures. In turn, incorporational rhetoric invites scholars concerned with these broad social constructs to consider taking up rhetorical frameworks to supplement their own inquiries.

However, as a specific study of film, this work has also expanded the "rhetoric of economics" to the visual. The work to understand these films—as a genre of film, as historical documents, as rhetorical objects, is still in fledgling form and proffers a rich untapped area for rhetorical criticism. And so I move to the third question asked of the hearings.

What role have appeals to size and interconnectivity played in this perception that economic institutions have become "too big" (and what does this designation mean for our collective imaginaries of the power of the nation-state)?

The rhetorics that these institutions used to produce these narratives can be studied using a configuration of rhetorical terms that already exist but are in some cases renewed by attention to connection and coordination. As a history of rhetorical events, chapters have explored how Ford used the similitudes (arguments to convenience, emulation, analogy), *topoi*, interstitiality, *theoros*, amplitude, *megethos*, and strategic omission in its films to connect and combine. However, these traditional rhetorical concepts were being executed via motion pictures, and so the project became an occasion to work at the intersections of film analysis and rhetorical theory.

Much like the various theories in this text that have sought to study the "skillful combinations," "relations," or "interstices" that exist in the world, this text has worked consistently to think through the benefits of working between disciplines. The most obvious way it has done so is by pairing the language of film analysis with the effects named by rhetorical theory. For rhetoricians seeking to study film, my hope is that these pairings introduce new resources in the study of texts from a rhetorical perspective. For film scholars, this work has sought to take a set of commonplace analytical frameworks that have been used to contemplate the artistic, the philosophical, and the historical and repositioned their effects in terms of the rhetorical interventions made possible by their use.

Mise-en-scène, for its attention to the combined visual effects at play in a single shot, has many potential rhetorical effects: simulating the "real," producing moments of sublimity, generating affiliations. The same is true for montage, which was studied for a number of its rhetorical properties—condensing time, drawing comparison, and overlapping material—in arguments about the nature of an economy. The various elements that produce motion in a motion picture—montage, perspective, and camera movement—can replicate the spatial logics by aligning material spaces with abstract ideological constructs. Rhetorically, these features can be instrumental in producing a fundamental feature of the postmodern world and capitalist world—interstitiality. Spectatorship, while a consistent feature of film, was studied here as a historically embedded point for rhetorical action. When pressed, corporate actors sought to change the public's relationship to corporate capitalism by invoking a particular kind of audience position that has been called the *theoros*, the *flaneur*. These names reference an audience that is a passive receiver of the images produced on-screen. From a rhetorical perspective, however, this passivity is neither an inherent feature of watching a film nor a purely ideological confluence of film and viewer needs. Rather, a rhetorical understanding of spectatorship asks what particular effects films muster that encourage the viewer to suspend their critical capacities. The effects used to do so in Ford's films relied on size, speed, and quantity as these features could be produced and circulated via film.

These various cinematic-rhetorical features function by producing wholes from parts—by creating affiliations and equivalences between previously disparate objects, by addressing common topics and shared spaces, and by advocating for uniform publics. Each of these theories draws out a similar point, however. Far from the notion of "mere ornamentation" that can detract from the pure rational debate that purportedly guides the appropriate rhetorical process, the "look of things" is often a matter of aligning particular sensibilities with much more expansive configurations of values, economic systems, and struggles over power. I follow Dennis Dake in encouraging scholars to recognize that "aesthetics is not about 'things' but about systems of ecological relationships and the processes that create these relationships and aid in their interpretation."[5] But it is important to note that this has only drawn on a sliver of rhetorical frameworks and ideas that might be combined with the many elements of film analysis that were not addressed in this book.

While the three CEOs certainly called attention to the size and interconnectedness of their companies in defending the bailouts, these appeals were a century in the making. Countless connections and affiliations that tied the American corporation to both the economic and the social heart of the nation contributed not just to that single decision in 2008 but to the many decisions individuals make each day as they work within, and sometimes contemplate, economic realities. These connections, however, leave a trace. For this reason, economies can be usefully studied using the various analytical frameworks that work to understand how objects and ideas get affiliated. In this framework the ability to spread an aesthetic network to increasingly wide objects and ideas, the ability to unsettle settled spaces and draw new connections, and the breakdown of economic relations into a set of representations and transformations of the way one economic topic aligns with the next are all important rhetorical processes.

Finally, I have attempted to craft this work as part of the ongoing project to expand histories of rhetoric, particularly as questions of visual rhetoric intervene in conventional understandings of persuasion and identification. The visual techniques made available (and eventually mass distributed) by film had, as I have explored them, profound effects on the public's understandings of knowledge, of economy, of their own position as spectators. These shifts in perception, however, were not neutral but enacted powerful shifts that aligned with the rise of Fordist industrial reason. This also, however, means looking forward to what developments are "incorporating" the world at present.

Much changed in the fifty years separating the last films in the Ford film archive and the bailout hearings that opened this book—the core of the American economy now lies in a combination of energy, retail, finance, and health care. The globalizing initiatives after the war would ultimately lead to Fordism's relative demise—first at the hands of Toyotaism and then to more wholesale shifts away from manufacturing that (never fully escaping from the company's shadow) has been called post-Fordism.

At the same time, the general institution of the corporation has only grown in stature and influence. A 2011 study of the global economy revealed that just 147 corporations account for 40 percent of global wealth, and the top 1,500 own more than 80 percent of global wealth. Just six mass conglomerates control nearly 90 percent of media options in the United States. Children, psychologists have suggested, recognize and understand the nature of corporate logos before they can read.[6] Legal scholars have been grappling with whether corporations function on par with individual persons in the eyes of the law—and by extension have been exploring the philosophical quandaries about the boundaries of personhood in the process.

We live, as Fredric Jameson has argued, in a world in which "the corporate fact and the corporate style is somehow no longer merely an aberrant business subculture, but some deeper, quasi-ontological law of the social world itself," one so thoroughly saturated by the corporate that even "forms of opposition" to the massive economic institutions "are today also collective and organized." The process by which we have arrived at this quasi-ontological state has been, I have argued, structured in part by a system of rhetorical activity that has consistently worked to incorporate elements of life within the ideological structures of corporate capitalism. Eventually, these contested points simply become a part of the day-to-day lives of millions.[7]

Notes

Introduction

1. Gary Ackerman, one of the congressmen at the first hearing, suggested that "[t]here is a delicious irony in seeing private luxury jets flying into Washington, D.C., and people coming off of them with tin cups in their hand, saying that they're going to be trimming down and streamlining their businesses ... couldn't you all have downgraded to first class or jet-pooled or something to get here? It would have at least sent a message that you do get it." Levs, "Big Three," n.p.
2. *Hearing Before the Committee on Banking, Finance, and Urban Affairs*, 38.
3. Ibid., 42.
4. U.S. Department of the Treasury, Office of Financial Stability, Citizen's Report, 5.
5. Banham, *Ford Century*, 99.
6. Raushenbush, *Fordism*, 6.
7. Galbraith, *Liberal Hour*, 119.
8. Jessop, "Post-Fordism," 62.
9. Paz et al., "Capitalisms, Crises, and Cultures I," 10.
10. Sklar, "Woodrow Wilson," 53.
11. Ford Motor Company, "Facts from Ford," 47.
12. Bray, *Guide*, 1.
13. The appraiser's language speaks openly to the challenges of the collection and is worth passing along more directly. In an archived draft of the films' appraisal before submission to the National Archives, the anonymous appraiser wrote, "There is no adequate catalog or index to the contents. Those guides that now exist are hopelessly disarranged and out of date due to the loss or discard of films ... the more difficult job of arranging and indexing the negative film was not touched." Instead, the appraiser simply noted that there is "approximately 600,000 feet of positive print film" and 1,345,000 feet of negative nitrate film. The films were, however, "by almost any criterion, priceless." Rather than provide a definitive cost, the appraiser suggested that "someone would have to determine what is useful and someone else would have to determine what is useable. In other words, it would be necessary to have an expert technician work with an expert historian in the decisions that would have to be made before the film could be duplicated and subsequently cataloged and indexed." The guide that was produced explains that the money that was "[g]iven with the motion pictures was a grant to be used for copying them on safety-base film, for describing and cataloging their contents, and for publishing a guide." A quick note on the 1904 date listed in the official archival finding aid: while Ford started producing film in 1914, the oldest film in the archive is a Thomas Edison–produced motion picture titled *The Great Train Robbery*, produced in 1903. What the film was doing in Ford's collection is unclear, but it certainly suggests both the influence of Edison on the Ford Motion Picture Laboratory and that the Laboratory was aware of its contemporaries. Bray, *Guide*, 1; "Ford Motor Company Historical Film Vault Survey," 3–4.
14. Zarefsky, "Four Senses," 20.
15. Ibid., 24.

16. Warner, *Publics and Counterpublics*, 69.
17. Gramsci, *Prison Notebooks*, 302.
18. Ibid., 302.
19. Ibid., 571.
20. Ibid., 165.
21. Williams, *Marxism and Literature*, 103.
22. Ibid., 103.
23. Ibid., 136.
24. Trachtenberg, "'The Incorporation of America' Today," 760.
25. Ibid.
26. Ibid., 758–59.
27. Shumway, "Incorporation," 757.
28. Laclau, *Rhetorical Foundations*, 63.
29. Kaplan, "Rhetoric of Hegemony," 274 (emphasis in original).
30. Stewart, *Henry Ford's*, 8.
31. Orgeron et al., *Learning*, 15.
32. Brown, *Corporate Eye*, 1.
33. Grieveson, *Cinema and the Wealth of Nations*, 2.
34. *Ford Times*, "Silent Celluloid Salesman," 534.
35. Bollman and Bollman, *Motion Pictures*, 23.
36. Prelinger, *Field Guide*.
37. Taking a small sampling of these entries, the *Ford Times* in 1914 reported on an exhibition that took place in San Francisco where "throngs of interested visitors" watched "both instructive and interesting are the stories told to thousands each day by the Ford Motion Picture Department through its exhibit in the Palace of Education." The story "Remarkable Ford Films" originated in the *Ford Times* but appears in a June 4, 1915, edition of *The Graham Guardian* located out of Safford, Arizona; it reported that "[t]he Ford Motor Company has recently added some remarkable films to the nation-wide service of the Ford Animated Weekly. One of the most interesting of these is the scene showing the military ceremonies conducted by the United States Engineering Department on the occasion of the filling of the last gap in the million-and-a-half-dollar sea-wall in Galveston Bay." Providing some insight into the circulation of these films, the article continues by explaining that "these films will be shown in Safford Monday and Tuesday nights; Pima, Wednesday night, and Thatcher, Thursday night." A May 9, 1920, copy of the *Morning Tulsa Daily World* contained a "YMCA Notes" section explaining that "[a]rrangements have been made to the educational department to secure the *Ford Educational Weekly*, a 1,000-foot reel produced by the Ford Motor Company." The June 22, 1923, edition of the *Ford News* ran an article titled "Safety Education Aided by the Motion Picture" which explained that "43,000 men have been shown the new Ford Safety reel, entitled 'A Study in Ford Safety' . . . accompanied by a comedy picture." The article further reveals that "a 'Movie Room' with a seating capacity of 200 has been recently installed in the River Rouge Plant." *Ford News*, "Safety Education," 7; *Ford Times*, "Ford Exhibits," 455; *Graham Guardian*, 1; *Morning Tulsa Daily World*, 14.
38. Lewis, *Public Image*, 117.
39. Cited in Prelinger, *Field Guide*, 35.
40. Galbraith, *Liberal Hour*, 121.
41. Ibid., 119.
42. Saker Woeste, *Henry Ford's*, 2.
43. Ford Motor Company Archives, "Reminiscences of E.G. Liebold," 512.

44. Brinkley, *Wheels for the World*, 421.
45. Lewis, *Public Image*, 12.
46. In a mailing to dealers, the company presented "the following subjects available on 35 mm and 16 mm non-inflammable film through the United States Department of the Interior, Division of Motion Pictures." These films, averaging 30 minutes in length, included *A Visit to Yellowstone National Park, Waterton Glacier International Peace Park, Nature's Cameo: Zion National Park*, and *Rainbow in the Desert: Bryce National Park*. Films available from the company included sound versions of all four national park films (averaging ten minutes in length). The company also offered, however, a collection of films dedicated to spectacle: *Rhapsody in Steel; Ford and a Century of Progress; Fair in the West; New Roads to Roam; On the Job; Adventure Bound; The Rouge Plant: The Story of Men, Methods, and Motor Cars; News from Dearborn; The Making of Safety Glass; The Harvest of the Years; Science Rules the Rouge; Scenes from the World of Tomorrow; Review of a Preview;* and *The Peak of Riding Comfort*. New releases for 1940 included *How Do They Do It, Symphony in F, Keep This Under Your Hood, While the City Sleeps,* and *The New York World's Fair in 1940*. Ford Motor Company, "Educational Pictures," 1.
47. Ford Motor Company, "Comparative Branch Record."
48. *New York Times*, "Industry Telling Stories," 2.
49. Dunn, "Ford Motor Company," 11.
50. Cara Finnegan and Jiyeon Kang have called for greater attention to the "scene of circulation" surrounding texts in order to better understand how meanings travel. Taking this a step further, Catherine Chaput has argued that rhetoric itself might be understood as a "circulation of exchanges, the whole of which govern our individual and collective decisions." Pushing this to a level largely designed for the more easily tracked digital age, Laurie Gries has called for studying texts through their "eventfulness." Eventfulness is the combination of distribution—the deliberate dissemination of materials—and circulation—a "dynamic network of distributed, unfolding, and unforeseeable becomings." Film scholars have similarly called for the study of a text's *Medeinverbund*. For Thomas Elsaesser and Malte Hagener, *Medeinverbund* is "a network of competing, but also mutually interdependent and complementary media practices, focused on a specific location, a professional association, or even a national or site initiative." Chaput, "Rhetorical Circulation," 8; Elsaesser and Hagener, *Film Theory*, 32; Finnegan and Kang, "'Sighting' the Public," 396; Gries, Laurie, *Still Life*, 335.
51. Warner, *Publics and Counterpublics*, 90.
52. Olson, *Constitutive Visions*, 56.
53. Acland and Wasson, *Useful Cinema*, 6.
54. Beller, *Cinematic Mode*, 2.
55. Hediger and Vonderau, *Films at Work*, 11.
56. Similar claims have appeared in two more edited collections since 2011: Devin Orgeron, Marsha Orgeron, and Dan Streible's *Learning with the Lights Off* and Charles Acland and Haidee Wasson's *Useful Cinema*. In addition to these edited collections, there are also a number of manuscript-length texts studying the development of the medium: Elspeth H. Brown's *The Corporate Eye: Photography and the Rationalization of American Commercial Culture*, Jennifer Peterson's *Education in the Field of Dreams: Travelogues and Early Nonfiction Film*, Paolo Bonifazio's *Schooling in Modernity: The Politics of Sponsored Films in Postwar Italy*, Lee Grieveson's *Cinema and the Wealth of Nations*, and Kelly Ritter's *Reframing the Subject: Postwar Instructional Film and Class-Conscious Literacies*. Ibid.
57. Hawhee and Messaris, "What's Visual," 211.
58. Gaillet, "Archival Survival," 28.
59. Finnegan, *Picturing Poverty*, vii.

60. Bazerman, "Orders," 378.
61. Derrida, *Archive Fever*, 2–3
62. Derrida, *Archive Fever*, 2.
63. Ibid., 12 (emphasis added).
64. Packer, 90.
65. Derrida, *Archive Fever*, 7.
66. Foucault, "The Archaeology of Knowledge," 45.
67. Foucault, *Birth of Biopolitics*, 3.
68. Flynn, "Foucault's Mapping of History," 30.

Chapter 1

1. Dewey, *Democracy in Education*, 142.
2. Herbert David Croly argued that "if Progressivism is to be constructive rather than merely restorative, it must be prepared to replace the old order with a new social bond, which will be no less secure than its predecessor, but which will serve still more effectually as an impulse, an inspiration and a leaven. The new system must provide, that is, not merely a new method, important as a new method may be, but a new faith, upon the rock of which may be built a better structure of individual and social life. Returning to the subject later in the work, Croly suggests that any "genuinely national system must possess unity as well as inclusiveness; and the unity can be obtained only by active cooperation of its different parts for the realization of a common purpose." Croly, *Progressive Democracy*, 25, 121.
3. Hahner, *To Become an American*, xv–xvi; Crick and Engels, "The Effort of Reason," 286–87; Quirke, *Eyes on Labor*, 5.
4. Porter, "Rhetoric," 107.
5. Singer, *Aesthetic Reason*, 1.
6. *Ford Times*, "Assimilation."
7. Marquis, "The Ford Idea in Education," 910.
8. Bushnell, "Give Men a Chance," 155.
9. Ford and Crowther, *My Life and Work*, 128.
10. Spring, *Education*, 1.
11. Cited in Hodsdon, "The Mystique of Mise en Scene," 68.
12. In this early format, a film would be sent to a Ford dealer, who would arrange to show it in local theaters, YMCAs, prisons, churches, and really anywhere that would seem an appropriate community partner in the process of social reformation. The dealers would then send the reel back to the parent company in Dearborn, where it would be shipped to another dealer/theater. *Honolulu Star-Bulletin*, 3.
13. *Arizona Republican*, n.p.
14. Ford Motor Company, "Facts from Ford," 33.
15. *Washington Standard*, n.p.
16. *New York Times*, "Written on Screen," 43.
17. In two separate listings in the December 26, 1919, edition of the *Clinch Valley News* of Tazewell, Virginia, these "rumors" are taken up directly. In the first ad, the manager of the New Theatre, F. T. Witten, addressed the rumor generally, assuring patrons that the theater was not paying for the reels. Taking this a step further, the Tazewell Motor Company also took out space in the same issue to declare that the rumors "circulated for the purpose of injuring the Ford Motor Company and the Ford business in general. The Ford films are produced by the Ford Motor Company and distributed throughout the United States for the

purpose of educating the people along certain lines which they are unable to obtain except by this method. These films are sent to the various theatres throughout the country and no charge is made for the film itself." *Clinch Valley News*, "Notice," n.p.; *Clinch Valley News*, "To the Patrons," n.p.

18. *Omaha Daily Bee*, n.p.
19. "Ford Educational Library," 39.
20. *Ford News*, "Ford Educational Library Awakens," n.p.
21. While his main focus was placed on four rhetorical figurations, Foucault added a number of terms subsumed within the four broader categories: "*Amicitia, Aequalitas (contractus, consensus, matrimonium, societas, pax, et similia), Consonantia, Concertus, Continuum, Paritas, Proportio, Similtudo, Conjunctio, Copula.*" Foucault, *Order of Things*, 17, 25.
22. Kress and Van Leeuwen, 154.
23. Ibid., 140.
24. Justice, "Visual Instruction," 15–18.
25. A cover story from the *Ford News* in May 1921 publicized, for example, the travelogues *Yosemite Valley* and *Old Mexico of Today* as opportunities to escape the confines of local mentalities and see something of the nation and world. The same can be said of *Cherry Blossom Time* (shot in Japan) or the *Panama Canal*. Rather than functioning as pure travelogues in the traditional sense of presenting primarily leisure and splendor, the films worked as a hybrid genre featuring elements of the travelogue alongside visual tours of places according to their symbols of modernity and industrial progress—public services, industry, and infrastructure. In *Old Mexico of Today*, for example, this meant establishing that "[t]he reader who believes that the romantic Mexico of old with its fabulous wealth still exists is doomed to disappointment for the Capital today is like any other modern city."
26. Foucault, *Order of Things*, 19, 21.
27. Ibid., 117–18.
28. *The Stroller's Weekly and Douglas Island News*, "PTA Meeting Tuesday Night," 1.
29. Grieveson, *Cinema and the Wealth of Nations*, 116.
30. Dewey, *Democracy and Education*, 374.
31. Ibid., 401.
32. Dewey and Dewey, *Schools of To-Morrow*, 236–38.
33. This use of the model school on film was not exclusive to the training of the young male worker (reimagined as a performed capitalist masculinity). The company also produced "A Day at the Merrill-Palmer School"—at an all-girl school dedicated to teaching practical skill—in 1927. The film opens with a quote from Merrill-Palmer's will, which declares that "the welfare of any community is divinely, and hence inseparably, dependent upon the quality of its motherhood, and the spirit and character of its homes." Extending beyond the immediately American context as well, a press release by N.W. Ayer and Son Inc. explained that "[t]rade schools closely patterned after the two divisions of the Henry Ford Trade School for Boys located at Highland Park, Michigan, are soon to be established in England and Russia, it was learned today ... The Russian school is to be built and maintained by the Soviet government at Nijni Novogovod and will be adjacent to 'Autostroy' ... The British school as an extension of the soon-to-be-completed Dagenham plant." N.W. Ayer and Son, Inc., "Four New Movies."
34. Foucault, *Order of Things*, 20–21.
35. Stafford, *Visual Analogies*, 9.
36. Dewey, *Democracy and Education*, 24–25.
37. Dewey, "Policy of Industrial Education," 94.
38. Dewey, *Individualism*, 21.

39. Lagemann, "Plural Worlds," 185; Labaree, "Progressivism," 279; Bowles and Gintis, *Schooling*, 181.

40. Lee Grieveson terms this films'"operational aesthetic," which "sequences on the movement of materials through factories, by means of roads, bridges, canals, sewage systems, and the circulation of information abound" (124). Lisa Gitelman has pointed out the collapsing distinctions between a number of previously separated concepts as the rise of technologies at the turn of the century led to "combining the nonverbal and verbal, know-how and knowing, *techne* and *logos*." Grieveson, *Cinema and the Wealth of Nations*, 124; Gitelman, *Scripts*, 7.

41. Gartman, *From Autos to Architecture*, 11.

42. Ewen and Ewen, *Channels of Desire*, 139.

43. Trachtenberg, *The Incorporation of America Today*, 69.

44. According to Martin, mise-en-scène has existed in classical form, in a post-structural form, as shorthand for the art of the long take. Martin, *Mise en Scène*, 87.

45. For Ott and Keeling, for example, "this means attending to the ways that elements such as pacing, movement, color, lighting, sound, and tactility invite particular affects or "immediate modes of sensual responsiveness to the world characterized by an accompanying imaginative dimension." Ott and Keeling, "Cinema," 367.

46. Foucault, *Order of Things*, 24.

Chapter 2

1. *Hood River Glacier*, n.p.; *Vernon Parish Democrat*, n.p.
2. Wilson and Hale, *New Freedom*, 7–10.
3. De Cock et al., "Financial Phantasmagoria," 154.
4. Hunter, *Critiques of Knowing*, 92.
5. Olson, *Constitutive Visions*, 6.
6. Ibid., 9.
7. Boyle, "Shape of Labor," 54.
8. This diagram appears in Spivak, "Scattered Speculations," 77.
9. Connolly, "Habermas," n.p.
10. Eisenstein, *Film Form*, 249.
11. Deleuze, *Cinema 1*, 8
12. Ibid., 30.
13. Ibid., 15.
14. Ibid., 10–20.
15. Josephson, *The Robber Barons*, 315.
16. Ibid., 30–31.
17. Ibid., 30.
18. Beckert, *Imagined Futures*, 271.
19. Marx, *Capital, Volume 1*, 174.
20. There have been many reiterations of Marx's point over the years. Mark Garret Longaker has argued that "John Locke, Adam Smith, Hugh Blair, and Herbert Spencer all imagined their 'material process of history'" (and asked their readers to imagine as well) before engaging in economic theorization. Arjo Klamer suggested that the economic process of "abduction," central to the contemporary field of economics, is "a matter of imagination." Ronald Walter Greene has argued that "neo-liberalism encourages people to imagine themselves and others as value-producing subjects." Greene, "Rhetorical Capital," 330; Klamer, "Visualizing the Economy," 259; Longaker, *Rhetorical Style*, 5.

21. McKeon, "Creativity and the Commonplace," 199.
22. Marx, *Grundrisse*, 103.
23. Arendt, *Human Condition*, 111.
24. Deleuze, *Cinema 1*, 31.
25. Adorno and Horkheimer, *Dialectic of Enlightenment*, 54.
26. Ibid., 62.
27. Ibid., 68.
28. Plett, "Rhetoric and Intertextuality," 328.
29. Polanyi, *Great Transformation*, 65.
30. Ibid., 171.
31. Arrighi, *Long Twentieth Century*, 5.
32. Ibid., 263.
33. Murphy and de la Fuente, *Aesthetic Capitalism*, 2.
34. Bordwell, "Idea of Montage," 9.
35. The *Ford News* article "New Picture Shows Complete Method of Ford Production" outlines the power of these narratives to sway public perceptions of the economy, reporting that "no pains were spared to fulfill the intention that the film should portray fully and clearly the wonders of science and machinery used in the production of Ford Cars" and that these films achieved the "highest attainments of the motion picture photographer's art. The touch of the master hand is evidenced by the artistry of the title and subtitles as well as the varied succession of 'shots.'" A month later, the *Ford News* once again reported that at least one of these films (*The Ford Age*) was "proving a drawing card of the first magnitude, and that the film is being kept in constant use. In many cities it appeared at the finest local theaters as the program feature." Providing some sense of the geographical reach of the films, the *Ford Age* was played in Cleveland, Atlanta, Cincinnati, Louisville, New Orleans, Kansas City, and Denver." *Ford News*, "New Picture Shows."
36. Deleuze, *Cinema 1*, 11.
37. Haraway, *Primate Visions*, 361.
38. Ross, *Working-Class Hollywood*, 12.

Chapter 3

1. Ford, "My Philosophy," 5, 19.
2. Urry, *Tourist Gaze*, 2.
3. Seiler, *Republic of Drivers*, 2–3; Wollen and Kerr, *Autopia*, 23; Flink, *Automobile Age*, 281.
4. McClintock, "Maidens, Maps, and Mines," 46.
5. Conley, *Cartographic Cinema*, 1.
6. Rice, *Digital Detroit*, 160.
7. Bhabha, *Location of Culture*, 13.
8. Ibid., 143.
9. Ibid., 217.
10. Flaxman, *Brain Is the Screen*, 6.
11. *Farm News*, "Farm Motion Pictures," 2.
12. In a 1904 Bulletin of the American Geographical Society titled "Good Roads in the United States," for example, Albert Perry Brigham argued that "if America be the most progressive nation in the world, her citizens will not much longer endure medieval discomforts when they go out to mingle with their fellows and market the fruits of their labor." Brigham, "Good Roads," 735.

13. Hiltzik, *New Deal*, 421.
14. De Certeau, *Practice of Everyday Life*, 36.
15. Henry Ford, reflecting in 1924 on the initial launch of the village-industries project, wrote that within these villages, "all the men live within a few miles of the plant and come to work by automobile." Highlighting one particularly ideal scenario, Ford pointed out that "[o]ne worker operates a farm which requires him to have two trucks, a tractor, and a small closed car." Cited in Segal, *Recasting the Machine Age*, 143–44.
16. The village-industries serve as the background for a number of films in the Ford collection. *The Story of a Little River* was first produced in 1919 amid the initial push for *Good Roads* but also to highlight the more expansive plans for the River Rouge plant, which broke ground two years earlier. The film was originally created to present the processes involved in harnessing hydroelectric power to run the smaller production factories, but a second version of the film was produced and distributed in 1930 to reframe the villages with the completion of the plant in 1928. In 1940, the company produced *Review of a Preview*, which used the village-industries as a backdrop for showcasing the 1940 line of Ford cars.
17. Deleuze, *Cinema 1*, 20.
18. Ibid., 22.
19. Ibid., 23.
20. Ford Motor Company, "Famous Ford Firsts," 17.
21. Simpson, *Trafficking Subjects*, 92.
22. Flink, *Automobile Age*, 169.
23. Aron, *Working at Play*, 238.
24. Leopold, "Letter to Edsel Ford."
25. Krausman, "Response."
26. Cheadle, "Letter to Edsel B. Ford."
27. In a letter dated February 16, 1939, from M. F. Leopold, a safety engineer at the Department of the Interior's Bureau of Mines reported the specific number of showings of a different film but added that he was recently "informed by the National Park Service that the demand for the National Park's films sponsored by the Ford Motor Company is so large that many of the copies are booked 6 months in advance. It occurred to me that the above information might be of interest to you." Leopold, "Letter to Edsel Ford."
28. The MotorCities National Heritage Area Partnership. "Welcome to MotorCities National Heritage Area," www.motorcities.org.
29. Reynolds, *Geographies of Writing*, 16.
30. LeFebvre, *The Production of Space*, 6.
31. Soja, *Thirdspace*, 10–11.
32. Ibid., 40.
33. Ibid., 41.
34. Bhabha, *Location of Culture*, 143.

Chapter 4

1. Lenthall, *Radio's America*, 10.
2. Houck, *Rhetoric as Currency*, 8.
3. McLane, *New History of Documentary Film*, 102–105.
4. Böger, *People's Lives*, 211.
5. Finnegan, *Picturing Poverty*, 169.
6. Bird, "Better Living," 5.

7. Crowther, *Critical Aesthetics*, 15.
8. "Official Guide Book," 1.
9. Ganz, *1933 Chicago World's Fair*, 1.
10. "Official Guide Book."
11. Ibid.
12. "Ford Exposition," 1.
13. Nye, *American Technological Sublime*, xiii.
14. Ibid., 199.
15. Benjamin, *Arcades Project*, 7.
16. Ibid., 18.
17. Debord, *Society of the Spectacle*, 14.
18. Ibid., 32.
19. Kellner, *Media Spectacle*, 2.
20. Gotham and Krier, "From the Culture Industry," 160.
21. Farrell, "Weight of Rhetoric," 467.
22. Sutherland, "Populism and Spectacle," 335.
23. Ibid., 333.
24. Gotham and Krier, 161 (emphasis in original).
25. Benjamin, *Arcades Project*, 21.
26. Panfilio, "Awakening," 248.
27. Aristotle, *Rhetoric and the Poetics of Aristotle*, 1358b2–3.
28. Dimitrova, *Theroi*, 12–14.
29. "Official Guide Book," 149.
30. Longinus, *On the Sublime*, 22–25.
31. Van Eck, Bussels, and Delbeke, *Translations of the Sublime*, 1.
32. Longinus, *On the Sublime*, 24.
33. Dake, "Aesthetics Theory," 27.
34. Chatman, *Coming to Terms*, 44.
35. *Evening Star*, "Low First Cost."
36. N.W. Ayer and Son, Inc., "World's Fair."
37. N.W. Ayer and Son, "Four New Movies."
38. "The movie swings from fantasy to actual pictures in color of various manufacturing processes at the Rouge, with comments by Wells on scenes in the steel mill, glass plant, plastics division, motor assembly building, tire plant, fabrics division and on the final assembly line." A second press release suggests the following: "In vivid color, it reveals the magnitude and scope of Ford's world-wide operations . . . The audience is taken to forests, farms and mines to see these materials gathered, then back to the 1200-acre Rouge plant here to see them converted into finished automobiles, trucks and tractors." As these releases suggest, *Symphony in F* was produced to generate an immense act of mental compression on its audiences, remaking workers, materials, and spaces into a single unified understanding of how production works in the Fordist regime. The music was composed by Edwin E. Ludig and performed by members of the New York Philharmonic. David Lewis writes, "Although a Ford News release hailed 'Symphony in F' as a 'masterpiece of industrial photography,' company executives were less enthusiastic." "It sounds like a puzzling combination of 'Snow White' and an educational, industrial reel," publicist George F. Pierrot declared, adding that "it's as though we hadn't decided whether to appeal to the intelligentsia or the proletariat and consequently, we fall somewhere in between." *Amplitude*, as a concept, offers up one explanation for why this intermediary nature was effective rhetorically. Combining *Snow White* and an industrial production picture allowed for an overwhelming cinematic experience, and that was just the first half of the offering. The audience

wasn't meant to land in a definitive site, they were meant to escape from any discernible conclusions. N.W. Ayer and Son, Inc. "World's Fair"; Lewis, "At the 1939–1940 World's Fair," 15.

39. Black, "Attendance," 3.

40. Rice, Jenny, *The Rhetorical Aesthetics of More*, 32; Balzotti and Crosby, "Diocletian's Victory Column, 330; Olson, "American Magnitude," 381.

41. Polan, "'Above All Else,'" 130, 137.

42. Ford Motor Company, "Educational Pictures," n.p.

43. A mailing to dealers at the time reveals a number of its offerings including the series "available on 35 mm and 16 mm non-inflammable film through the United States Department of the Interior, Division of Motion Pictures." These films, averaging 30 minutes in length, included *A Visit to Yellowstone National Park*, *Waterton Glacier International Peace Park*, *Nature's Cameo: Zion National Park*, and *Rainbow in the Desert: Bryce National Park*. Films listed as available from the company included sound versions of all four national park films (averaging ten minutes in length) as well as *Rhapsody in Steel*, *Ford and a Century of Progress*, *Fair in the West*, *New Roads to Roam*, *On the Job*, *Adventure Bound*, *The Rouge Plant*, *News from Dearborn*, *The Making of Safety Glass*, *The Harvest of the Years*, *Science Rules the Rouge*, *Scenes from the World of Tomorrow*, *Review of a Preview*, and *The Peak of Riding Comfort*. New releases for 1940 included *How Do They Do It*, *Symphony in F*, *Keep This Under Your Hood*, *While the City Sleeps*, and *The New York World's Fair in 1940*. Ibid.

44. Ford Motor Company, "Comparative Branch Record."

45. Blakesley, *Terministic Screen*, 13.

46. A number of contemporary scholars have shifted the core of film spectatorship from hypothetical arguments about desire and positionality to empirical research that maps literal spectators' reactions to films. I follow Linda Williams in arguing that "no amount of empirical research into the sociology of actual audiences will displace the desire to speculate about the effects of visual culture, and especially moving images, on hypothetical viewing subjects." As such, attending to the work of "gaze theory," a theory that interrogates how typified and produced responses to the visual produce particular ideological effects en masse, is crucial to cinematic rhetoric. Williams, *Viewing Positions*, 4.

47. Plantinga, *Moving Viewers*, 18.

48. Roosevelt, "Fireside Chat."

Chapter 5

1. Sorensen and Williams, *My Forty Years*, 273.
2. Nelson, *National Manhood*, 15.
3. Columpar, "Gaze," 43.
4. Honey, *Creating Rosie the Riveter*, 5.
5. Lewis, *The Public Image of Henry Ford*, 380–81.
6. Althusser, *On the Reproduction of Capitalism*, 180.
7. Jack, *Acts of Institution*, 287, 299.
8. Ferguson, "One Thousand Planes a Day," 151.
9. Weber, *Theory of Social and Economic Organization*.
10. *Reconsolidation*.
11. Ford Motor Company (Egypt) S.A.E., *Memento*.
12. *New York Times*, "Egyptian Ford."
13. Nancy, *Creation of the World*, 44.
14. Mitchell, "World Pictures," 251.

15. Galbraith, *New Industrial State*, 59, 61, 74.
16. Hardt and Negri, *Empire*, 4.
17. Ibid., 245.
18. Lipietz, *Mirages and Miracles*, 145.
19. Foucault suggests that for nearly two centuries "the concepts of money, price, value, circulation, and market" were part of "a rigorous and general epistemological arrangement." Foucault, *Order of Things*, 166.

Conclusion

1. Anna Kornbluh suggest that, using *metalepsis*, Victorian economic writers "substitute[ed] psychological effects for causes" to allow for "psychologism . . . to supplant the structural critique of finance that had predominated in the mid-Victorian period" so that "the very idea of 'fictitious capital' was replaced by that of fickle subjects." For Mark Garrett Longaker, scholars of the "British Enlightenment wove [economics, style, and ethics] into a cohesive vision of free market capitalism, rhetorical style, and bourgeois virtue" using varying degrees of tropological reason from "Locke's injunctions against tropes" to "Smith's celebration of sentimental figures" to Blair's advice to "avoid [tropes'] use when the situation or the subject does not warrant such a locution." For Arjo Klamer economics must evolve to recognize more than just its use of induction and deduction but also "abduction" or "reasoning by means of analogy, or metaphor." For Deirdre McCloskey, contemporary economics' might be understood through the metaphors of Robert Solow. We have, then, a robust set of theories in economic rhetoric about written tropes—how they were used and theorized—in order to form the intellectual climate surrounding an economy. Kornbluh, *Realizing Capital*, 23; Longaker, *Rhetorical Style*, 2; Houck, *Rhetoric as Currency*; Klamer, "Visualizing the Economy," 258; McCloskey, "Rhetoric."
2. Codeluppi, "The Integrated Spectacle," 51.
3. Shiller, *Narrative Economics*, xi.
4. Dake, "Aesthetics Theory," 6.
5. McAlister and Cornwell, "Children's Brand Symbolism," 203.
6. Jameson, *The Geopolitical Aesthetic*, 60.

Bibliography

Acland, Charles R., and Haidee Wasson, eds. *Useful Cinema*. Durham: Duke University Press, 2011.
Adorno, Theodor W. *The Culture Industry: Selected Essays on Mass Culture*. New York: Psychology Press, 2001.
———. *The Schema of Mass Culture*. New York: Routledge, 1991.
Adorno, Theodor W., and Max Horkheimer. *Dialectic of Enlightenment*. New York: Verso, 1997.
Agamben, Giorgio, and Marilene Raiola. *Homo Sacer*. Stanford, CA: Stanford University Press, 1998.
Althusser, Louis. *On the Reproduction of Capitalism: Ideology and Ideological State Apparatuses*. New York: Verso, 2014.
Arendt, Hannah. *The Human Condition*. Chicago: University of Chicago Press, 2013.
Aristotle. *Rhetoric and the Poetics of Aristotle*. 1st ed., New York: Random House, 1984.
Arizona Republican. "'A Poor Relation' with Will Rogers at Columbia." December 22, 1921.
Aron, Cindy Sondik. *Working at Play: A History of Vacations in the United States*. Oxford: Oxford University Press, 2001.
Arrighi, Giovanni. *The Long Twentieth Century: Money, Power, and the Origins of Our Times*. New York: Verso, 1994.
Balzotti, Jonathan Mark, and Richard Benjamin Crosby. "Diocletian's Victory Column: Megethos and the rhetoric of spectacular disruption." *Rhetoric Society Quarterly* 44, no. 4 (2014): 323–42.
Banham, Russ. *The Ford Century: Ford Motor Company and the Innovations That Shaped the World*. New York: Artisan Books, 2002.
Barkan, Joshua. *Corporate Sovereignty: Law and Government under Capitalism*. Minneapolis: University of Minnesota Press, 2013.
Bazerman, Charles. "The Orders of Documents, the Orders of Activity, and the Orders of Information." *Archival Science* 12, no. 4 (2012): 377–88.
Beckert, Jens. *Imagined Futures*. Cambridge, MA: Harvard University Press, 2016.
Beller, Jonathan. *The Cinematic Mode of Production: Attention Economy and the Society of the Spectacle*. Lebanon, NH: University Press of New England, 2012.
Benjamin, Walter. *The Arcades Project*. Cambridge, MA: Harvard University Press, 1999.
———. *The Work of Art in the Age of Mechanical Reproduction*. London: Penguin UK, 2008.
Bhabha, Homi K. *The Location of Culture*. London: Psychology Press, 1994.
Bird, William L. *"Better Living": Advertising, Media, and the New Vocabulary of Business Leadership, 1935–1955*. Evanston, IL: Northwestern University Press, 1999.
Black, F. L. "Attendance New York World's Fair 1939." Edsel B. Ford Office Papers 1903–1945, Accession 6, Box 245, File: 1939 New York World's Fair. Benson Ford Research Center, Detroit, MI.
Blakesley, David. *The Terministic Screen: Rhetorical Perspectives on Film*. Carbondale: Southern Illinois University Press, 2007.

Böger, Astrid. *People's Lives, Public Images: The New Deal Documentary Aesthetic*. Tübingen: Gunter Narr, 2001.
Bollman, Gladys, and Henry Bollman. *Motion Pictures for Community Needs: A Practical Manual of Information and Suggestion for Educational, Religious and Social Work*. New York: Holt, 1922.
Bordwell, David. "The Idea of Montage in Soviet Art and Film." *Cinema Journal* 1, no. 2 (1972): 9–17.
Bowles, Samuel, and Herbert Gintis. *Schooling in Capitalist America: Educational Reform and the Contradictions of Economic Life*. Chicago, IL: Haymarket Books, 2011.
Boyle, Casey. "The Shape of Labor to Come." In *Topologies as Techniques for a Post-Critical Rhetoric*, 51–73. Cham: Palgrave Macmillan, 2017.
Braverman, Harry. *Labor and Monopoly Capital: The Degradation of Work in the Twentieth Century*. New York: New York University Press, 1998.
Bray, Mayfield. *Guide to the Ford Film Collection in the National Archives*. No. 70. Washington, DC: National Archives, 1970.
Brigham, Albert Perry. "Good Roads in the United States." *Bulletin of the American Geographical Society* 36, no. 12 (1904): 721–35.
Brinkley, Douglas. *Wheels for the World: Henry Ford, His Company, and a Century of Progress, 1903–2003*. New York: Viking, 2003.
Brown, Elspeth H. *The Corporate Eye: Photography and the Rationalization of American Commercial Culture, 1844–1929*. Baltimore: Johns Hopkins University Press, 2005.
Brummett, Barry. *Rhetoric of Machine Aesthetics*. Westport, CT: Greenwood Publishing Group, 1999.
Burke, Kenneth. *Attitudes Toward History*. Berkeley, CA: University of California Press, 1984.
———. *A Grammar of Motives*. Berkeley, CA: University of California Press, 1969.
Bushnell, Sarah. "Give Men a Chance—Not Charity." *National Magazine*, July 1920.
Chaput, Catherine. *Market Affect and the Rhetoric of Political Economic Debates*. Columbia, SC: University of South Carolina Press, 2019.
———. "Rhetorical Circulation in Late Capitalism: Neoliberalism and the Overdetermination of Affective Energy." *Philosophy & Rhetoric* 43, no. 1 (2010): 1–25.
Chatman, Seymour Benjamin. *Coming to Terms: The Rhetoric of Narrative in Fiction and Film*. Ithaca, NY: Cornell University Press, 1990.
Cheadle, C. C. "Letter to Edsel B. Ford. Departmental Communication." June 21, 1937. Public Relations Fairs and Exhibits Accession 450, Box 5, File: Government Pictures. Benson Ford Research Center, Detroit, MI.
Clinch Valley News. "Notice to the Public." December 26, 1919.
———. "To the Patrons of the New Theater." December 26, 1919.
Codeluppi, Vanni, and Briziarelli, Marco. "The Integrated Spectacle: Towards Aesthetic Capitalism." In *The Spectacle 2.0: Reading Debord in the Context of Digital Capitalism*, 51–66. London: Westminster University Press, 2017.
Columpar, Corinn. "The Gaze as Theoretical Touchstone: The Intersection of Film Studies, Feminist Theory, and Postcolonial Theory." *Women's Studies Quarterly* 30, no. 1/2 (2002): 25–44.
Conley, Tom. *Cartographic Cinema*. Minneapolis: University of Minnesota Press, 2007.
Connolly, William E. "Habermas, Deleuze, and Capitalism." *Theory & Event* 11, no. 4 (2008): n.p.
Crick, Nathan, and Jeremy Engels. "'The Effort of Reason, and the Adventure of Beauty': The Aesthetic Rhetoric of Randolph Bourne." *Quarterly Journal of Speech* 98, no. 3 (2012): 272–296.

Croly, Herbert David. *Progressive Democracy*. London: Routledge, 2017.
Crowther, Paul. *Critical Aesthetics and Postmodernism*. London: Oxford University Press, 1996.
Dake, Dennis. "Aesthetics Theory." In *Handbook of Visual Communication*, 25–44. London: Routledge, 2004.
Debord, Guy. *Society of the Spectacle*. N.p.: Bread and Circuses Publishing, 2012. Kindle.
de Certeau, Michel. *The Practice of Everyday Life*. Translated by Steven Rendall. Berkeley: University of California Press, 2011.
De Cock, Christian, Max Baker, and Christina Volkmann. "Financial Phantasmagoria: Corporate Image-Work in Times of Crisis." *Organization* 18, no. 2 (2011): 153–72.
Deleuze, Gilles. *Cinema 1: The Movement-Image*. Translated by Hugh Tomlinson and Barbara Habberjam. Minneapolis: University of Minnesota Press, 1986.
Derrida, Jacques. *Archive Fever: A Freudian Impression*. Chicago: University of Chicago Press, 1996.
Dewey, John. *Democracy and Education, 1916*. Edited by Jo Ann Boydston and Patricia Baysinger. Carbondale: Southern Illinois University Press, 1985.
———. *Individualism Old and New*. Amherst, NY: Prometheus Books, 1999.
———. "A Policy of Industrial Education." In *The Middle Works, 1899–1924*, vol. 7, *1912–1914*, edited by Jo Ann Boydston, 93–97. Carbondale: Southern Illinois University Press, 2008.
Dewey, John, and Evelyn Dewey. *Schools of To-morrow*. London: Dent, 1915.
Dimitrova, Nora Mitkova. *Theoroi and Initiates in Samothrace: The Epigraphical Evidence*. Princeton, NJ: The American School of Classical Studies at Athens, 2008.
Dunn, Robert O. "Ford Motor Company Captures Annual Film Audience of 64,000,000." *Public Relations Journal*, December 1961, 11.
Eisenstein, Sergei. *Film Form: Essays in Film Theory*. New York: HMH, 2014.
Elsaesser, Thomas, and Malte Hagener. *Film Theory: An Introduction through the Senses*. London: Routledge, 2015.
Evening Star (Washington, DC). "Low First Cost." Advertisement. September 6, 1934.
Ewen, Stuart, and Elizabeth Ewen. *Channels of Desire: Mass Images and the Shaping of American Consciousness*. Minneapolis: University of Minnesota Press, 1992.
Farrell, Thomas B. "The Weight of Rhetoric: Studies in Cultural Delirium." *Philosophy & Rhetoric* 41, no. 4 (2008): 467–487.
Ferguson, Robert G. "One Thousand Planes a Day: Ford, Grumman, General Motors, and the Arsenal of Democracy." *History and Technology* 21, no. 2 (2005): 149–75.
Finding Aid to Accession 1940. Reconsolidation of Foreign Operations Records, 1946–1955. Benson Ford Research Center, Detroit, MI.
Finnegan, Cara A. *Picturing Poverty: Print Culture and FSA Photographs*. Washington, DC: Smithsonian Books, 2003.
Flaxman, Gregory, ed. *The Brain Is the Screen: Deleuze and the Philosophy of Cinema*. Minneapolis: University of Minnesota Press, 2000.
Flink, James J. *The Automobile Age*. Cambridge, MA: MIT Press, 1990.
Flynn, Thomas. "Foucault's Mapping of History." In *The Cambridge Companion to Foucault*. 29–48. Cambridge: Cambridge University Press, 2006.
Ford, Henry. *My Philosophy of Industry: An Authorized Interview by Fay Leone Faurote*. New York: Coward-McCann, 1929.
Ford, Henry, and Samuel Crowther. *My Life and Work: In Collaboration with Samuel Crowther*. New York: Doubleday, 1922.
"Ford Educational Library." *Visual Education* 2 (January 1921): 39.

"Ford Exposition, A Century of Progress." Brochure, 1934.
Ford Motor Company. "Comparative Branch Record of Mass Selling Activity, 25 April 1941." Sales Dealer Films, Accession 446, Box 4, File: Reports. Benson Ford Research Center, Detroit, MI.
———. "Educational Pictures Sponsored by the Ford Motor Company." 1940, Sales Dealer Films, Accession 446, Box 4, File: General Letters. Benson Ford Research Center, Detroit, MI.
———. *Facts from Ford*. 4th ed. Detroit, MI: Ford Motor Co., 1920.
———. "Famous Ford Firsts Advertisement." *Life Magazine*. June 25, 1945.
Ford Motor Company (Egypt) S.A.E. *A Memento for Our Friends. To Commemorate the Laying of the Corner Stone of the Company's New Plant at Smouha, Alexandria*. September 1948.
Ford Motor Company Archives. *The Reminiscences of E.G. Liebold (part one)*. Oral History Transcript, January 1953.
"Ford Motor Company Historical Film Vault Survey, 4/23/62." Archives and Vertical File: Photography and Film File. Benson Ford Research Center, Detroit, MI.
Ford News. "Farm Motion Pictures." March 1, 1921.
———. "Ford Educational Library Awakens 'Sleeping Beauty.'" December 8, 1923.
———. "New Picture Shows Complete Method of Ford Production." June 22, 1923.
———. "Remote Sections Have Motion Pictures: Ford Truck Equipped with Cinema Outfit Will Tour Southwestern U.S. and Mexico; To Meet Long-Felt Need." October 15, 1923.
———. "Safety Education Aided by the Motion Pictures." June 22, 1923.
Ford Times. "Assimilation through Education: A Motto Wrought into Education." April 1916.
———. "Ford Exhibits Popular at San Francisco." March 3, 1914.
———. "The Silent Celluloid Salesman." July 1916.
Foucault, Michel. "The Archeology of Knowledge." In *Foucault Live: Interviews*. 57–65. New York: Semiotext(e), 1989.
———. *The Birth of Biopolitics: Lectures at the Collège de France, 1978–79*. New York: Palgrave Macmillan, 2008.
———. *The Order of Things*. New York: Vintage Books, 1994.
Gaillet, Lynée Lewis. "Archival Survival: Navigating Historical Research." In *Working in the Archives: Practical Research Methods for Rhetoric and Composition*. 28–39. Carbondale: Southern Illinois University Press, 2010.
Galbraith, John Kenneth. *The Liberal Hour*. London: Hamish Hamilton, 1960.
———. *The New Industrial State*. Princeton, NJ: Princeton University Press, 2007.
Ganz, Cheryl R. *The 1933 Chicago World's Fair: A Century of Progress*. Champaign-Urbana, IL: University of Illinois Press, 2012.
Gartman, David. *From Autos to Architecture: Fordism and Architectural Aesthetics in the Twentieth Century*. New York, NY: Princeton Architectural Press, 2012.
Gitelman, Lisa. *Scripts, Grooves, and Writing Machines: Representing Technology in the Edison Era*. Stanford, CA: Stanford University Press, 1999.
Gotham, Kevin, and Daniel A. Krier. "From the Culture Industry to the Society of the Spectacle: Critical Theory and the Situationist International." In *No Social Science without Critical Theory*. 155–92. Bingley, UK: Emerald Group Publishing Limited, 2008.
Graham Guardian. "Remarkable Ford Films." June 4, 1915.
Gramsci, Antonio. *Prison Notebooks*. Vol. 2. New York: Columbia University Press, 1992.
Greene, Ronald Walter. "Rhetorical Capital: Communicative Labor, Money/Speech, and Neo-liberal Governance." *Communication and Critical/Cultural Studies* 4, no. 3 (2007): 327–31.

Gries, Laurie. *Still Life with Rhetoric: A New Materialist Approach for Visual Rhetorics.* Boulder, CO: University Press of Colorado, 2015.
Grieveson, Lee. *Cinema and the Wealth of Nations: Media, Capital, and the Liberal World System.* Chicago: University of Chicago Press, 2018.
Hahner, Leslie A. *To Become an American: Immigrants and Americanization Campaigns of the Early Twentieth Century.* East Lansing: Michigan State University Press, 2017.
Haraway, Donna J. *Primate Visions: Gender, Race, and Nature in the World of Modern Science.* London: Routledge, 2013.
Hardt, Michael, and Antonio Negri. *Empire.* Cambridge, MA: Harvard University Press, 2001.
Hawhee, Debra, and Paul Messaris. "What's Visual about 'Visual Rhetoric'?" *Quarterly Journal of Speech* 95, no. 2 (2009): 210–23.
Hearing Before the Committee on Banking, Finance, and Urban Affairs: Examining the State of the Domestic Automobile Industry—Part II. 110th Congress, 2nd session, December 4, 2008.
Hediger, Vinzenz, and Patrick Vonderau. *Films at Work.* Amsterdam: Amsterdam University Press, 2008.
Hodsdon, Barrett. "The Mystique of Mise en Scene Revisited." *Continuum: Journal of Media & Cultural Studies* 5, no. 2 (1992): 68–86.
Honey, Maureen. *Creating Rosie the Riveter: Class, Gender, and Propaganda during World War II.* Amherst: University of Massachusetts Press, 1984.
Honolulu Star-Bulletin. "Getting 12,000 Feet of Movies for Henry Ford." February 20, 1917.
Hood River Glacier. "Big Industrial Caravan Coming Soon." July 13, 1922.
Houck, Davis W. *Rhetoric as Currency: Hoover, Roosevelt and the Great Depression.* College Station: Texas A&M University Press, 2001.
Hunter, Lynette. *Critiques of Knowing: Situated Textualities in Science, Computing and the Arts.* London: Routledge, 2002.
———. "From Cliché to Archetype." In *Towards a Definition of Topos,* 199–227. London: Palgrave Macmillan, 1991.
Jack, Jordynn. "Acts of Institution: Embodying Feminist Rhetorical Methodologies in Space and Time." *Rhetoric Review* 28, no. 3 (2009): 285–303.
Jameson, Fredric. *The Geopolitical Aesthetic: Cinema and Space in the World System.* Bloomington: Indiana University Press, 1995.
Jessop, Bob. "Post-Fordism and the State." In *Post-Fordism: A Reader,* 251–79. Somerset, UK: Wiley, 1994.
Josephson, Matthew. *The Robber Barons: The Great American Capitalists, 1861–1901.* Vol. 47. New York: Houghton Mifflin Harcourt, 1962.
Justice, W. Arthur. "Visual Instruction in the Public Schools of Evanston." *Visual Education* 1 January 1920: 12–22.
Kaplan, Michael. "The Rhetoric of Hegemony: Laclau, Radical Democracy, and the Rule of Tropes." *Philosophy & Rhetoric* 43, no. 3 (2010): 253–83.
Kellner, Douglas. *Media Spectacle.* London: Routledge, 2003.
Klamer, Arjo. "Visualizing the Economy." *Social Research: An International Quarterly* 71, no. 2 (2004): 251–62.
Kornbluh, Anna. *Realizing Capital: Financial and Psychic Economies in Victorian Form.* Oxford, UK: Oxford University Press, 2013.
Krausman, A. M. "Response: Bryce and Zion National Park Silent Films Made with the Co-operation of the United States Department of the Interior, Washington D.C." April 4, 1938. Sales Dealer Films Accession 446, Box 7, File: Bryce Canyon and Zion National Park. Benson Ford Research Center, Detroit, MI.

Kress, Gunther R., and Theo Van Leeuwen. *Reading Images: The Grammar of Visual Design*. London: Routledge, 1996.
Labaree, David F. "Progressivism, Schools, and Schools of Education: An American Romance." *Paedagogica Historica* 41, no. 1–2 (2005): 275–88.
Laclau, Ernesto. *The Rhetorical Foundations of Society*. London: Verso Books, 2014.
Latour, Bruno. *Reassembling the Social*. Oxford, UK: Oxford University Press, 2007.
Lefebvre, Henri. *The Production of Space*. Oxford: Blackwell, 1991.
Lenthall, Brian. *Radio's America: The Great Depression and the Rise of Modern Mass Culture*. Chicago: University of Chicago Press, 2007.
Leopold, M. F. Letter to Edsel Ford, February 16, 1939. Edsel B. Ford Office Papers, General Correspondence 1903–1945, Accession 6, Box 147. Benson Ford Research Center, Detroit, MI.
Levs, Josh. "Big Three Auto CEOs Flew Private Jets to Ask for Taxpayer Money." cnn.com. January 4, 2008.
Lewis, David. "At the 1939–1940 New York World's Fair." *Bulb Horn*. July–August 1973. Accession 1117, Box 5. Benson Ford Research Center, Detroit, MI.
———. *The Public Image of Henry Ford: An American Folk Hero and His Company*. Detroit, MI: Wayne State University Press, 1976.
Life Magazine. "Famous Ford Firsts Advertisement." June 25, 1945.
Lipietz, Alain. *Mirages and Miracles*. London: Verso, 1987.
———. "Post-Fordism and Democracy." In *Post-Fordism: A Reader*. 338–57. New York: Wiley, 1994.
Longaker, Mark Garrett. *Rhetorical Style and Bourgeois Virtue: Capitalism and Civil Society in the British Enlightenment*. University Park: Penn State University Press, 2015.
Longinus. *On the Sublime*. Translated by H. L. Havell. New York: Gottfried and Fritz, 1927.
Marquis, Samuel Simpson. "The Ford Idea in Education." *National Education Association of the United States. Journal of proceedings and addresses*, 1916, 910–912.
Martin, Adrian. *Mise en Scène and Film Style: From Classical Hollywood to New Media Art*. Basingstoke, UK: Palgrave Macmillan, 2014.
Marx, Karl. *Capital, Volume I*. Translated by Ben Fowkes. New York: Penguin, 1976.
———. *Grundrisse*. New York: Penguin, 1993.
McAlister, Anna R., and T. Bettina Cornwell. "Children's Brand Symbolism Understanding: Links to Theory of Mind and Executive Functioning." *Psychology & Marketing* 27, no. 3 (2010): 203–228.
McClintock, Anne. "Maidens, Maps, and Mines: The Reinvention of Patriarchy in Colonial South Africa." *The South Atlantic Quarterly* 87, no. 1 (Winter 1988), 147–192.
McCloskey, Deirdre N. *The Rhetoric of Economics*. Madison, WI: University of Wisconsin Press, 1998.
McGee, Michael Calvin. "The 'Ideograph': A Link between Rhetoric and Ideology." *Quarterly Journal of Speech* 66, no. 1 (1980): 1–16.
McKeon, Richard. "Creativity and the Commonplace." *Philosophy & Rhetoric* (1973): 199–210.
McLane, Betsy A. *A New History of Documentary Film*. New York: Bloomsbury Publishing USA, 2013.
Mitchell, W. J. T. "World Pictures: Globalization and Visual Culture." *Neohelicon* 34, no. 2 (2007): 49–59.
Morning Tulsa Daily World. "YMCA Notes." May 9, 1920.
The MotorCities National Heritage Area Partnership. "Welcome to MotorCities National Heritage Area," www.motorcities.org. Accessed: November 16, 2019.
Murphy, Peter, and Eduardo de la Fuente. *Aesthetic Capitalism*. Leiden: Brill, 2014.

Nancy, Jean-Luc. *The Creation of the World, or, Globalization*. Albany, NY: SUNY Press, 2007.
Nelson, Dana D. *National Manhood*. Durham, NC: Duke University Press, 1998.
Nevins, Allan, and Frank Ernest Hill. *Ford: Expansion and Challenge, 1915–1933*. New York: Scribner, 1957.
New York Times. "Egyptian Ford Co. Gets Yugoslav Order." June 12, 1947.
———. "Industry Telling Stories by Movie." January 24, 1954.
———. "Written on the Screen." January 5, 1919.
N. W. Ayer and Son, Inc. "Four New Movies Released by Ford." Press release, 7-18-1940. Public Relations Fairs and Exhibits Accession 450, Box 5, Files: News Releases, General, 1940. Benson Ford Research Center, Detroit, MI.
———. "World's Fair Color Film Shown at Ford Rotunda." Press release, 7-3-40. Accession 447, Box 1, File: Film, Series: Public Relations News Releases 1938–1941. Benson Ford Research Center, Detroit, MI.
Nye, David E. *American Technological Sublime*. Cambridge, MA: MIT Press, 1996.
"Official Guide Book of the Fair, 1933." Chicago: A Century of Progress Administration Building, 1933.
Olson, Christa J. "American Magnitude: Frederic Church, Hiram Bingham, and Hemispheric Vision." *Rhetoric Society Quarterly* 48, no. 4 (2018): 380–404.
———. *Constitutive Visions: Indigeneity and Commonplaces of National Identity in Republican Ecuador*. University Park: Penn State University Press, 2014.
———. "Performing Embodiable Topoi: Strategic Indigeneity and the Incorporation of Ecuadorian National Identity." *Quarterly Journal of Speech* 96, no. 3 (2010): 300–23.
Omaha Daily Bee. "Ford to Furnish Films for U.S. Propaganda in Europe." February 10, 1918.
Orgeron, Devin, Marsha Orgeron, and Dan Streible, eds. *Learning with the Lights Off: Educational Film in the United States*. Oxford, UK: Oxford University Press, 2011.
Ott, Brian L., and Diane Marie Keeling. "Cinema and Choric Connection: *Lost in Translation* as Sensual Experience." *Quarterly Journal of Speech* 97, no. 4 (2011): 363–86.
Packer, Jeremy. "What Is an Archive?: An Apparatus Model for Communications and Media History." In *Media History and the Archive*, pp. 97–113. London: Routledge, 2014.
Panfilio, Kenneth Michael. "Awakening from the Nightmarish Slumber of Phantasmagoria: Meditations on Walter Benjamin and the Arcades Project." *Philosophy & Social Criticism* 39, no. 3 (2013): 243–61.
Paz, Octavio, et al. "Capitalisms, Crises, and Cultures I: Notes Toward a Totality of Fragments." In *Reworking Modernity: Capitalisms and Symbolic Discontent*. 1–20. New Brunswick, NJ: Rutgers University Press, 1992.
Plantinga, Carl. *Moving Viewers: American Film and the Spectator's Experience*. Berkeley: University of California Press, 2009.
Plett, Heinrich F. "Rhetoric and Intertextuality." *Rhetorica: A Journal of the History of Rhetoric* 17, no. 3 (1999): 313–29.
Polan, Dana B. "'Above All Else to Make You See': Cinema and the Ideology of Spectacle." *Boundary 2* (1982): 129–44.
Polanyi, Karl. *The Great Transformation: The Political and Economic Origins of Our Time*. Boston: Beacon Press, 1944.
Porter, James. "Rhetoric, Aesthetics, and the Voice." In *The Cambridge Companion to Ancient Rhetoric*. 92–108. Cambridge, UK: Cambridge University Press, 2009.
Prelinger, Rick. *The Field Guide to Sponsored Films*. San Francisco, CA: National Film Preservation Foundation, 2006.

Quirke, Carol. *Eyes on Labor: News Photography and America's Working Class.* Oxford, UK: Oxford University Press, 2012.

Raushenbush, Carl. *Fordism, Ford and the Workers, Ford and the Community.* Ann Arbor, MI: League for Industrial Democracy, 1937.

Ray, Larry, and Michael Reed. *Organizing Modernity: New Weberian Perspectives on Work, Organization, and Society.* London: Routledge, 2002.

Reynolds, Nedra. *Geographies of Writing: Inhabiting Places and Encountering Difference.* Carbondale: Southern Illinois University Press, 2007.

Rice, Jeff. *Digital Detroit: Rhetoric and Space in the Age of the Network.* Carbondale: Southern Illinois University Press, 2012.

Rice, Jenny. "The Rhetorical Aesthetics of More: On Archival Magnitude." *Philosophy & Rhetoric* 50, no. 1 (2017): 26–49.

Roosevelt, Franklin D. "Fireside Chat on National Security, 12/29/1940." Collection: FDR-PPF: Papers as President, President's Personal File, 1933–1945. U.S. National Archives, Washington, DC.

Ross, Steven J. *Working-Class Hollywood: Silent Film and the Shaping of Class in America.* Princeton, NJ: Princeton University Press, 1999.

Saker Woeste, Victoria. *Henry Ford's War on Jews and the Legal Battle against Hate Speech.* Stanford, CA: Stanford University Press, 2012.

Segal, Howard P. *Recasting the Machine Age: Henry Ford's Village Industries.* Amherst: University of Massachusetts Press, 2008.

Shiller, Robert J. *Narrative Economics: How Stories Go Viral and Drive Major Economic Events.* Princeton, NJ: Princeton University Press, 2019.

Shumway, David R. "Incorporation and the Myths of American Culture." *American Literary History* 15, no. 4 (2003): 753–58.

Simpson, Mark. *Trafficking Subjects: The Politics of Mobility in Nineteenth-Century America.* Minneapolis: University of Minnesota Press, 2005.

Singer, Alan. *Aesthetic Reason: Artworks and the Deliberative Ethos.* University Park: Penn State University Press, 2010.

Sklar, Martin J. "Woodrow Wilson and the Political Economy of Modern United States Liberalism." In *A New History of Leviathan: Essays on the Rise of the American Corporate State.* 7–66. New York: Dutton, 1972.

Soja, Edward W. *Thirdspace: Journeys to Los Angeles and Other Real-and-Imagined Places.* Cambridge, MA: Blackwell, 1996.

Sorensen, Charles E., and Samuel T. Williams. *My Forty Years with Ford.* Detroit, MI: Wayne State University Press, 2006.

Spivak, Gayatri Chakravorty. "Scattered Speculations on the Question of Value." *Diacritics* 4, no. 14 (1985): 73–93.

Spring, Joel H. *Education and the Rise of the Corporate State.* Boston: Beacon Press, 1972.

Stafford, Barbara Maria. *Visual Analogy: Consciousness as the Art of Connecting.* Cambridge, MA: MIT Press, 2001.

Stewart, Phillip W. *Henry Ford's Moving Picture Show: An Investigator's Guide to the Films Produced by the Ford Motor Company, Volume One: 1914–1920.* Crestview, FL: PMS Press, 2011.

Stroller's Weekly and Douglas Island News (Juneau, Alaska). "PTA Meeting Tuesday Night." December 3, 1921.

Sutherland, Meghan. "Populism and Spectacle." *Cultural Studies* 26, no. 2–3 (2012): 330–45.

Trachtenberg, Alan. "'The Incorporation of America' Today." *American Literary History* 15, no. 4 (2003): 759–764.

Urry, John. *The Tourist Gaze.* 2nd ed. London: Sage Publications, 2002.

U.S. Dept. of the Treasury, Office of Financial Stability. *Citizens' Report on the Troubled Asset Relief Program (TARP): Summary of Performance and Financial Results*. Washington, DC: U.S. Dept. of the Treasury, 2009.
van Eck, Caroline A., Stijn Bussels, Maarten Delbeke, and Jürgen Pieters, eds. *Translations of the Sublime: The Early Modern Reception and Dissemination of Longinus' Peri Hupsous in Rhetoric, the Visual Arts, Architecture and the Theatre*. Vol. 24. Leiden: Brill, 2012.
Vernon Parish Democrat (Leesville, Louisiana). "New Constitution for State This Year." January 13, 1921.
Warner, Michael. *Publics and Counterpublics*. New York: Zone Books. 2014.
Washington Standard. "Ten Million See Ford Pictures Weekly." January 16, 1920.
Weber, Max. *The Theory of Social and Economic Organization*. New York: Simon and Schuster, 2009.
Williams, Linda. *Viewing Positions: Ways of Seeing Film*. New Brunswick, NJ: Rutgers University Press, 1995.
Williams, Raymond. *Marxism and Literature*. Oxford, UK: Oxford Paperbacks, 1977.
Wilson, Woodrow, and William Bayard Hale. *The New Freedom: A Call for the Emancipation of the Generous Energies of a People*. New York: Doubleday, 1918.
Wollen, Peter, and Joe Kerr. *Autopia: Cars and Culture*. London: Reaktion Books, 2002.
Zarefsky, David. "Four Senses of Rhetorical History." In *Doing Rhetorical History: Concepts and Cases*, 19–32. Tuscaloosa: University of Alabama Press, 1998.

Film Bibliography

Are You a Piker? series FC-FC-579, 1920–1921. Collection FC: Ford Motor Company Collection, ca. 1903–ca. 1954; Series: Motion Picture Films Relating to the Ford Motor Company, the Henry Ford Family, Noted Personalities, Industry, and Numerous Americana and Other Subjects, compiled ca. 1903–ca. 1954; National Archives at College Park, College Park, MD.
Around the World with Ford Motor Company, FC-FC-4262-4265, 1948. Collection FC: Ford Motor Company Collection, ca. 1903–ca. 1954; Series: Motion Picture Films Relating to the Ford Motor Company, the Henry Ford Family, Noted Personalities, Industry, and Numerous Americana and Other Subjects, compiled ca. 1903–ca. 1954; National Archives at College Park, College Park, MD.
Bubbles, I'm Forever Using Soap, FC-FC-2461, 1919. Collection FC: Ford Motor Company Collection, ca. 1903–ca. 1954; Series: Motion Picture Films Relating to the Ford Motor Company, the Henry Ford Family, Noted Personalities, Industry, and Numerous Americana and Other Subjects, compiled ca. 1903–ca. 1954; National Archives at College Park, College Park, MD.
Century of Progress Exposition, FC-FC-4107, 1934. Collection FC: Ford Motor Company Collection, ca. 1903–ca. 1954; Series: Motion Picture Films Relating to the Ford Motor Company, the Henry Ford Family, Noted Personalities, Industry, and Numerous Americana and Other Subjects, compiled ca. 1903–ca. 1954; National Archives at College Park, College Park, MD.
A Day at the Merrill-Palmer School. FC-FC-121-123, 1927. Collection FC: Ford Motor Company Collection, ca. 1903–ca. 1954; Series: Motion Picture Films Relating to the Ford Motor Company, the Henry Ford Family, Noted Personalities, Industry, and Numerous Americana and Other Subjects, compiled ca. 1903–ca. 1954; National Archives at College Park, College Park, MD.

BIBLIOGRAPHY

As Dreams Come True, FC-FC-4014, 1921. Collection FC: Ford Motor Company Collection, ca. 1903–ca. 1954; Series: Motion Picture Films Relating to the Ford Motor Company, the Henry Ford Family, Noted Personalities, Industry, and Numerous Americana and Other Subjects, compiled ca. 1903–ca. 1954; National Archives at College Park, College Park, MD.

Democracy in Education: Penmanship, FC-FC-2460-2461. Collection FC: Ford Motor Company Collection, ca. 1903–ca. 1954; Series: Motion Picture Films Relating to the Ford Motor Company, the Henry Ford Family, Noted Personalities, Industry, and Numerous Americana and Other Subjects, compiled ca. 1903–ca. 1954; National Archives at College Park, College Park, MD.

Fair in the West, A Visit to the California Pacific International Exposition, FC-FC-4144, 1935. Collection FC: Ford Motor Company Collection, ca. 1903–ca. 1954; Series: Motion Picture Films Relating to the Ford Motor Company, the Henry Ford Family, Noted Personalities, Industry, and Numerous Americana and Other Subjects, compiled ca. 1903–ca. 1954; National Archives at College Park, College Park, MD.

Fairy Fantasies in Stone: Bryce National Park, FC-FC-4483, 1941. Collection FC: Ford Motor Company Collection, ca. 1903–ca. 1954; Series: Motion Picture Films Relating to the Ford Motor Company, the Henry Ford Family, Noted Personalities, Industry, and Numerous Americana and Other Subjects, compiled ca. 1903–ca. 1954; National Archives at College Park, College Park, MD.

The Ford Age, FC-FC-139, 1923. Collection FC: Ford Motor Company Collection, ca. 1903–ca. 1954; Series: Motion Picture Films Relating to the Ford Motor Company, the Henry Ford Family, Noted Personalities, Industry, and Numerous Americana and Other Subjects, compiled ca. 1903–ca. 1954; National Archives at College Park, College Park, MD.

Ford and a Century of Progress, FC-FC-4115-4118. Collection FC: Ford Motor Company Collection, ca. 1903–ca. 1954; Series: Motion Picture Films Relating to the Ford Motor Company, the Henry Ford Family, Noted Personalities, Industry, and Numerous Americana and Other Subjects, compiled ca. 1903–ca. 1954; National Archives at College Park, College Park, MD.

Ford Motor Company Alexandria, Egypt, FC-FC-4635, 1948. Collection FC: Ford Motor Company Collection, ca. 1903–ca. 1954; Series: Motion Picture Films Relating to the Ford Motor Company, the Henry Ford Family, Noted Personalities, Industry, and Numerous Americana and Other Subjects, compiled ca. 1903–ca. 1954; National Archives at College Park, College Park, MD.

Ford Motor Company Bombay, India, FC-FC-4639, 1948. Collection FC: Ford Motor Company Collection, ca. 1903–ca. 1954; Series: Motion Picture Films Relating to the Ford Motor Company, the Henry Ford Family, Noted Personalities, Industry, and Numerous Americana and Other Subjects, compiled ca. 1903–ca. 1954; National Archives at College Park, College Park, MD.

Ford Motor Company Stockholm, Sweden, FC-FC-4157, 1948. Collection FC: Ford Motor Company Collection, ca. 1903–ca. 1954; Series: Motion Picture Films Relating to the Ford Motor Company, the Henry Ford Family, Noted Personalities, Industry, and Numerous Americana and Other Subjects, compiled ca. 1903–ca. 1954; National Archives at College Park, College Park, MD.

The Ford Year, FC-FC-1120-1130, 1935. Collection FC: Ford Motor Company Collection, ca. 1903–ca. 1954; Series: Motion Picture Films Relating to the Ford Motor Company, the Henry Ford Family, Noted Personalities, Industry, and Numerous Americana and Other Subjects, compiled ca. 1903–ca. 1954; National Archives at College Park, College Park, MD.

Glacier National Park, FC-FC-964, 1939. Collection FC: Ford Motor Company Collection, ca. 1903–ca. 1954; Series: Motion Picture Films Relating to the Ford Motor Company, the Henry Ford Family, Noted Personalities, Industry, and Numerous Americana and Other Subjects, compiled ca. 1903–ca. 1954; National Archives at College Park, College Park, MD.

Good Roads, FC-FC-3139, 3139. Collection FC: Ford Motor Company Collection, ca. 1903–ca. 1954; Series: Motion Picture Films Relating to the Ford Motor Company, the Henry Ford Family, Noted Personalities, Industry, and Numerous Americana and Other Subjects, compiled ca. 1903–ca. 1954; National Archives at College Park, College Park, MD.

Harvest of the Years, FC-FC-1107-1110, 1938. Collection FC: Ford Motor Company Collection, ca. 1903–ca. 1954; Series: Motion Picture Films Relating to the Ford Motor Company, the Henry Ford Family, Noted Personalities, Industry, and Numerous Americana and Other Subjects, compiled ca. 1903–ca. 1954; National Archives at College Park, College Park, MD.

The Henry Ford Trade School, FC-FC-151-154. Collection FC: Ford Motor Company Collection, ca. 1903–ca. 1954; Series: Motion Picture Films Relating to the Ford Motor Company, the Henry Ford Family, Noted Personalities, Industry, and Numerous Americana and Other Subjects, compiled ca. 1903–ca. 1954; National Archives at College Park, College Park, MD.

Mirror of America, FC-FC-2103, 1963. Collection FC: Ford Motor Company Collection, ca. 1903–ca. 1954; Series: Motion Picture Films Relating to the Ford Motor Company, the Henry Ford Family, Noted Personalities, Industry, and Numerous Americana and Other Subjects, compiled ca. 1903–ca. 1954; National Archives at College Park, College Park, MD.

Old Mexico of Today, FC-FC-2415, 2415. Collection FC: Ford Motor Company Collection, ca. 1903–ca. 1954; Series: Motion Picture Films Relating to the Ford Motor Company, the Henry Ford Family, Noted Personalities, Industry, and Numerous Americana and Other Subjects, compiled ca. 1903–ca. 1954; National Archives at College Park, College Park, MD.

Oranges and Olives, FC-FC-348, 1922. Collection FC: Ford Motor Company Collection, ca. 1903–ca. 1954; Series: Motion Picture Films Relating to the Ford Motor Company, the Henry Ford Family, Noted Personalities, Industry, and Numerous Americana and Other Subjects, compiled ca. 1903–ca. 1954; National Archives at College Park, College Park, MD.

Ordinance for Victory/Women on the Warpath, FC-FC-4331, 1943. Collection FC: Ford Motor Company Collection, ca. 1903–ca. 1954; Series: Motion Picture Films Relating to the Ford Motor Company, the Henry Ford Family, Noted Personalities, Industry, and Numerous Americana and Other Subjects, compiled ca. 1903–ca. 1954; National Archives at College Park, College Park, MD.

Panama Canal, FC-FC-329, 1919. Collection FC: Ford Motor Company Collection, ca. 1903–ca. 1954; Series: Motion Picture Films Relating to the Ford Motor Company, the Henry Ford Family, Noted Personalities, Industry, and Numerous Americana and Other Subjects, compiled ca. 1903–ca. 1954; National Archives at College Park, College Park, MD.

Paper Making, FC-FC-326, 1920. Collection FC: Ford Motor Company Collection, ca. 1903–ca. 1954; Series: Motion Picture Films Relating to the Ford Motor Company, the Henry Ford Family, Noted Personalities, Industry, and Numerous Americana and Other Subjects, compiled ca. 1903–ca. 1954; National Archives at College Park, College Park, MD.

BIBLIOGRAPHY

Paving the Way to Success, FC-FC-138, 1921. Collection FC: Ford Motor Company Collection, ca. 1903–ca. 1954; Series: Motion Picture Films Relating to the Ford Motor Company, the Henry Ford Family, Noted Personalities, Industry, and Numerous Americana and Other Subjects, compiled ca. 1903–ca. 1954; National Archives at College Park, College Park, MD.

The Power Thought Built, FC-FC-4002-4004, 1922. Collection FC: Ford Motor Company Collection, ca. 1903–ca. 1954; Series: Motion Picture Films Relating to the Ford Motor Company, the Henry Ford Family, Noted Personalities, Industry, and Numerous Americana and Other Subjects, compiled ca. 1903–ca. 1954; National Archives at College Park, College Park, MD.

Rhapsody in Steel, FC-FC-4339-4441. Collection FC: Ford Motor Company Collection, ca. 1903–ca. 1954; Series: Motion Picture Films Relating to the Ford Motor Company, the Henry Ford Family, Noted Personalities, Industry, and Numerous Americana and Other Subjects, compiled ca. 1903–ca. 1954; National Archives at College Park, College Park, MD.

Road to Happiness, FC-FC-114-116, 1926. Collection FC: Ford Motor Company Collection, ca. 1903–ca. 1954; Series: Motion Picture Films Relating to the Ford Motor Company, the Henry Ford Family, Noted Personalities, Industry, and Numerous Americana and Other Subjects, compiled ca. 1903–ca. 1954; National Archives at College Park, College Park, MD.

Scenes from the World of Tomorrow, FC-FC-4451, 1940. Collection FC: Ford Motor Company Collection, ca. 1903–ca. 1954; Series: Motion Picture Films Relating to the Ford Motor Company, the Henry Ford Family, Noted Personalities, Industry, and Numerous Americana and Other Subjects, compiled ca. 1903–ca. 1954; National Archives at College Park, College Park, MD.

The Source of the Ford Car, FC-FC-951, 1932. Collection FC: Ford Motor Company Collection, ca. 1903–ca. 1954; Series: Motion Picture Films Relating to the Ford Motor Company, the Henry Ford Family, Noted Personalities, Industry, and Numerous Americana and Other Subjects, compiled ca. 1903–ca. 1954; National Archives at College Park, College Park, MD.

Story of a Little River, FC-FC-317, 1931. Collection FC: Ford Motor Company Collection, ca. 1903–ca. 1954; Series: Motion Picture Films Relating to the Ford Motor Company, the Henry Ford Family, Noted Personalities, Industry, and Numerous Americana and Other Subjects, compiled ca. 1903–ca. 1954; National Archives at College Park, College Park, MD.

Sugar Cane Growing, Louisiana, FC-FC-547, 1920. Collection FC: Ford Motor Company Collection, ca. 1903–ca. 1954; Series: Motion Picture Films Relating to the Ford Motor Company, the Henry Ford Family, Noted Personalities, Industry, and Numerous Americana and Other Subjects, compiled ca. 1903–ca. 1954; National Archives at College Park, College Park, MD.

Sweetness, Giving You a Taste of the Sugar Industry, FC-FC-2448, 1919. Collection FC: Ford Motor Company Collection, ca. 1903–ca. 1954; Series: Motion Picture Films Relating to the Ford Motor Company, the Henry Ford Family, Noted Personalities, Industry, and Numerous Americana and Other Subjects, compiled ca. 1903–ca. 1954; National Archives at College Park, College Park, MD.

Symphony in F, FC-FC-4355, 1940. Collection FC: Ford Motor Company Collection, ca. 1903–ca. 1954; Series: Motion Picture Films Relating to the Ford Motor Company, the Henry Ford Family, Noted Personalities, Industry, and Numerous Americana and Other Subjects, compiled ca. 1903–ca. 1954; National Archives at College Park, College Park, MD.

Thirty Years of Progress, FC-FC-323, 1932. Collection FC: Ford Motor Company Collection, ca. 1903–ca. 1954; Series: Motion Picture Films Relating to the Ford Motor Company, the Henry Ford Family, Noted Personalities, Industry, and Numerous Americana and Other Subjects, compiled ca. 1903–ca. 1954; National Archives at College Park, College Park, MD.

Village-Industries, FC-FC-356-359, 1936. Collection FC: Ford Motor Company Collection, ca. 1903–ca. 1954; Series: Motion Picture Films Relating to the Ford Motor Company, the Henry Ford Family, Noted Personalities, Industry, and Numerous Americana and Other Subjects, compiled ca. 1903–ca. 1954; National Archives at College Park, College Park, MD.

Yellowstone National Park, FC-FC-1106, 1940. Collection FC: Ford Motor Company Collection, ca. 1903–ca. 1954; Series: Motion Picture Films Relating to the Ford Motor Company, the Henry Ford Family, Noted Personalities, Industry, and Numerous Americana and Other Subjects, compiled ca. 1903–ca. 1954; National Archives at College Park, College Park, MD.

Yosemite Valley, FC-FC-2414, 1920. Collection FC: Ford Motor Company Collection, ca. 1903–ca. 1954; Series: Motion Picture Films Relating to the Ford Motor Company, the Henry Ford Family, Noted Personalities, Industry, and Numerous Americana and Other Subjects, compiled ca. 1903–ca. 1954; National Archives at College Park, College Park, MD.

Index

Page numbers in *italics* refer to figures.

Ackerman, Gary, 193n1
Acland, Charles R., 18
aemulatio, 53
aesthetics
    Fordism and, 59
    industrial, 59, 122
    machine, 58
    manufacturing, 82
    operational, 197n107
    as rhetorical practice, 28
agglutination, 17, 18
agriculture, 83
    industry importance to, 147
    interconnection with industry, 94, 105
    interstitiality and, 26
    village-industries and, 109
allegories, 66
All Out for Victory (film), 157
Althusser, Louis, 153, 158, 160, 164
Americanism, 6
Americanization, 30, 31
The American Road (film), 90
amplitude, 139–44
analogy, 37
    model schools and, 53–57
    similitude and, 53
anti-Semitism, 14, 23
Archive Fever (Derrida), 21
Arendt, Hannah, 79
Are You a Piker? (film series), 102
Aristotle, 10, 130
Around the World with Ford Motor Company (film), 26, 165–77, *168*, *178*, *183*
Arrighi, Giovanni, 84
"Arsenal of Democracy" speech (Roosevelt), 153–55
assembly lines, 59, 81–82, 146
    positioning of, 43
"Assimilation through Education" (*Ford Times*), 28
Associated Films, Inc., 16

bailout hearings, 1, 185, 193n1
Baker, Max, 66
Balzotti, Jonathan Mark, 144
Battle of the Overpass, 14
Bazerman, Charles, 21
Beckert, Jens, 76
Beller, Jonathan, 18
Benjamin, Walter, 26, 128, 130
Bennett, Harry, 14, 23
Benson Ford Research Center, 22
Bhabha, Homi, 95, 121
Bingham, J. R., 16
Bird, William, Jr., 124, 125
Blakesley, David, 18, 150
Bollman, Gladys, 12
Bordwell, David, 89
Bowles, Samuel, 58
Boyle, Casey, 67
Brinkley, Douglas, 15
British Enlightenment, 202n254
Brown, Elspeth, 11
Brummett, Barry, 58, 59
Bryce Canyon National Park, 115, *116*
Buenos Aires, Argentina, 172
Building for Quality (film), 90
Burbank, Luther, 34
Bureau of Public Roads, 102
Burke, Edmund, 127, 129
Burke, Kenneth, 9, 10

California-Pacific International Exposition, 126
capital, 67
    conglomeration and, 85
    cultural, 119
    As Dreams Come True and, 65, 84–89
    exchangeable, 85
    patriotic, 86
    rhetorical account of, 84
    transformation and, 85, 87
capitalism, 15
    corporate, 189

capitalism (continued)
    economic *topoi* and, 67
    free-market, 187
    Great Depression and, 123
    ideologies of, 7
    industrial, 32, 77, 111, 121
    interstitiality and, 189
    late, 67, 96, 187
    managerial, 21, 154
    managerial gaze and, 156
    projections produced by, 128
    spectatorship of, 150
    thirdspaces and, 121
Capra, Frank, 156
car culture, 102
car-mediated tourism, 120
channels, 17
Chaput, Catherine, 151, 195n50
Chatman, Seymour Benjamin, 140
Cheadle, C. C., 115
Chevrolet Leader News, The, 12
chiasmus, 9
Chicago World's Fair of 1934, 125–26
    on-screen, 130–39
Chrysler, 1, 15, 126
cinematic century, 18
cinematic mobility, 25
cinematic montage, 68
cinematic tourism, 111
circulation, 195n50
cities, visual rubric of, 45
collapse of value, 85
"Collection FC: Ford Motor Company Collection, ca.1903-ca.1954," 4
collective action, 27
collective imaginary, 189
colonialism, 98
color
    lighting and, 40–41
    mise-en-scène and, 39
Columbia River Parkway, The (film), 112
commerce
    connections and, 101
    international, 166
communities, interstitiality between, 106
conglomeration
    capital and, 85
    implications of, 138
    media, 191
    montage and, 85
Congressional Banking, Housing, and Urban Affairs Committee, 1

Conley, Tom, 95
Connolly, William, 68
conspicuous consumption, 84
consubstantiation, 9
containment, 149
convenientia, 36–37, 53, 54
    industrial knowledge and, 38–46
    lack of color and, 39
    similitude and, 45
    visual, 44–45
convergent montage, 74
corporate archives, 20–24
corporate capitalism, 189
corporate communication, 12–13
corporate film, rise of, 10–18
corporate image of society, 31–32
corporations, 6
    economy nature shifted by, 124–25
    growth of institution, 191
    as integral to society, 186
    positioning, 2
Courtis Standard Practice Tests in Handwriting, 51
craft labor, devaluing of, 44
creative destruction, 3, 76
Crick, Nathan, 27
critical scholarship, 151
Croly, Herbert David, 27, 196n69
Crosby, Richard Benjamin, 144
Crowther, Paul, 124
cultural capital, 119
cultural superiority, 98
Cut and Dried: The Lumber Industry (film), 62

Dake, Dennis, 139, 190
Dearborn Independent (film), 14
Debord, Guy, 26, 128–30
decentralization, 17, 26, 92, 94, 103–12
decentralized production, 109
de Certeau, Michel, 103
De Cock, Christian, 66
de la Fuente, Eduardo, 84
Deleuze, Gilles, 69–70, 74, 81, 90, 93, 104–5
Democracy and Education (Dewey), 46, 47
Democracy in Education: Penmanship (film), 46–56
Department of the Interior, U.S., 94
depictions of labor, 82–83
Depression Era, 123
Derrida, Jacques, 21, 23
Dewey, John, 25, 27
    Ford Motor Company emulating, 46–47
    on three Rs, 50, 52, 58

documentary decade, 123
As Dreams Come True (film), 25, 63–67, 75, 99, 187
    capital and, 65, 84–89
    Fordist economy and, 124
    imagined futures and, 71–79
    labor as links in chain, 80–84
    montage and, 69, 70
    rhetorical economy and, 90–91

economic activity, naturalization of, 79
economic ideology, 14
economic imaginaries, 78–79
economic individualism, 164
economic interstitiality, 95–96
economic narratives, 76, 90
economic persuasion, 187
economic rhetoric, 187
economic space, 119–21
economic *topoi*, 66–68, 78, 91
economic transformation, 87
economic world system, Fordism and, 155
economization, 123
economy
    corporations shifting nature of, 124–25
    defining, 66
    Fordist, 65
    imagined ideals of, 76
    mass, 92
    reconfiguration of, 62
    rhetorical, 63, 65, 78, 82, 90–91, 164
Edison, Thomas, 10, 193n13
editing choices, 178–81
Edsel: West to the Tetons (film), 112
education, 48, 49
    corporate image of society and, 32
    Ford, H., and, 30, 71–72
    informal, 73
    public, 50, 58
    trade schools, 53–57, 86
    work and, 54
educational films
    distribution of, 33–34
    effectiveness of, 44
    Ford Motor Company turn to, 33–38
Eisenstein, Sergei, 69
elasticity, 42
emulation, 37, 45
    industrial knowledge spread and, 46–53
Engels, Jeremy, 27
escape, 139–44
eventfulness, 195n50
Ewen, Elizabeth, 59

Ewen, Stuart, 59
exchangeable capital, 85

Fair in the West (film), 131
Fairy Fantasy in Stone: Bryce National Park (film), 116, 118
Farm Security Administration, 123
Farrell, Thomas, 129
femininity, 161
feminism, 161
Ferguson, Robert G., 163
film
    See also specific topics
    corporate, 10–18
    Fordism and, 11, 13
    industrial, 16, 24–25
    management training, 164–65
    wartime propaganda, 156
Film and Photo League, 123
filmic space, 95
film rhetoric, 18–20
Film World and A-V News, 13
Finnegan, Cara, 21, 22
fireside chats, 153
Firestone, 157
Fitzpatrick and McElroy, 34
flaneurs, 130, 189
Flaxman, Gregory, 96
Flink, James J., 113
Ford, Clara, 89
Ford, Edsel, 150
Ford, Henry, 10, 86–87, 89, 96, 157
    anti-Semitism, 14, 23
    death of, 110
    As Dreams Come True and, 63–66, 71, 77
    education and, 71–72
    on Sociology Department, 31
    vision for society of, 30
Ford, Henry, II, 165, 166, 175
Ford, William Clay, 4
Ford Age, The (film), 90
Ford Alexandria, Egypt, 180
Ford and a Century of Progress (film), 131, 132, 133, 135, 137
Ford Animated Weekly, The (film series), 11–13
Ford Australia, 169–70
Ford Bombay, India, 179
Ford Canada, 169, 171
Ford Cycle of Production exhibit, 144
Ford Educational Library (film series), 33–34, 36, 38, 39, 46, 51
Ford Educational Weekly (film series), 13, 33, 38, 46, 48

Ford Egypt, 174, 175, 179
Ford English School, 12
Ford Exposition, 138, 140
Ford Exposition Hall, 126
Ford India, 178
Fording the Lincoln Highway (film), 102
Fordism, 3, 5, 6, 15, 21
  aesthetics and, 59
  appearance of, 32
  decline of, 190
  As Dreams Come True and, 65, 77–78
  economic ideology and, 14
  as economic system, 78
  economic world system and, 155
  film and, 11, 13
  global, 175, 182–84
  labor and, 77, 82
  managerial capitalism and, 154
  managerial gaze and, 155
  marketplace and, 101
  mise-en-scène and, 32
  national parks and, 94
  rhetorical economy and, 78
Fordist economy, 65, 124
Fordist global process, 174
Fordist production, 138, 199n148
  As Dreams Come True and, 80
  topoi and, 67
Fordist world-picture, 184
Ford Motor Company, 1, 9, 91, 92, 160
  See also Industrial Sociology Department; Motion Picture Laboratory; Sociology Department
  Chicago World's Fair of 1934 and, 125–26
  circulation and distribution of films of, 17
  As Dreams Come True and, 65
  early educational films, 33–38
  in Europe, 173
  global spread and, 165–77
  Great Depression and, 14–15
  Harvest of the Years on, 148
  history of, 2–5
  media created by, 4, 5, 11–12
  montage used by, 70
  public archives of, 21–22
  public education and, 58
  technology investments by, 11
  World War I and, 85–86
Ford Motor Company English School, 28, 30, 31
Ford News, 34, 96
Ford Pavilion, 134, 139
Ford Times (newspaper), 12, 28, 194n37

Ford Way of Mining Coal, The (film), 62
Ford Year, The (film), 90
Foucault, Michel, 3, 24, 32, 45, 186
  on similitude-based appeals, 36–37, 53
  on sympathies, 60
free-market capitalism, 187
Frigidaire, 156

Gaillet, Lynée, 20
Galbraith, John Kenneth, 3, 13, 182, 183
Ganz, Cheryl R., 125
Gartman, David, 59
gaze, 25, 26, 154
  managerial, 155, 165–77, 180, 182
  spectatorship and, 177
  tourist, 94, 112
gaze theory, 155, 162, 202n231
General Agreement on Tariffs and Trade, 166
General Motors (GM), 1, 13, 15–16, 125–26, 156, 163
geometrical composition, 41–42
Gintis, Herbert, 58
Gitelman, Lisa, 197n107
"Give Men a Chance—Not Charity" (*National Magazine*), 30
Glacier National Park, 120
global bureaucracy, 165–77
global expansion, 165–77
global Fordism, 175, 182–84
globalization, 6, 25, 190
global marketplace, 165–66, 176
global North, 167
global South, 167
Goldwyn Distributing Corporation, 33
"Good Citizenship" Progressives, 27
Good Roads (film), 93, 97–103, 113
Good Roads Congress, 97
Good Roads Movement, 93, 97, 99, 117
Goodyear Newsreel, The 12
Gotham, Kevin, 129
Gramsci, Antonio, 6, 7, 10
Great Depression, 25
  capitalism and, 123
  film impact on interpretations of, 19
  Ford Motor Company and, 14–15
  mass culture and, 5, 122
  reconstruction after, 120
  road construction during, 102
  village-industries and, 93, 103
  World's Fairs and, 126
Greenfield Village, 21–22, 93

Gries, Laurie, 195n50
Grieveson, Lee, 11, 46, 197n107

Hahner, Leslie A., 27
hailing, 153
handwriting, 48, 51
Haraway, Donna, 91
Hardt, Michael, 183
Harvest of the Years (film), 144–49, 148
Hawhee, Debra, 19
Hayden Mills, 106
Hearon, Fanning, 115
Hediger, Vinzenz, 19
hegemonic crisis, 184
hegemony, 6–8
  rhetoric and, 9, 10, 185
Henry Ford Trade School, 57, 64, 86, 134, 197n100
Henry Ford Trade School, The (film), 53–57, 55, 56
Highland Park plant, 80, 167
historiography, 7
homogeneity, 29
homogenizing masculinity, 154
Houck, Davis, 123
Human Ford, The (film), 140, 143
Hunter, Lynette, 66
hyperbole, 144–49

identification, 9
ideological constructs, lived world and, 60
ideology
  capitalism and, 7
  economic, 14
  hegemony and, 8
  rhetoric and, 9
imagined dream *topos*, 74
imagined futures, 71–79, 176
imago, of laborer, 83
incorporation, 8
  process of, 186
incorporational rhetoric, 6–10, 19, 185, 188
Incorporation of America Today, The (Trachtenberg), 8, 182
individualism, economic, 164
industrial aesthetics, 59, 122
industrial capitalism, 32, 77, 111
  thirdspaces and, 121
  World War I and, 86
industrial competency, 27, 28
industrial development, depictions of, 38–39
industrial films, 16, 24–25
Industrial Hour, The (Galbraith), 182
industrialism, 163

industrial knowledge, 73
  convenientia and experience of, 38–46
  emulation and spread of, 46–53
  Fordism and, 77
industrial managers, 164
industrial production, 54
industrial realism, 59
Industrial Sociology Department, 12
industry
  See also village-industries
  agriculture and importance of, 147
  interconnection with agriculture, 94, 105
  interstitiality and, 26
informal education, 73
interconnection, 44, 94, 105
  appeals to, 189–91
Interior Department, U.S., 115–16
international commerce, 166
International Monetary Fund, 166
interstitiality, 26, 93, 189
  between communities, 106
  economic, 95–96
  movement-images and, 104–5
interstitial reconfiguration, 111

Jack, Jordynn, 161
Jameson, Fredric, 191
Jam Handy, 13
Jefferson, Thomas, 48
Jessop, Robert, 3
Jewett, Ambrose B., 10

Kant, Immanuel, 127, 129
Kaplan, Michael, 9
Kellner, Douglas, 129
Kimberly-Clark, 156
King, Lloyd L., 96
Klamer, Arjo, 202n254
knowledge
  acquisition of, 54
  industrial, 38–53, 73, 77
  mechanical, 57, 73
  public, 46
Krausman, A. M., 115
Kress, Gunther, 41, 43
Krier, Daniel, 129
Kuhn, Thomas, 3

Labaree, D. F., 58
labor
  depictions of, 82–83
  as economic topic, 79

labor (*continued*)
    Fordism and, 77, 82
    individual, 81
    as links in chain, 80–84
    mass-mediated, 77
    social constructs and depictions of, 83
laborer, imago of, 83
labor history, 44
labor relations, 79
Laclau, Ernesto, 9
Lagemann, E. C., 58
landscape, movement-images and, 105–6
late capitalism, 67, 96, 187
LeFebvre, Henri, 121
Lenthall, Bruce, 122
Leopold, M. F., 115
Lewis, David L., 157, 201n223
Liebold, E. G., 14
lighting, color and, 40–41
Lincoln Motors, 87
Lipietz, Alain, 184
literacy, 48, 52
lived spaces, 119
lived world, ideological constructs and, 60
Locke, John, 79, 202n254
Longaker, Mark Garrett, 202n254
Longinus, 127, 129
Ludig, Edwin E., 201n223

machine aesthetics, 58
management training films, 164–65
managerial capitalism, 21, 154
managerial function, 77
managerial gaze, 155, 165–77, 180, 182
    capitalism and, 156
Manifest Destiny, 98
manufacturing, national security and, 86
manufacturing aesthetic, 82
marketplace
    Fordism and, 101
    global, 165–66, 176
    mass production, 97, 109
    nationalized, 93, 99, 101
Marquis, Samuel, 30
Marshall Plan, 166
Martin, Adrian, 60
Marx, Karl, 3, 6, 76, 79, 198n133
mass economy, 92
mass-mediated labor, 77
mass production, 122, 181
    marketplace and, 97, 109

mass selling, 150
McClintock, Anne, 95
McCloskey, Deirdre, 202n254
McKeon, Richard, 77
mechanical knowledge, 57, 73
mechanical production, 76
megethos, 143, 144–49
Melting Pot ceremonies, 28–29
Melting Pot Pageant, 29–30
mental maps, 93
Merrill-Palmer School, 197n100
Messaris, Paul, 19
metalepsis, 202n254
metaphor, 146, 202n254
metonymy, 9
Mexico City, 172
Mirror of America (film), 90
mise-en-scène, 5, 20, 25, 45, 189
    analysis and, 37
    color and, 39
    Fordism and, 32
    Ford Motor Company use of, 37–38
    rhetoric and, 60
Mitchell, W. J. T., 182
Model A, 2
model schools, 197n100
    analogy and, 53–57
Model T, 2, 74, 80
montage, 68, 69–71, 90, 189
    conglomeration and, 85
    convergent, 74
    in exposition films, 136, 138
    in *Harvest of the Years*, 146
    industrial rhetoric and, 145
    of office scenes, 171
    parallel alternate, 81, 99
    rhetorical economy rules and, 82
    topoi and, 70
montage rhetoric, 26
montage theory, 25
motion, 42, 43, 189
Motion Picture Laboratory, 10–13, 33, 37, 93, 113, 193n13
    closing of, 124
    Good Roads Movement and, 97
    montage and, 69
    renewal of, 165
Motor Cities National Heritage area, 120
movement-images, 20, 93, 104, 120
    landscape and, 105–6
MPO Productions, 165

Mullaly, Alan, 1
Murphy, Peter, 84
My Life in Industry (film), 96
"My Philosophy of Industry" (Ford, H.), 92

Nancy, Jean-Luc, 182
Nardelli, Bob, 1
narrative economics, 188
National Education Association, 30, 46
National Highway Association, 97
national identity, car culture and, 102
nationalism, 27
nationalized marketplace, 93, 99, 101
National Magazine, 30
National Park films, 94
national parks, consumption of, 117
National Park System, 113, 120, 121, 186
national security, manufacturing and, 86
national space, 102
nations, 6
Native Americans, 98
nature, rhetorical consumption of, 112–19
Negri, Antonio, 183
Nelson, Dana D., 154
New Deal, 15, 105, 154
    road building and, 102
New Deal films, 123
New York Times
    on Ford Egypt, 175
    on Ford Motor Company films, 33
    on industrial films, 16
noneconomic *topoi*, 84
non-representable concepts, 66
nonsense, 139–44
Nye, David E., 127

Office of War Information (OWI), 157
Old Faithful Geyser, 114
Olson, Christa, 17, 66
omission, 178–81
operational aesthetic, 197n107
organizational structures, 6
Organization Man, The (Whyte), 182
OWI. *See* Office of War Information

Pacific International Exhibition, 126
pacing, 144–49
Packer, Jeremy, 23
Panfilio, Kenneth Michael, 130
panoramas, 147
papwerwork, 171

parallel alternate montage, 81, 99
paternalism, 31
patriotic capital, 86
patriotism, 158
Paving the Way to Success (film), 102
perspective, 42–43
phantasmagoria, 128, 129
Pierrot, George F., 201n223
Plantinga, Carl, 151
Platt, Heinrich, 83
Polan, Dana B., 149
Polanyi, Karl, 84
Porter, James, 28
post-Depression era, visual culture in, 123
post-Fordism, 190
postmodern world, 189
poverty, rhetoric of, 123
Power That Thought Built, The (film), 90
procedural continuity, 42
production
    decentralized, 109
    Fordist, 67, 80, 138, 199n148
    industrial, 54
    mass, 122, 181
    mechanical, 76
    wartime, 163
product planning narratives, 181–82
professional manhood, 154
Progressive education, 27, 47, 186
Progressive Era, 5, 25, 27
Progressives
    constructiveness and, 196n69
    visual culture and, 28
projections, capitalism producing, 128
pseudo-Longinus, 139
public education, 50, 58
public knowledge, 46

quality control, 171
quantitative appeals, 147
quantitative data, 171
Quirke, Carol, 28

racism, 98
rationalization, 164
Reconsolidation of Foreign Operations Records, 166
Recovery Act, 102
Remillard, Sam, 96
representation, 67–68
Rhapsody in Steel (film), 140–41, 142, 143

rhetoric, 4, 5, 17
    aesthetic as practice of, 28
    economic, 187
    film, 18–20
    hegemony and, 9, 10, 185
    ideology and, 9
    incorporational, 6–10, 19, 185, 188
    mise-en-scène and, 60
    montage and, 26, 145
    of poverty, 123
    spatial, 25, 26, 96, 104
    spectacular, 125–30
    visual, 60
rhetorical analysis, 25
rhetorical consumption of nature, 112–19
rhetorical crisis, 185
rhetorical criticism, 9
rhetorical economy, 63, 65, 78, 90–91, 164
    montage and, 82
Rice, Jeff, 95
Rice, Jenny, 144
Rivera, Diego, 126, 134
River Rouge plant, 79, 127, 147, 149, 201n223
Rivette, Jacques, 32
road building, 92
roads, 96–103
Road to Happiness (film), 102
Roosevelt, Franklin D., 153–55, 163
Rosie the Riveter, 161
Ross, Steven J., 91
Roundup on the U (film), 62

Sao Paolo, Brazil, 172, 178
scale, in exposition films, 136, 138
scene of circulation, 195n50
Scenes from the World of Tomorrow (film), 131, 144
Schumpeter, Joseph, 3
Scientific Films, Inc., 124
seeing-as-knowing, 36
self-control, 52
self-direction, 51
self-interest, 84
self-regulation, 84
Shiller, Robert, 188
shop theory, 56, 57
Shumway, David R., 8, 9
Sigler, Fred, 171
similitude, 25, 32, 59
    analogy and, 53
    appeals based on, 36–37, 53
    convenientia and, 45
    defining, 36

Simpson, Mark, 112
Singapore, 170, 179
Singer, Alan, 28
Situationists, 129
size
    appeals to, 188–91
    expertise and, 148
Sklar, Martin, 4
social constructs, depictions of labor and, 83
social development, 7
society, corporations integral role in, 186
"The Society of Spectacle" (Debord), 128
Sociology Department, 30, 31
Soja, Edward, 121
Soldiers of the Soil (film), 157
Solow, Robert, 202n254
Sorenson, Charles, 154
Sousa, John Philip, 22
space
    cinematic uses of, 42
    economic, 119–21
    filmic, 95
    lived, 119
    national, 102
    national park consumption and, 117
    subjectivity connected to, 99
    thirdspaces, 121
space films, 95
spatial configurations, 42
spatial consumption, 113
spatial infrastructure, 103
spatial narratives, 103
spatial patterns, 106
spatial relations, 92
spatial rhetoric, 25, 26, 96, 104
spectacularization, 129
spectacular rhetoric, 125–30
spectatorship, 18, 20, 25, 26, 189
    Around the World with Ford Motor Company and, 177
    of capitalism, 150
    film study and, 151, 202n231
    gaze and, 177
    importance of, 149–52
    positioning, 151
Spivak, Gayatri, 67, 68, 83
Spring, Joel, 31–32
Stafford, Barbara, 53
statistics, 171
stock market crash of 1929, 122
stop-motion animation, 141
strategy of containment, 149

subjectivity, space connected to, 99
sublime, 125–30
    technological, 140
suburbanization, 17
Sugar Cane Growing, Louisiana (film), 62
Sutherland, Megan, 129
sympathies, 37, 60
Symphony in F (film), 144, 201n223
synecdoche, 9

technological sublime, 140
Texas Centennial Exposition, 126
Thatcher, Margaret, 7
theoros, 130–31, 151, 189
These Are the People (film), 156
These People (film series), 156
thirdspaces, 121
Thirty Years of Progress (film), 90
Thomas Aquinas, 10
three Rs, 48–50
topoi, 66–68, 78, 91
    imagined dream, 74
    montage and, 70
    noneconomic, 84
tourism, 94, 111, 112–19
    car-mediated, 120
tourist gaze, 94, 112
Toyotaism, 190
Trachtenberg, Alan, 8, 59, 182
trade schools, 53–57, 86
transformation, 67–68
    capital and, 85, 87
    economic, 87
travelogues, 94, 112–19
Trip to the San Diego Fair (film), 131
Troubled Asset Relief Program, 1

uniformity, 29
urbanization, 92
Urry, John, 94
U.S. National Archives, 4, 11, 16, 21, 22, 193n13
    village-industry footage in holdings of, 104

Van Leeuwen, Theo, 41, 43
Veblen, Thorstein, 84
village-industries, 103–12, 199nn166–67
Village-industries (film), 103–6, 107, 108, 109–10, 113
Visit to the California Pacific International Exhibition, A (film), 131
Visit to Yellowstone National Park, A (film), 113, 114, 115

visual associations, 110
visual consonance, 176
visual *convenientia*, 44–45
visual conventions, 48–50
    overhead views, 105
visual coordination, 60
visual culture
    in post-Depression era, 123
    Progressives and, 28
Visual Education (Fitzpatrick and McElroy), 34, 44
visual logic, 139–40
visual rhetoric, 60
Volkmann, Christina, 66
Vonderau, Patrick, 19

Wagoner, Rick, 1
Warner, Michael, 6, 17
wartime production, 163
wartime propaganda films, 156
Wasson, Haidee, 18
Waterton Glacier International Peace Park (film), 113
Weber, Max, 3, 164
Western Union, 12
While the City Sleeps (film), 90
White, Randal, 115
Whyte, William H., 182
Why We Fight (film series), 156
Wilding Picture Productions, 165
Williams, Linda, 202n231
Williams, Raymond, 8, 186
Willow Run plant, 157, 160
Wilson, Woodrow, 62
Women on the Warpath (film), 26, 157, 158–65, 159, 161, 162
work, education and, 54
Works Progress Administration, 102
world-picture, Fordist, 184
World's Fairs, 5, 26, 124, 125–30, 153, 186
    amplitude and, 139–44
    films of, 130–39, 143
World War I, 85–86
World War II, 25, 153, 154
    film impact on interpretations of, 19
    as industrial war, 16

Yellowstone National Park, 113, 114, 115

Zion National Park, 115

www.ingramcontent.com/pod-product-compliance
Lightning Source LLC
Chambersburg PA
CBHW022051290426
44109CB00014B/1056